Theorising ... and the Mundane: Precarious Positions

Theorising Normalcy and the Mundane:
Editorial Board

Theorising Normalcy and the Mundane: Precarious Positions

Edited by

Rebecca Mallett, Cassandra A. Ogden

and Jenny Slater

University of Chester Press

First published 2016
by University of Chester Press
University of Chester
Parkgate Road
Chester CH1 4BJ

Printed and bound in the UK by the
LIS Print Unit
University of Chester
Cover designed by the
LIS Graphics Team
University of Chester

ISBN 978-1-908258-20-5

*We dedicate this book to all
who have encountered the hostility of a
world increasingly governed by normalcy*

CONTENTS

ACKNOWLEDGEMENTS

This publication would not be possible without the help and support of our colleagues, friends and family who have advised, contributed and put up with us. Firstly we would like to thank our fellow members of the *Theorising Normalcy and the Mundane Conference* team, which continues to gain in numbers as the years pass by. These include: Anat Greenstein, Dan Goodley, Nick Hodge, Rebecca Lawthom, Kirsty Liddiard, Marek Mackiewicz, Katherine Runswick-Cole and Jill Smith. Equally, we want to thank the motley crews that come along and participate, making Normalcy what it is – a critical space where we can debate issues such as those explored in these pages. Thanks for helping to create that space!

Many thanks to the University of Chester Press for providing us with a way of publishing affordable academic texts. Special thanks to Sarah Griffiths who has provided us with answers to our endless queries as well as allowing us extensions to deadlines. Also thanks go to our editorial panel, some of whom have acted as anonymous reviewers to chapters in this book, offering invaluable and insightful comments and suggestions.

As Game and Metcalfe (1996, p. 118) have noted "[a]cknowledgements often admit what the title page denies, that no one can write a book alone". As all authors know, it is often mundane acts of support which matter the most. In this spirit, allow us some unconventional and yet hugely heartfelt thank-yous. Cassie would like to thank everyone close to her who occasionally witnesses her rants and outrages at the various injustices in the world. Jen, Em and Scotty have borne the brunt of this project and deserve many treats. For Rebecca, thanks go to all those who, in times of need, make her hot cups of caffeinated liquid and, sometimes, magically rustle up a jammy doughnut.

References

Game, A., & Metcalfe, A. (1996). *Passionate Sociology*. London, United Kingdom: Sage.

NOTES ON CONTRIBUTORS

Kathy Boxall is Professor of Social Work and Disability Studies at Edith Cowan University's South West Campus in Bunbury, Western Australia. Kathy is from the UK and moved to Australia in August 2014, having been employed previously at the University of Sheffield. Before moving into higher education Kathy worked with people with intellectual disabilities and their families in social work, adult education, employment and advocacy roles. Kathy has also been a mental health service user herself and draws upon this experience in her teaching and research. Kathy's research interests are in the areas of intellectual disability and mental health. Her research, undertaken jointly with service users, explores service users' perspectives on barriers to inclusion in the mainstream and approaches to barrier removal.

Jess Bradley was a founding member of Students for Sensible Drug Policy UK, a UK-based network of student and youth activists taking action for harm reduction and drug policy reform, and Youth Organisations for Drugs Action, a Europe-wide network of youth and student organisations working for similar goals. She is now a director of Action for Trans Health, a grassroots network of trans and gender variant activists organising for democratic patient-worker control of transgender healthcare. Jess is currently a PhD candidate at the University of Manchester working in the field of Planning and Environmental Management, and also conducts independent gender and disability studies research. Her research interests include; queer geographies, posthumanism, normalcy, hegemony/counter-hegemony, drug user studies, and urban studies. Her work with Greta Williams-Schultz focuses on the histories of drug user activists and disabled people.

Sue Chantler has a professional background in primary education, where she worked as a teacher and as a headteacher, and as an academic in the Autism Centre at Sheffield Hallam University. Her work within schools enabled her to appreciate the intellectual style associated with the label of autism. Through working with many children and their families over the years, she gained understanding of some of the ways in which this style of thinking and learning might impact on a child's way of "being in the world", and to recognise the fact that for many children with the label of autism, the mainstream school environment was not always accessible. As a headteacher and then as a Senior Lecturer at Sheffield Hallam University she explored ways in which education professionals develop their professional knowledge and understanding, in particular how they perceive their ability to create an accessible classroom for children whose style of thinking and learning challenges the normalising standards of the English national curriculum.

Harriet Cooper is currently based in the Department of English and Humanities at Birkbeck, University of London, where she is funded as a Wellcome Trust ISSF Researcher to work on publications in the field of medical humanities. Harriet is interested in theorising the making of disabled and "rehabilitated" subjectivities. In her work she uses a conceptual framework informed by medical humanities, critical disability studies and psychoanalysis to investigate the ways in which cultural anxieties about impairment come to be embodied and lived by disabled subjects.

Steve Graby is a PhD candidate in Disability Studies at the University of Leeds, focusing on personal assistance for disabled people in a context of critiques of waged work and capitalism. Autonomy and (in(ter))dependence are core concepts in his research. He has also written and presented about autism, neurodiversity and the relationship between the categories of mental distress and disability. Steve has also been active over the last decade in Disabled People's Movement organisations, including formerly the Disabled People's Direct Action Network (DAN) and now Disabled People Against Cuts (DPAC) and Greater Manchester Coalition of Disabled People (GMCDP). As a disabled activist-academic, his aims include bridging the divide between academic theory and grassroots political action, and bringing disability and neurodiversity perspectives to anti-state and anti-capitalist movements and vice versa.

Anat Greenstein is a Senior Lecturer in Inclusive Education and Disability Studies at Manchester Metropolitan University. Her main research interests include using creative methods to work in partnership with disabled children and adults, exploring the connections and tensions between critical pedagogy and inclusive education, and exploring social movements, and in particular the disabled people's movement as sites of learning and education. She has previously worked as a lecturer in Learning Disability Studies at the University of Manchester and has a professional background as a speech and language therapist. Anat is the author of several academic papers and her book *Radical Inclusive Education: Disability, Teaching and Struggles for Liberation* has recently been published by Routledge.

Naomi Lawson Jacobs has an MA in Disability Studies from the University of Leeds and is a PhD candidate at SOAS, University of London in the Department of the Study of Religions. Her current research focuses on the involvement of disabled people in Christian churches, and how their reception is impacted by Christian discourses of disability and the body. Her work is framed by an accessible and participatory approach to research. Her other research interests include normalcy in Christianity, embodiment and the Christian healing movements, emancipatory research paradigms, and the inclusion and exclusion of disabled researchers in higher education. Recent conference papers have included *Reinforcing Normalcy: Christian Churches and Faith Healing* (*Lancaster Disability Conference*, 2014), *Stories and Silence: Disabled Women in the Bible* (*Gender and Disability Conference*, University of Sheffield, 2014) and *Cripping Up: The Politics of Visibility and Invisibility for Disabled People* (*Disrupting Visibility: The Politics of Passing* conference, Goldsmiths, 2015). She is currently writing about the experiences of autistic academics at conferences. Naomi is a book reviewer for the *Disability and Society* journal, and a member of the British Sociological Association and the International Association for the Study of Religion and Gender.

Rebecca Mallett is a Principal Lecturer at the Sheffield Institute of Education (Sheffield Hallam University, UK). Her main areas of research include "disability" in popular culture, the constitution and regulation of interpretative strategies within cultural disability studies and, more recently, the commodification of impairment. She is on the editorial board of *Disability and Society*, is a fellow of the Higher Education Academy, and co-coordinates the Disability Research Forum (www.disabilityresearchforum.wordpress.com).

Cassandra A. Ogden is Senior Lecturer and Programme Leader for Sociology at the University of Chester. Her PhD thesis explored the experiences of children with Inflammatory Bowel Disease, which fuelled her interest in exploring the social disgust of particular bodies and the stigma people face due to perceived differences of the body. Much of Cassandra's current work utilises a critical disability studies perspective but she has also published and co-published on disability hate crime, childhood illness experiences, the social and legal responses to smoking in public and its impact upon the incarcerated, quality of life research, the narrative inquiry technique and the use of food banks in Cheshire.

Lucia Radcliffe considers herself to be a bit of an academic nomad as she is still figuring out what she wants to be when she grows up (and everything that entails). She is currently looking for new ways to change the world, or at least her little corner of it. She has been known to do adult things, like get a first class degree in Education and Disability Studies, get married and become a parent. However, her inner child prefers taking photos and thinking outside the box.

Katherine Runswick-Cole is Senior Research Fellow in Disability Studies and Psychology at Manchester Metropolitan University, Manchester, UK. She has published extensively in the area of Critical Disability Studies and has a particular focus on participatory research with disabled children, young people and their families and allies as well as working alongside people labelled with learning disabilities (www.bigsocietydis.word press.com).

Jenny Slater is a Senior Lecturer in Education and Disability Studies at Sheffield Hallam University. Her doctoral studies involved spending time with two youth groups in the north of England as well as with young disabled women running Iceland's first and only user-led independent living centre. Her research explores youth and disability as social, cultural and political constructs. She is particularly interested in thinking about "youth" and "disability" alongside gender, sexuality and the body. In her latest research she is working with disabled, queer and trans people's organisations to think about "access", "identity" and toilets (https://aroundthe toilet.Wordpress.com).

Greta Williams-Schultz is a disabled activist with a strong academic interest in disability history. They organised the 2013 Disability and the Cuts Community Conference and are active in organising against cuts to disability benefits as well as ongoing casework with individuals most affected by those cuts. They are a director of Action for Trans Health, a transgender healthcare organisation. They study part time at University of Manchester and have written publicly about the impact on disabled people of the First World War. They have also produced research on modern queer and trans* technological history. Their previous work with Jess Bradley has included broader analysis of disability history and trans* history which has been presented at various conferences. Their research interests include modern social histories, disability history, disability studies, and technology studies.

INTRODUCTION

You are the Reasonable Teacher with your reasonable rules, reasonable exams and reasonable lesson plans. The teacher that believes it is only reasonable to stratify and separate children out from the moment they enter the school grounds; punishing those who refuse to conform (Davis and Watson, 2001). You are the Reasonable Careers Advisor whose lecture I left [...] when she asserted that if we did not "speak properly", dared to utter an "erm" or an "um" in a job interview, we would remain unemployed. You are the Reasonable Academic who told me this was "just the way it is" when I pointed out the ableism of that careers advice. You are the Reasonable Boss that told my Mum she needed to "man up and grow some balls" in order to survive work in the public sector: the workplace will not change to accommodate you, so you must change to accommodate it. You are the Reasonable Landlord, the Reasonable Councillor and the Reasonable Politician that live dogmatically by the reasonable, bureaucratic rules of Western neoliberal individualism (Titchkosky, 2011). (Slater, 2013, p. 11)

Normalcy imagines – "sees" – no other possibility of human life than itself, and thus, ironically, does not "see" itself. The centre understands itself as the only legitimate space of human habitation and, like all spaces, the centre has its causalities. (Titchkosky and Michalko, 2009, p. 7)

Things Don't Always Get Better: The Persistent Relevance of Normalcy

In 2010, the UK's Equality Act gave protection, under civic law, to nine "protected characteristics" (age; disability; gender reassignment; marriage and civil partnership; pregnancy and maternity; race; religion and belief; sex; and sexual orientation). Barely two years later, in 2012, as part of the Conservative-Liberal Democrat Coalition's *Red Tape Challenge*, the Act became the focus of a series of consultations and reviews which aimed to "simplify" the legislation. Hepple (2013) was not alone in characterising these moves as being part of wider attempts to scale down specific employment and equality rights and, furthermore, to consider those attempts as ideologically motivated. Commenting that they marked "a return to the market fundamentalism championed by the Conservative Thatcher and Major governments in the 1980s and 1990s", Hepple (2013, p. 206) places the *Red Tape Challenge* firmly in its historical context, highlighting further the increasingly precarious position of those relatively recent and certainly hard-won equality protections.

By 2013 broader worries over the direction of global social and economic inequalities were increasing. The *4th Annual International Conference of Theorising Normalcy and the Mundane*, on which this book is based, sought to take such "precarious positions" as its focus. The event took place on 3–4 September 2013 and witnessed a wide range of people coming together in Sheffield (hosted at Sheffield Hallam University, UK) to discuss and debate. In many ways, we would have liked those discussions to be part of our past – memories of a time gone by. However, and sadly, the discussions remain as relevant today as they were then.

In September 2015, as we write this Introduction, we are two years on from the conference, and Britain is facing (at least) five more years of austerity. Within the first few months of power, the recently elected Conservative government has already attacked legislation which aims to protect the most vulnerable in society; the July budget promised cuts to welfare and housing benefits, by, amongst other proposals, reducing household benefit caps and restricting entitlement to certain benefits for young adults whilst also announcing the reduction of corporation tax and the cutting of student maintenance grants (HM Treasury, 2015). In the name of reducing "red tape" or making services "more efficient", it can be argued that a regime of stigmatising and punishing people in poor, dependent and vulnerable positions continues to flourish.

While this sad, frustrating and uncomfortable reality can be easily laid at the feet of capitalism, neo-conservatism and Western neoliberalism, the piece of the jigsaw which is rarely acknowledged on a wider scale is normalcy. As "the only legitimate space of human habitation" (Titchkosky and Michalko, 2009, p. 7), normalcy sketches out the do-able and the say-able, it cajoles, polices and decides, sometimes with mundane, and sometimes with devastating consequences. Its increasing casualty count has motivated us to work with some of the presenters from the 2013 conference to edit a collection intended to further provoke discussions and debate. What is of specific concern to many of our contributors is that tolerance, it seems, only lasts as long as there is enough room and resources for difference to be accommodated. In times of austerity, being anything other than "neoliberally normal" places you in extremely precarious positions. Whether you are on the sharp end of welfare reforms or face budgets cuts to your local services/provision, being (or at least, passing as) healthy, wealthy and wise seems to be your best bet to survive.

The 2013 conference offered spaces to discuss and explore the precarious positions "normal", and its operating system "normalcy" (Davis, 2010), create, present us with and, more often than not, force us into. The wide-ranging chapters in this book are written by activists, students, practitioners and academics and offer related but diverse approaches to ponder the ways in which "normal" and "normalcy" (Davis, 2010) present clear and present dangers and opportunities to individual and collective futures. However, and importantly, the conference also asked: what if increasingly precarious encounters with, and positions of, marginality and non-normativity offers us a chance (perhaps *the* chance) to critically explore the possibilities of "imagining otherwise"? From questioning the privileged position of "non-normativity" in youth (Slater, Chapter 1), to unpacking the expectation of the "normal" student in higher (Radcliffe, Chapter 2) and primary education (Chantler, Chapter 3); from using the position of transable people to push the boundaries of "disability" (Ogden, Chapter 6), to interrogating the psycho-emotional disablism (Reeve, 2002) of box-ticking bureaucracy (Cooper, Chapter 5) and the "urge to know" impairment (Mallett and Runswick-Cole, Chapter 4); from cross-movement and cross-disciplinary work around disability and drug use (Bradley and Williams-Schultz, Chapter 7) and the Bible (Lawson Jacobs, Chapter 8), to ways forward with relational autonomy (Graby and Greenstein, Chapter 9) and (perhaps controversially), reinstating "normal" (Boxall, Chapter 10) this book continues in this vein by paying attention to the opportunities presented amongst the fissures of critique and defiance.

Before we introduce these chapters more fully, we first turn to introduce normalcy.

Theorising Normalcy
The term "normalcy" is perhaps most widely attributed to the work of Lennard Davis (1995, 2002, 2010). Mallett and Runswick-Cole (2014, pp. 23–24) explain Davis's concept of normalcy as follows:

> Davis contends that in order to understand 'disability', we must begin by examining the idea of 'normal'. Indeed, he draws our attention to what he describes as the hegemony, or dominance, of the 'world of norms' (1995, p. 23). The world of norms is one in which intelligence, height, weight and many other aspects of the body are measured in comparison to the 'normal'. In some disciplines, such as psychology and medicine, the 'normal' range is often depicted on a bell-shaped graph that offers a visual representation and statistical description of the limits of normal.

Introduction

The original aim of the *Theorising Normalcy and the Mundane International Conference* series was to take attention away from studies of disabled bodies and minds, to instead unpick the systemic working of the "norm". Goodley (2009, p. x) writes that "normality and normalcy is achieved through an unsaying: an absence of descriptions of what it is to be normal". The conference series, and indeed this book, aims to pay attention to "the everyday", to denaturalise "common-sense", to notice what often goes unnoticed. Davis (1995, p. 24) helps here by unsettling the taken-for-granted nature of "normal". "A common assumption would be that some concept of the norm must have always existed [...] But the idea of a norm is less a condition of human nature than it is a feature of a certain kind of society." He moves to historically contextualise the concept by highlighting the rather late entry into the English language of the current usage of the word "normal". Pinpointing the mid-1800s as the time when "normal" changed from meaning "perpendicular" (in relation to carpentry) to its modern meaning as "constituting, conforming to, nor deviating or different from, the common type or standard, regular, usual" (Davis, 1995, p. 24), Davis (1995) points out that before the concept of the "norm" took hold, ideas pertaining to "ideal" were in currency and often related to aspirational "perfect" bodies which could never be attained by humans. Indeed, the ideal body remains as often perceived *outside* the norm: fetishised as it is pedestalled but also scrutinised, chastised and considered in some way "freakish" (Slater, 2012). An interrogation of the projected ideal crops up in several places in this collection: perhaps most readily in Chapter 6 as Ogden interrogates "the ideal body" through exploring contradictory societal reaction to accepted forms of body modification and reactions and responses to transableism.

In order to demonstrate how "normal" came to enter, and indeed pervade, English language and society, Davis (1995) considers the rise of two particular areas of "science": statistics and eugenics. He notes that the word "statistik" was first used in 1749 by Gottfried Achenwall in relation to compiling information about the state (Davis, 1995, p. 26) and goes on to outline how, by 1829, Bisset Hawkins had defined medical statistics as "the application of numbers to illustrate the natural history of health and disease" (Porter, 1986 cited in Davis, 1995, p. 26). Around this time, in France, statistics were being used in public health to measure the health of the nation. French statistician Adolphe Quetelet developed the concept of "l'homme moyen" (the average *man*) which acted as an abstract concept of the "average" human, both physically and morally. Here the science of statistics justified the middle and the average as the "normal", and thus began to deal with "individual types". Of course, through the creation of a perceived "norm" we also infer its opposition: the abnormal. From here the question begins to arise: what should *we* do with deviations, extremes and abnormalities? As Davis (1995, p. 30) writes, statisticians had an answer for this and reveals a particularly telling historical detail: "The rather amazing fact is that almost all the early statisticians had one thing in common: they were eugenicists."

Davis (1995) argues that statistics not only gave eugenicists a valid, legitimate norm to look for but also a way of identifying deviations from that norm. This, in effect, creates the concept of the non-normal, deviating, disabled body and returns us to Davis's (1995, p. 23) fundamental contention, that "[t]o understand the disabled body, one must return to the concept of the norm, the normal body".

It becomes clear from the chapters herein that we shouldn't: (a) be too quick to position eugenic thinking as only historical; and (b) consider disability separately from other forms of oppression. The valuing of some bodies over others continues, yet, it could be argued, in a post-political, neoliberal time, it happens more covertly than during the period of time to which Davis refers. Legislation today may supposedly protect us from discrimination yet it arguably only protects the most assimilated (normal) of us, and perhaps even this is limited (Conrad, 2014). Normalcy creeps up on us differently dependent upon time, place and social context. Today, in Britain for example: it is *normal* for people living in poverty to be regularly accessing food banks in order to survive (Spencer, Ogden, and Battarbee, 2015); it is *normal* when nobody is prosecuted for the murdering of black people by the police, and although the most high-profile cases are in the USA, it is by no means an "American issue" (Black Lives Matter, 2015; Inquest, 2015); it is *normal* that immigration policies decide which bodies are legitimate to cross borders and when the prison industrial complex relegates those that contend with social problems (homelessness, unemploy-ment, drug addiction, mental illness and illiteracy) to cages (Davis, 2003); it is *normal* that pharmaceutical companies sell drugs deemed dangerous in the minority world to those in the majority world in pursuit of profit (Mills, 2014) and; it is *normal* that the average age of a black trans woman in the USA is just 35 years old (Black Lives Matter, 2015).

Left un-interrogated, normalcy allows for (unnoticed) oppressive cultures catering only for those perceived to sit neatly within the bell curve (the white, middle-class, non-disabled, cisgender[1] and heterosexual male). Importantly, and particularly pertinent to a discussion of eugenics, the disabled body is always living at the intersections of many other forms of oppression (and privilege); and it is not only disabled people that are threatened under conditions of normalcy. In fact, Mingus (2011, para. 11)

---

[1] Cisgender is used to refer to people who identify with the gender that they were assigned at birth.

argues that disability has always been socially constituted by other forms of perceived abnormality:

> Ableism cuts across all of our movements because ableism dictates how bodies should function against a mythical norm – an able-bodied standard of white supremacy, heterosexism, sexism, economic exploitation, moral/ religious beliefs, age and ability. Ableism set the stage for queer and trans people to be institutionalized as mentally disabled; for communities of color to be understood as less capable, smart and intelligent, therefore "naturally" fit for slave labor; for women's bodies to be used to produce children, when, where and how men needed them; for people with disabilities to be seen as "disposable" in a capitalist and exploitative culture because we are not seen as "productive;" for immigrants to be thought of as a "disease" that we must "cure" because it is "weakening" our country; for violence, cycles of poverty, lack of resources and war to be used as systematic tools to construct disability in communities and entire countries.

Detailing this Book

This book asks then, what (everyday) encounters with liminality and/or marginalisation reveal about the limits of normalcy. In Chapter 1, for example, Slater grapples with age, race, class, gender, sexuality and disability to consider how the common-sense assumption that youth is a time of non-normativity applies to only a privileged few. Indeed, the moral panics surrounding youth in particular, offer a moral imperative to society to provide a framework (strait-jacket) for "normal" to reduce the risk involved in being otherwise. Radcliffe's and Chantler's chapters (2 and 3) both use the arena of educational institutions to explore what normalising discourses serve to restrict and limit the experiences of students and pupils. Radcliffe's discourse analysis of higher education (HE) prospectuses unpacks the expectation of the "normal" student in HE and how "risky" students are kept

8

Introduction

out through various discourses apparent in prospectus and application marketing literature. Chantler's work turns the focus more to primary education and the structural limitations to ensuring "inclusion" (and resisting normalcy) and the teachers' roles in these processes. Both Radcliffe's and Chantler's chapters speak about particular times in British political history and while policy specifics may have changed, as we explored at the beginning of this Introduction, underpinning ideologies and economic realities remain relevant long after the policy briefings have been shredded.

As we move further into the book, we begin to ask how abnormality becomes defined; and what it becomes defined against. Cooper and Mallett and Runswick-Cole's chapters (5 and 4), for example, think about the bureaucracy and limits of definition in relation to impairment. Whereas Cooper draws on personal narrative to interrogate the psycho-emotional disablism (Reeve, 2002) of box-ticking bureaucracy, Mallett and Runswick-Cole delve into an eclectic range of sources to explore the "urge to know" impairment and, thereby, reveal the power (and the pitfalls) of the "normal-abnormal". Furthermore Ogden's work (Chapter 6) interrogates the limitations of medical/professional understandings of transable people and their experiences and through a queering of dis/abled dichotomies demonstrates how transability can trouble ideas of "authentic" disabled identities. Cooper's and Ogden's chapters (5 and 6) together call for a reformation of understandings of impairment, and in doing so accept fluid and different understandings of corporeal experiences. From these three chapters we begin to question categorisation and whether such categorisations (e.g. autism, ADHD, depression) are being used (and abused) in the race to export "normal" (Western) ways of being. Do these characterisations of "abnormality" in fact serve to ensure the continued protection of "normal"?

9

From here, the book further looks beyond the topic of disability to understand the negative impact of "normalising" deviant labels that impact upon drug users and the way that "normalcy" functions within the Christian church. In their chapter, Bradley and Williams-Schultz (Chapter 7) consider the similar (historical and current day) social positioning of drug users and disabled people. Through this chapter they grapple with one of the original questions asked in the conference call: is contexualising normalcy (historically, culturally, spatially) is the best (the only?) way to reveal its illusionary nature? What do we gain by doing this, and where do we go from here? The chapter offers one way forward as looking back at the origins of Disability Studies: Bradley and Williams-Schultz explore what an activist-led "drug user studies" would look like. They also highlight that to those rendered abnormal through a positioning in opposition to "the norm", normalcy is not as illusionary as some in more powerful positions would like it to appear.

Like this book, the *Theorising Normalcy and the Mundane Conference* continues to make the unnoticed, noticed. Lawson Jacobs (Chapter 8), continues this work in Chapter 8 in relation to the specific use of concepts of "health" and "wholeness" within the pentecostal-charismatic Christian healing movement. Lawson Jacobs outlines how these concepts have been challenged by disability theologians and disabled people with a view to exploring the potential marginalising and oppressive effects for disabled people both within and outside Christian churches. Like many of the subjects in this book, and like the "normal" body itself, this chapter takes as its subject an area of life which is rarely questioned or critiqued.

In the penultimate chapter, Graby and Greenstein (9) explore the concept of "autonomy" and its relationship to disability and feminist studies and activism. They argue that the conflation of "autonomy" with "independence" (a "normalcy taboo" which indeed needs some interrogation!), has meant that Disability Studies critiques of independence, have, at times, erred towards denying disabled people's autonomy. They therefore argue for a relational view of autonomy as something that no individual ever "has", but that we should all collectively be striving towards. In the second half of their chapter they productively give examples of relational autonomy in action. Through this chapter then Graby and Greenstein illustrate how critiques of normalcy, such as the pedestalling of independence, need to be done with some care. This theme continues (more explicitly) into Boxall's chapter (10), on which we end the book. Here Boxall asks whether we are being too fast to reject normal. Drawing on Wolfensberger, and particularly considering the place of those with labels of learning difficulties and psychiatric system survivors, Boxall asks whether the rejection of normal as a privileged position could harm those most marginalised. Echoing back to Slater's chapter (1) on which we began, it is certainly safer for some to reject normal than it is for others. Although perhaps controversial given the focus of the book therefore, Boxall's chapter (10) in fact reflects a tension that runs throughout: for those living in precarious positions forced on them through neoliberal capitalism, the safest option can be to argue oneself "normal". Yet, as previous chapters have shown, for others, proving themselves "normal" is not an option on offer.

The ten chapters in this book therefore work at this slippery border between normal and abnormal, and begin to unpick some of the illusionary and often contradictory conditions of normalcy. We invite you to join the debate at future *Theorising Normalcy and the Mundane Conferences*.

References

Black Lives Matter. (2015). Retrieved 21 May 2015, from http://blacklivesmatter.com

Theorising Normalcy and the Mundane

Conrad, R. (Ed.). (2014). *Against equality: Queer revolution not mere inclusion*. Edinburgh, United Kingdom; Oakland, CA: AK Press.

Davis, A. Y. (2003). *Are prisons obselete?* New York, NY: Seven Stories Press.

Davis, L. J. (1995). *Enforcing normalcy: Disability, deafness and the body*. London, United Kingdom; New York, NY: Verso.

Davis, L. J. (2002). *Bending over backwards: Disability, dismodernism, and other difficult positions*. New York, NY; London, United Kingdom: New York University Press.

Davis, L. J. (2010). Constructing normalcy. In L. J. Davis (Ed.), *The disability studies reader* (3rd ed., pp. 3–19). New York, NY; London, United Kingdom: Routledge.

Goodley, D. (2009). Foreword. In K. F. Campbell (Ed.), *Contours of ableism* (pp. ix–xiv). Basingstoke, United Kingdom; New York, NY: Palgrave.

Hepple, B. (2013). Back to the future: Employment law under the Coalition government. *Industrial Law Journal, 42*(3), 203–223.

HM Treasury. (2015). *Summer budget 2015: Key announcements*. Retrieved 3 August 2015, from https://www.gov.uk/government/news/summer-budget-2015-key-announcements

Inquest. (2015). BAME deaths in police custody. Retrieved 15 June 2015, from http://www.inquest.org.uk/statistics/bame-deaths-in-police-custody

Mallett, R., & Runswick-Cole, K. (2014). *Approaching disability: Critical issues and perspectives*. London, United Kingdom: Routledge.

Mills, C. (2014). *Decolonizing global mental health: The psychiatrization of the majority world*. London, United Kingdom; New York, NY: Routledge.

Mingus, M. (2011, 22 August). Moving toward the ugly: A politic beyond desirability. *Femmes of Color Symposium* keynote speech, Oakland, CA (21 August 2011). Retrieved 4 October 2015, from http://leavingevidence.wordpress.com/2011/08/22/moving-to toward-the-ugly-a-politic-beyond-desirability/

Reeve, D. (2002). Negotiating psycho-emotional dimensions of disability and their influence on identity constructions. *Disability and Society, 17*(5), 493–508.

Introduction

Slater, J. (2012). Youth for sale: Using critical disability perspectives to examine the embodiment of "youth". *Societies, 2*(3), 195–209.

Slater, J. (2013). *Constructions, perceptions and expectations of being young and disabled: A critical disability perspective.* (Doctoral thesis, Manchester Metropolitan University, Manchester, United Kingdom).

Spencer, A., Ogden, C., & Battarbee, L. (2015). #cheshirehunger Understanding emergency food provision in West Cheshire. Retrieved 3 August 2015, from http://westcheshire.food bank.org.uk/resources/documents/Cheshire_Hunger_March_201 5_Full_Report_Final.pdf

Titchkosky, T., & Michalko, R. (2009). Introduction. In T. Titchkosky & R. Michalko, *Rethinking normalcy: A disability studies reader* (pp. 1–15). Toronto, Canada: Canadian Scholars' Press Inc.

CHAPTER 1

THE (NORMAL) NON-NORMATIVITY OF YOUTH

Jenny Slater

Summary

Youth unnerves us. Awkwardly bridging the space between "child" and "adult", we are delivered demonising depictions of young people (hoodies and hooligans), and working out how to deal with these not-quite children but not-quite-adults is high on policy makers' agendas (Slater, 2013b). On the other hand, the non-normativity of "teenage rebellion" is considered an "identity forming" rite of passage for young people to cross the border zone between child and adult (Lesko, 2002). We hear, in fact, young people scorned for their apolitical, apathetic acceptance of normativity – the youth today a pale reflection of their predecessors (Bennett, 2008). Even our ever-so reasonable politicians tell us that they "[did] things that teenagers do", before they "pulled [themselves] up and headed in the right [direction]" (Cameron in Watt, 2009).

This chapter will explore how, through youth, "non-normativity" emerges as a place allowed, indeed expected, as a stage of "normative development". I will argue, however, that it is a stage only permissible to young people fitting neatly into other culturally privileged positions. Furthermore, it must be played out by meeting other societal expectations ("masculinity" – lads will be lads; first heterosexual encounters, and so on) which set young people on the path to normative adulthood. Commercialised and commodified "what it is to be young", I argue, is an illustration of the required flexible neoliberal subject; it is okay to be "non-normative" if "non-normativity" can be compartmentalised, as a phase to be grown-out of, and later periodically bought into. Drawing on fieldwork with disabled young people alongside other cultural and media representations of "youth" and "youth culture", I will argue that perceived "non-normativity" leaves young people not fitting into other culturally privileged positions much more precariously positioned.

The (Normal) Non-Normativity of Youth

Introduction: A Normative Imagination

Susan, Dawn and Linda sit around discussing their children. Dawn, worrying about her teenage daughter, begins:

> "I don't understand her, Susan. She just won't talk to me."
> "I wouldn't worry about it," Susan – the voice of experience – replies, "they're all like that as teenagers. God – I remember how my two were."
> Linda chips in: "Yeah, I'm dreading our Sarah hitting thirteen!"
> Susan ends the conversation, by reassuring the group: "You've just gotta remember they'll grow out of it. There's no *point* trying to understand teenagers! Here, have another biscuit."

That everyday conversation comes from my imagination, based upon things I've heard and seen. Through their claims to not understand "youth", Susan, Dawn and Linda are reiterating some of the most "well-known" messages delivered to us about young people: the rational adult mind will never understand the irrationality of the teenage brain and that, in time, the irrational teenage mind would develop into the mind of a rational adult (Payne, 2010). As Susan reassures the others: "abnormal" teenage behaviour is just a "normal" part of growing up (Elman, 2014).

You may or may not be able to picture yourself as part of that conversation: either as a teenager being discussed, or as a concerned parent. You may already feel there are problems within the script. You may be troubled for those implicated within the messages being delivered. On the other hand, you may feel concerned that your past or present self, or your loved ones, are excluded from this particular narrative of youth. This chapter interrogates the kinds of talk about and around youth that may go on over a cup of tea and a biscuit. I do this through a consideration of the strange relationships between categories of "youth" and concepts of "normal". I will contextualise in order to ask where these common-sense knowledges of youth come

15

from, before arguing that they are not inclusive to many young people's lives. Furthermore, I will wonder, if not inclusive, what purpose do they serve, and are there dangers hidden within them?

The way I approach the above task is by thinking about youth in three different ways. Firstly, I'll think about the discourse projected above: youth as "abnormals-becoming-normal". Secondly, I will draw on Lesko (2012) to think about youth as a border zone between child and adult; and finally I'll consider the relationships between youth, normal and the (commodified) neoliberal subject. I explore each of these (re)conceptualisations separately, using academic literature from critical psychology, youth studies, critical studies of neuroscience, and disability studies, to interrogate popular culture. I conclude that the (sometimes) expected abnormality of youth, can only be safely played out by the most normative and privileged of people.

(Re)-Conceptualising Youth (1): Abnormals-Becoming-Normal
I begin with the discourse of youth as "abnormals-becoming-normal", depicted by Figure 1. In the bottom left-hand corner of this sketch are the figures of a man, woman and child – a normative representation of the family. The emphasis here is on the child, and these figures are labelled the "relative stability of childhood" (Wyn and White, 1997). The child stands between the mother and father, the small size represents the narrative and often materiality of childhood dependence upon his/her parents. An arrow then leaves this family, moving towards the top right-hand corner, where there is a figure of a single man – the most normative representation of adulthood (Slater, 2015) – labelled "stable adulthood". Before reaching adulthood, however, the arrow, representing the person's growth passes through this in-between, messy and turbulent stage of youth.

16

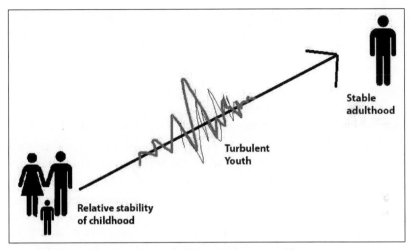

Figure 1: Youth as "abnormals-becoming-normal".

Teenage Evolution: Bodies and Minds

Susan's account, which began this chapter, fits with this depiction of youth as "abnormals-becoming-normal"; youth as a time of irrationality, which one outgrows as they become "adult". Interestingly this implicit and over-simplistic account in fact rests upon scientific knowledges, which are in turn reflected and perpetuated through the popular media (Elman, 2014). According to theorists of adolescence working in the early 1900s, youth parallels human evolution from savage to civilised being (Hall, 1904). There is a presumed progression, aided by a mixture of nature and nurture, from child, through youth, to adult (Burman, 2008). To unpick these supposed scientific "truths" of youth, Lesko (1996a, 1996b, 2002) traces the beginnings of discourse around youth in the USA. She highlights that this period saw a rise in disciplines such as anthropology, psychology and pedagogy, which paralleled the growth of each individual child with the development of human kind. It was also a time of American colonisation, and if we consider this context, it is not

17

surprising that this theory – known as recapitulation theory – became "hot stuff". Worries about America's nationhood and manhood meant studies of adolescence, projected as scientific and neutral, became the rationale for boys' education aiming "to produce young, masculine, Christians" (Lesko, 2002, p. 183); good colonial subjects, well suited for the building, protection and maintenance of Empire. With this, the entwined racism, sexism, dis/ablism and other prejudice of evolutionary theory was transferred to development theory; a threefold parallel developing where animals, "savages" and children were all presumed as equal. For example, on posture, one author writes:

> [S]avage races do not stand so erect as civilised races. Country people ... tend to bend forward, and the aristocrat is more erect than the plebeian. In this respect women appear to be nearer to the infantile [and apelike] condition than men.
> (Serres cited in Lesko, 1996b, pp. 140)

Although these ideas have since been heavily critiqued, we nevertheless see "youth as evolution" reiterated through the popular media. In one scene of animated film, *Persepolis* (Paronnaud and Satrapi, 2008), for example, we see the protagonist, Marjane, "transform from a girl into a woman overnight". In the voiceover to the scene (which can be viewed here: https://www.youtube.com/watch?v=2zncsnYFGGQand feature=youtu.be), Marjane tells us:

> This was a period of incredible ugliness. First, I grew eight inches taller. Then my face changed: my head got longer, my right eye bigger, and my chin followed. My right hand became enormous. Then my left foot. My nose tripled in size; my breasts inflated like balloons; then my butt expanded, restoring my centre of gravity. And last but not least, an enormous beauty mark provided the finishing touch.

Marjane depicts youth as being about changing bodies, from child, through a gawky teenage stage, to emerge as a young adult. However, as Susan, Dawn and Linda were aware, youth is also about changing minds. Harry Enfield's British sitcom/sketch show *Kevin the Teenager* depicts this well. Played by Enfield, Kevin first appeared as an energetic little boy in the show, *Harry Enfield's Television Programme* (Enfield, 1990–1992), annoying his elder brother. However, in Enfield's (1994–1998) later shows the sketch progresses as Kevin reaches his 13th birthday. From this point onwards the show documents the experiences of a family with a teenage boy portrayed as awkward, moody and selfish. The popularity of Kevin led to the later production of a feature length teen comedy film, *Kevin and Perry Go Large*. The moment I want to focus on now, however, is perhaps the most memorable of all moments of the Kevin stories; the stroke of midnight on his 13th birthday; the moment, to his parents' despair, that Kevin "becomes a teenager".

The clip (which can be viewed here: http://www.You tube.com/watch?v=dLuEY6jN6gY) begins with 12-year-old Kevin excitedly and innocently counting down the seconds until the clock turns midnight and marks his birthday. He's constantly distracted by thoughts of ice cream, and the presents he's hoping to receive the next day. Whilst Kevin paces the kitchen, his parents sit on the sofa, reminding him it's school the next day, to which he amicably responds "oh yeah! Duhhh brain!" On the strike of midnight, however, the mood changes. As the clock chimes, Kevin throws his hands in the air, shouting "yeah, I'm thirteen!" and begins singing "Happy Birthday" to himself. As the clock continues to chime, however, Kevin's animated "teenage evolution" begins. His movements become slower and more erratic, his posture becomes more bent forwards, and his arms hang down by his sides. As his parents observe the transformation, they observe:

Dad: Darling, he's losing the power of rational thought
Mum: ... and the use of his arms
Both: He's become ... a teenager!

As the clip continues, Kevin's mother's "happy birthday Kevin!" is responded to with an "Okay – stop going on about it, will you?!" After he searches in the fridge for ice cream ("Why's there no bloody ice cream?!"), we hear the first of Kevin's signature catchphrases (to be repeated throughout the series): "I hate you! It's so unfair!" The clip ends, however, much like the mothers' conversation over a cuppa earlier: Kevin's father reassures Kevin's mother that Kevin will grow out of the dreaded teenage years.

As Elman (2014) points out, cultural representations of teenagers often work to reproduce and secure developmental theory. In both these clips, like the conversation I started with, youth is as an uncomplicated, instantaneous shift from the innocence of childhood to the irrationality and *crisis* of adolescence (echoing the work of youth psychologist Erik Erikson). Moreover, "youth" is caricatured into a hollow character to laugh at but not to take seriously as a meaningful subjectivity. The humour in both clips works on the assumption that we all "know" youth ... and the reason we all know it – because we've all been there! Even the current UK Conservative Prime Minister, David Cameron (supposedly one of our most reasonable and responsible adults!), confirms that youth is a place of behaviour that deviates from the norm. Cameron, along with other powerful UK politicians such as Boris Johnson (elected Mayor of London) and George Osborne (Chancellor of the Exchequer), were all members of the Bullingdon Club, an elite society "notorious for very wealthy students from Oxford University trashing restaurants and participating [sic] outlandish, criminal behaviour" (Snowdon, 2015). Questioned about his youthful antics in an interview for *Grazia* magazine in

August 2009, Cameron tells us that as a young man he did "things that teenagers do". Yet he also makes it clear that although it is normal to be non-normative in youth, it is not necessarily desirable. Cameron soon realised that he was, "in some ways, heading in the wrong direction", so he "pulled [him]self up and headed in the right one" (Cameron in Watt, 2009). In another interview in 2011 Cameron tells us that "we all do stupid things when we're young and we should learn the lessons" (Cameron as quoted in Sparrow, 2011).

Studying the (Normal) Abnormality of Youth
The abnormality of youth, it seems so far, is both normal, yet undesirable. Furthermore, this undesirable normal abnormality continues to be an object of scientific intrigue. The most recent way youth – and the non-normativity we associate with it – has been approached is through neurology (Elman, 2014; Ortega and Choudhury, 2011; Payne, 2010). A BBC News headline in 2013 read, "Brain scan study to understand workings of teenage mind" (Ghosh, 2013a, 2013b). Again, in the report the representation of youth is of a stage that is both humorous, yet undesirable. In an accompanying news clip the reporter tells us:

> Teenage behaviour has been around since, well, teenagers. But, until recently, nobody has known what it comes down to, what they can do about it, or when it might end. […] Now, some may say thankfully, *The Wellcome Trust* has funded a £5 million project to try and understand how the teenage mind works.

To avoid a purely comical account, however, and assert the importance of this £5 million study, a professor explains the significance further (Ghosh, 2013a). He is interested in the study of – to use his words – "brain development and mental development in *normal* [sic] adolescence" (italics my own). Such an assertion is not unusual, as Elman (2014, p. 139) points out, neurological research has often concentrated on "visualizing and mapping the 'normal' brain" and from this making comparisons to the "abnormal". Moreover, the "teenage brain" is almost always envisioned as normally-abnormal, in its "unfinished" state (Elman, 2014). Ghosh, for example, tells us that as a person grows from child to adult, emotional, behavioural and cognitive changes occur which can be attributed to brain restructuring. He wants to understand two elements, which change between child and adult: learning how to control emotions in order to interact with people; and the ability of forward thought. Through this, he hopes to develop games, which could help speed up young people's development of their cognitive control. Like Cameron, the professor feels youth is a stage that should be passed through as quickly as possible.

Elman (2014) explores some of the material consequences of positioning young people as "unfinished brains". Perhaps unsurprisingly when we consider the targeted psychologisation of certain populations of people (Goodley and Lawthom, 2005; Mills, 2014; Tosh, 2014), these consequences differ dependent upon socio-cultural positioning. For example, Elman (2014) writes that neurological accounts have been used to explain the actions of white youth (particularly young men in relation to American high school shootings), yet for African American and Latino young men they are used to justify screening and intervention. Rather than recognising social-cultural and political context, however, the BBC report portrays neurology as scientific (that is: neutral, objective) knowledge which we could read into Susan and her pals talking about teenagers. Yet, the BBC reporter does admit that these studies are in their early stages. Payne (2010) explains, however, that despite the embryonic nature of neurological studies, they have nevertheless been widely taken up by policy makers, largely because they fit with early and mid-twentieth century notions of adolescence.

The website accompanying the BBC report confirms this when it explains Granville Stanley Hall's evolutionary model of adolescence not as historical, but as current theory. Proclaiming that:

> every individual rehearses the evolutionary history of their species.
> Emotions arise from more primitive brain regions and so according to this theory they develop more quickly than higher, more rational brain functions as a person grows up. The human brain [... is] carrying a lot of evolutionary baggage – which may be at the root of the difficulties of the teenage years. (Ghosh, 2013a)

We have already seen the prejudice inherent in conversations of recapitulation theory (Lesko, 2002; Slater, 2015); the supposed neutrality and possible consequences of neurological investigations therefore also need to come into question. As well as wanting to understand "normal adolescence", the professor involved in the study tells us that understanding the normal-abnormality of the teenage brain, may help us understand the abnormality of other brains deemed non-normative; those who have not, or it is assumed will not, grow out of the normal-abnormality of youth as, at this, alarms bells begin to ring.

Fine Lines of Normal and Abnormal Abnormality

That youth is "risky" is confirmed to us in a best-selling parenting book from 2003, *Yes, Your Teen is Crazy: Loving Your Kids Without Losing Your Mind*. In the opening chapter psychologist Michael Bradley seems to confirm the normal, yet undesirable, abnormality of youth. He explains to worried parents that although the mood swings of their teenagers may appear "uniquely crazy", they are in fact, just like those demonstrated by all other teenagers. To use his words, all teenagers are "commonly crazy". He tells us that:

23

> The good part is that these behaviours are not character flaws or signs of an evil nature. In adolescent children, this maddening behaviour is just the result of mixed-up brain wiring which will straighten out in time if, if, and only if we adults respond not with raging, hurtful punishments, but with carefully crafted responses intended to calmly but firmly teach brain-challenged children to become functional adults.
> (Bradley, 2003, p. 8)

The comparisons made in this text between the teenage brain and those labelled with "mental health problems" are overt. This is perhaps unsurprising when we consider the similarly loaded discourse youth and mental health share. Crowe (2000) highlights a lack of productivity, unity, moderation and rationality as recurring markers of "mental disorder" set out by *DSM-IV*. A similar set of homogenised behaviours is attributed to teenagers: young people are lazy and passive (there is a lack of productivity); they're scorned for their pack-like behaviour (identity crisis leading to lack of unity); and they're subject to mood swings (cognitive instability leading to a lack of moderation and irrationality) (Lesko, 1996b). Yet, unlike the temporary abnormality of youth, psychiatric and other brain-related labels stick; not only read as a sign of the individual's past and present, but also "dominating the future" (Crowe, 2000, p. 69). Therefore, although on first glance, Bradley appears to be reiterating the discourse we have been continuously delivered thus far: non-normative behaviour is normal during adolescence. He doesn't assume the "commonly crazy" time of youth will be grown-out of, but instead instils youth as a time of risk (Kelly, 2003; Ortega and Choudhury, 2011). For Kelly (2003), the next question to ask is, at risk of what …? Reconceptualising youth as border zones in the next section can help us to address this question.

(Re)-conceptualising Youth (2): Youth as Border Zones
Key to a forgiving albeit pathologising discourse of youth as abnormals-becoming-normal is an assurance that young people "grow-up" to meet the normality of adulthood. The risk, then, is that this adulthood normativity – dependent upon racialised, classed, gendered, ableist and hetero-normative assumptions of what "adults" should do and be (Slater, 2015) – will not be met. Youth as abnormal-becoming-normal, in fact, is a discourse which only works through dangerously pathologising those deemed Other. David Cameron can only justify his actions as "youthful stupidity" [*sic*] by marginalising people with labels of "intellectual impairment". Similarly, Bradley's (2003) reassurance that all teenagers are "commonly crazy" delivers harmful messages around what is normal and abnormal mental health.

Lesko's (2002) conceptualisation of youth as a border zone can help us see this more clearly. Lesko argues that technologies such as schools, families and youth services work in particular gendered, raced, sexualised, and ability dependent ways, to shape children, through youth, to meet the social, cultural and political adulthood requirements of a particular time and place (see Figure 2 overleaf). As in the depiction of youth as abnormals-becoming-normal, we see the same normative image of a family on the left – a female, male and child figure represented. A sole male adult figure again represents adulthood on the right-hand side. In between, however, labelled "border zone of youth" is a surveillance tower. There are numerous arrows going between the child and male adult figure. Some pass through the border zone directly, whilst others take a less direct route. Some aren't allowed to pass at all, either dwelling in border zones, or returning to childhood. Border zones can be dangerous places, and what the next part of the chapter will now go on to explore,

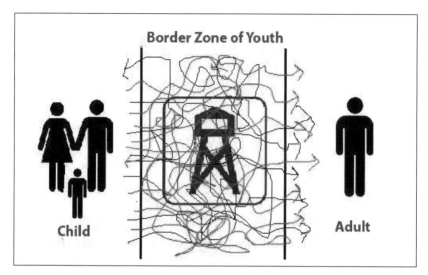

Figure 2: Border Zone of Youth.

is why the border zone of youth may be more dangerous for some than for others. The following three stories illustrate the potential dangers of border zones of youth.

Space to "Be Young"? Border Zones of Youth as Dangerous
The first story emerges from a one year auto/ethnography with young disabled people in the UK and Iceland which interrogated the meanings we associate with "youth", "adult", "disabled" and "able" (Slater, 2013c, 2015). Workshops over one year were spent with two disabled youth groups in England (27 young people with different genders, physical and intellectual impairment labels). Three months was then spent with two young disabled women running Reykjavik's Independent Living Cooperative. Data was collected using creative art-based methods, interviews and fieldwork notes. The term auto/ethnography was employed to highlight that although the aim of research was not to tell the author's story, the author's story was significant and tangled amongst the stories of others. The author's telling of stories is

thus treated as data in this chapter. The research was deemed ethically sound by a university ethics committee. Following this, all names from the fieldwork, except Freyja, who chose to be identified, are pseudonyms. More stories from this research project and details on methodology are included in Slater (2015).

A conversation taking place between a mother of a young man with a label of "intellectual impairment" and Freyja, one of my participants, went as follows:

> **Mother**: Bjarne was annoyed last night.
> **Freyja**: Oh dear, what about?
> **Mother**: I'm not sure. I kept asking him but never got to the bottom of it.
> **Freyja**: Sometimes we don't really know ourselves.
> **Mother**: Yeah but with Bjarne I constantly want a reason! Without a reason it's easy for other people to call it "challenging behaviour". I want to be able to say, "He's pissed off because you didn't let him choose his own dinner, you would be too!"... But he must get annoyed with my constant asking. I never do it with my other kids; they're allowed to just be moody teenagers.
> (Based on notes from research diary in Slater, 2013a, p. 203)

Socio-cultural accounts, backed up by developmental discourse and more recent neurological studies, have already told us about young people's mood swings. Yet, they've also told us not to worry, as young people will grow up into rational adults. Disability, however, is rarely associated with rationality (Slater, 2015). Disabled people's applications to be granted a passport of adulthood and cross border zones of youth, therefore, are likely to meet rejection. Bjarne's mother is aware of this. Rather than pathologised, but forgiven, as a temporary and "normal" part of adolescence, Bjarne's mother worries that Bjarne's moods will be read as a sign of his impairment. Considered outside of normative developmental discourse, a label of "challenging behaviour" has the potential to dominate Bjarne's life. Therefore, she felt she needed to argue Bjarne into a discourse of adulthood rationality in order to challenge the pathologisation of his "bad mood" as an impairment-thing. Yet, Bjarne's mother also worried that her actions may be denying him the opportunity to "be" a teenager in a bad mood; to "live" the non-normativity of youth.

Furthermore, it is not only disabled young people who may not feel able to dwell in border zones of youth for too long. Bringing together disability and critical race theory, Watts and Erevelles (2004) note the disproportionate number of black and Latino young people given labels associated with "intellectual impairment" or "mental health problems". We have already seen the racist roots of development theory, and we should not write off the racism of developmentalism as only historical. Boom (2014, para. 1), for example, writes of her struggles to feed her body as a young queer woman of colour. "To be a woman in the Western world", she writes, "is to understand that your worth stems from the ability to be thin, passive, agreeable, servile and beautiful." She goes on to frame becoming-woman as an attempt to become-white:

> When I was thirteen years old I began starving myself. I did so, in short, because I wanted so desperately to be thin. And by thin, I mainly meant white. I wished to be slimmer, smaller, slighter because that was the beauty I saw beamed at me from the TV shows I so desperately clung to in a bid to escape and from the magazines I pored over, fascinated by the lithe limbs and flawless milky skin of the models within their pages. When I saw these images I felt not just abnormal but abhorrent. An aberration. Furthermore, next to my svelte, slight, white friends I felt monstrous and vast, an expanse of disappointment next to their slim elegance. Their hair fell in straight sheens of silk and their skin shone like snow. My hair was unruly, disobedient and permanently reaching up to the sky. My skin felt dirty and dull pulled over swathes of myself that I wished would disappear. In

photos I loomed over them, broader, taller, darker. They seemed to obey the contours of their bodies, but I was spilling out of mine. I desperately tried to occupy less space, to shut my mouth, to flatten my hair with painful relaxers. Dismayed with the fullness of my lips and how I thought they betrayed my ancestry, I used to bite down into my bottom lip hard enough to let blood run, convinced that this would make them smaller. I stayed sullenly in the shade, wore Factor 50 suncream and only ever let myself sunbathe under layers of towels. I did not dare catch the light lest it accentuated my Otherness in the bright unrelenting white of my suburban surroundings. (Boom, 2014, para. 3)

We see here Boom feeling that an interlinked necessity of becoming-adult is to become-white. Furthermore, Dyson, commenting on the Trayvon Martin tragedy, points out the dangers of "youth" for black boys:

The fear for – and, unfortunately, of – our sons of color is paramount. It allows no room for black boys to be kids – to wear hoodies when it rains, to wear jeans that fall in line with the current fashion trends; mothers fear their growth spurts, facial hair, and voice changes. (Dyson, 2013, para. 14)

She quotes a mother's comment on an article titled "I'm Afraid to Raise a Little Black Boy":

My biracial son is 15. I made him cut his hair over the weekend to look less black. This fear you speak of is making me crazy. My own child didn't understand why I insisted on him keeping his hair short now. (Biddy commenting on Jefferson, 2013)

Whilst Boom's teenage-self felt that growing up meant she had to try to become-white, for this mother, the only way to keep her son safe is for him to "pass" as white. We understand this mother's logic when considering the numbers of black young men (and women, non-binary people and children) incarcerated

(Davis, 2003) or killed by the police (Black Lives Matter, 2015). For Elman (2014, p. 2), the anxieties around youth are clear: youth is "the possibility and peril of a future citizen who may yet be anything [this proto-citizen] may not turn out straight or gender-normative, may not be white, may not be nondisabled, may not be a productive worker who adheres to the economic and cultural values of U.S. capitalism." Young people are "unfinished projects". The space and freedom that youthful non-normativity is often presumed to allow, therefore, can only be played out by the most normative of young people, in the most normative of ways. Furthermore, what is striking about the above stories is the demand for young people and their families to be self-surveying.

Youth and Self-Surveillance
For Giroux (2009) to understand the positioning of young people today we need to note a neoliberal change in attitude towards young people. Although media rhetoric was not wholly positive, the post-war years were met with a desire to make a world "fit for heroic young soldiers". Aided by greater Western affluence and the development of the welfare state, this meant that young people were instilled with hopes and ideals of a future generation worth protection and investment (France, 2007). It is important to note that such a discourse was neither inclusive of all young people, nor without its own problems of assumed future adulthood normativity. Border zones of youth were rife (Lesko, 2002). Youth considered "at risk" were subject to intervention from various youth services (Kelly, 2003). Yet, this contrasts with a discourse presented to us today; with massive austerity cutbacks in the UK and elsewhere, youth services are under threat (Slater, 2015); the narrative therefore changes from one of protection and nurturing, to one of personal responsibility.

Youth and (Developing) Personal Responsibility: Considering the UK "Riots"

We see this narrative of personal responsibility if we look at discourse emerging after the so-named UK "riots" in summer 2011. Many of the people involved were young people of colour from poor neighbourhoods (Smith, 2011). Arguably *because* of this, media reports failed to see the action as a legitimate form of political resistance. Neither did most reports contextualise young people's actions in the uncertain futures and harsh political climates they were facing. The answer, even after the initial aftermath, wasn't to examine structural inequalities. Rather, a picture was painted of an uncontrollable "mindless mob" (Cavanagh and Dennis, 2012). News stories read under headlines such as "Battle for London" (*The Guardian*), "Rule of the Mob" (*The Telegraph*); "Yob Rule" (*Daily Mail*); and "Anarchy" (*The Sun*). Unable to resist tapping into the neurologically driven path, the *Daily Mail* ran a story under the headline "Rioters may have 'lower levels' of brain chemical that keeps impulsive behaviour under control" (*Daily Mail*, 2011). Yet, this impulsiveness wasn't attributed to a youthfulness that will be "naturally" grown-out of, but a diagnostic feature of *some* male brains linked to an equally un-contextualised and flippant comparison with "psychiatric disorders or substance dependence". Tellingly, a disclaimer was later added as the *Daily Mail* was asked to make clear that the study they were drawing on made no mention of "rioting". Nevertheless, this pathologisation of the teenage mind was used take focus away from any meaningful exploration of structural inequality, instead putting the focus on individuals.

Boris Johnson, Mayor of London, took to the streets; urging people to join him for a "Big Society" clean up. Blame was attributed to "broken families", a "lack of male role models", "moral collapse", and "social breakdown" (Smith, 2011). A

31

commentary in *The Guardian* was typical in its claim that the riots were a result of "allow[ing] our welfare system to prop up immoral lifestyles". The author claimed that, "[w]e have not taught young people that entitlement culture is wrong" (Bailey, 2011, para. 11). Rather than given any social or political context, young people were deemed an entitlement generation obsessed with the commodity (Brand, 2011).

Looking historically, this is not the first time that a moral panic has been sparked over the relationship between young people and the markets (Cohen, 2002). Similarly to its 2011 headline, "Yob Rule", in 1964 the *Daily Mail* reported the Margate Riots under the headline, "Wild Ones 'Beat Up' Margate". Although it is not an entirely undisputed notion (see France, 2007), for many the 1950s mark the first time that young people were recognised as consumers in their own right (Clarke, Hall, Jefferson, and Roberts, 2006; Hodkinson, 2008). With this came the rise of certain "youth subcultures" (France, 2007) and the claim that young people were being corrupted by the markets. A new discipline, youth subcultural studies emerged which aimed to challenge this, not by concentrating on individual psychologies or neurology, but contextualising young people's actions in social, political and cultural contexts (Hall and Jefferson, 2006). Largely this was done by considering relationships between youth, consumerism and the commodity. Young people's non-normativity was argued to be an act of resistance to the status quo. The arguments of youth subcultural theorists, therefore, are at least part of the reason that youth culture is largely projected as an identity-forming rite of passage (Bennett, 2008). For Bennett (2008), in fact, a hangover from the youth subcultural days leads us to another contradictory message delivered around young people today. We're told that young people are an apathetic generation, a pale reflection of our predecessors in the 1960s and 1970s (Bennett, 2008). Young people are just too normal!

Generational Differences: Youth as Not Abnormal Enough
An article appearing in *The Guardian* in July 2013 was typical of this as it juxtaposed teen idol Justin Bieber's conformity with the rebellion of The Rolling Stones (Hyde, 2013). Commenting on the article, one blogger wrote, "Perhaps these new kids could be given lessons on how to really behave disgracefully? Keith Richards could give them a few pointers at gun point" (comment by blogger, Strummered, in Hyde, 2013). What we're again lacking through the implicit and unthinking talk of youth in this comment is an updated social, political or cultural context. The author fails to point out that there were similarly manufactured bands in the 1960s and 1970s (The Monkees, The Osmonds and The Bay City Rollers, for example). Nor does he note the DIY music scenes that scatter the country today. Furthermore, since the time of the original subcultural work, the discipline has been criticised for focusing exclusively on public displays of white, male – and I'd add, non-disabled – youth (Dorn and South, 1999; McRobbie, 1980, 1990, 2000; Rattansi and Phoenix, 2005; Slater, 2015). McRobbie (1982), for example, argued in the 1980s that by focusing only on overtly public displays of young men, researchers excluded the more mundane, albeit just as real identity-forming experiences happening behind closed doors. There is no mention in this article of the other, less public ways young people are resisting the paths laid out for them. Perhaps most significantly, however, there is no acknowledgement of the demonising discourse and dangerous positions young people find themselves subject to when they do publicly rebel, such as during the riots. I turn now to another story from the fieldwork with young disabled people outlined above, which illustrates why, for many young people, embracing a youthful non-normativity is not an option.

A discussion with Colin, a young man and active disability activist about his job as a voluntary web designer for a local company went as follows:

> **Colin:** … no matter how ill I am I still struggle on.
> **Jenny:** I can imagine! Are you worried people will be like, it's 'cos he's a disabled person …
> **Colin:** Yeah. It hacks me off that people go out during the week, get absolutely hammered and then phone in sick the next day when there are people, disabled people out there, wanting to work and we can't get jobs. Recently, Philip Davis, the MP, said disabled people are scroungers … and that all the disability allowances get spent on trying to get things that non-disabled people have to work for – I don't agree.
> (Interview with Colin, 1 December 2011, cited in Slater, 2013a)

Colin told me that people's low expectations of him meant he was "sick of" having to prove himself above and beyond his peers, but also fearful of the consequences if he stopped. Reliant on expensive taxis for travel, Colin was more mobile during the week because his workplace subsidised his transport. One very obvious and immediate consequence of not proving himself adult enough to work would be to be physically restricted to his parental home. The choice was between forced dependency (akin to childhood), or self-disciplining adulthood responsibility – with little in between. Despite neurologists telling us that young people's underdeveloped pre-frontal cortex means they have little choice but to "live in the moment" (Payne, 2010), and sociologists telling us that youth is an "identity-forming rite of passage", Colin is allowed little freedom to embody the here-and-now non-normativity of youth. Not being allowed to pass through the border zone of youth could lead to paternalism and the denial of autonomy continuing into (chronological) adulthood (Baron, Riddell, and Wilson, 1999).

Furthermore, Colin also had structural barriers preventing him taking part in what we may consider "youthful activities". Going out for Colin, more than many of his peers, was an expensive feat. He told me stories of shelling out £40 for taxis, only to reach inaccessible venues. Ironically, gaining the "adult responsibility" of paid work could allow him periodical access to some practices that we might consider youthful, by increasing both his finances and autonomy. Yet, this could only happen on the assurance that the next day he could position himself once again as an adult worker.

Ironically, then, we see that for Colin, only by being accepted as adult, could he be allowed safe access (and periodical) access to youth. Furthermore, this passported access would have to be used carefully; dwell in the space of youthful non-normativity too long – miss a day at work, for example – and his opportunity to return back to adulthood may be denied.

(Re)-Conceptualising Youth (3): Youthful Non-Normativity Commodified

Through the stories told so far, our third relationship between youth and adulthood is beginning to emerge. Figure 3 (overleaf) shows the same figures of a family used in earlier sketches. However, on this occasion the family is repeated multiple times around the outside of a circle. Youth is not represented by a figure, but by a pound sign, placed in the centre of this circle, and next to it the words "non-normative youth commodified". This time the adult male in the family is the focus – the most normative representation of adulthood. He is circled in each depiction and an arrow leads him in and then back out of the circle, representing his ability to buy into, but then step back out of a commodified, compartmentalised youthful non-normativity. The youth-adult time binding is different: rather than an assumption that young people will grow out of a youthful non-normativity; there is a profit-driven expectation

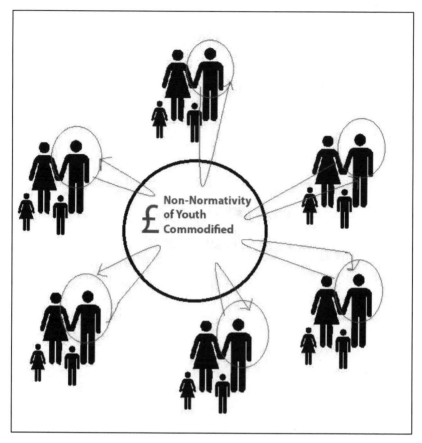

Figure 3: Non-Normativity of Youth Commodified.

that young people should be able to display the reasonableness and responsibility of adulthood, whilst periodically buying into, the non-normativity of youth. I turn now to choose a deliberately normative (i.e. white, middle-class, normatively gendered, heterosexist, minority world, ableist) example of the "student experience" to further illustrate the commodified non-normativity of youth.

The "Student Experience" and Commodified Youthful Non-Normativity

Considering the discourse of the student experience can help us understand how the strange contradiction of commodified and compartmentalised youthful non-normativity may play out in young people's lives. Prospective students at my own university are told on our website that they're "expected to study on [their] own much more than [they] might be used to" (Sheffield Hallam University, 2013). The rhetoric we as a team of lecturers employ on a daily basis is that students are "responsible" for their own learning, which should gradually become more "autonomous". The general message students are delivered is one of adulthood (Price, 2011; Slater, 2013b): you are not children (at school) any more – you're adults now, and should be able to take care of yourselves. Yet, Radcliffe (Chapter 2, this volume) highlights that although there is an expectation of future adulthood productivity, universities also expect (some – the most normative) students to want a *complete* "university experience"; and with this there is an expectation to be "social creatures". Although in the day students must demonstrate themselves as adults, on a night there is an engrained expectation to go out, get drunk, and embrace the identity-forming, non-normativity of youth.

A "school disco" themed student night local to my university, for example, plays up to its juxtaposition with the (adult) academic environment. Its promotional material reads:

> The Original Skool Disco, now celebrating over eight years of the finest lubrication of Sheffield's brightest young academic minds. Skools [*sic*] out, and it's time to do some serious Music and Biology revision at Sheffield's largest and loudest student night. Three rooms of musical mayhem unleash a massive party whatever your musical taste.
> (Corporation Nightclub, 2013)

There is a call to embrace what is considered the "natural" state of being which has to be (unnaturally) reined back during the day. Students are encouraged to "lubricate" in order to "unleash" animal instincts. Another student night, "Hallam Nation", conveys a similar message of "survival of the fittest" when it uses the words "harder ... better ... faster ... stronger" to sell itself (Embrace Nightclub, 2013). This commercialised and commodified discourse of a youthful non-normativity meshes cultural and evolutionary scripts of youth; presenting idealised and sexualised images of a youthful femininity to be lived up to, that many young people would not recognise themselves within. For Filipovic (2008, p. 19), such representation leads to a dangerous "boys will be boys" discourse where men are "expected to be aggressive sexual actors attempting to "get" sex from passive women who both hold and embody sex itself". We are taken right back to the beginning of this chapter as, despite being portrayed as a space of non-normativity, we once again see that youth is suffocated in dangerously normative rules.

Where Are We Left?
Lennard Davis (2010, p. 3) tells us "we live in a world of norms"; everything measured "along some conceptual line from subnormal to above average". In this chapter I have thought about how this claim sits with our perceptions of "youth"; a time, we are often told, that is anything but normal. My romp through various illustrative representations of youth, however, has left me inclined to agree with Davis. The only way to safely live a youthful non-normativity, it seems, is to fit into various other normative constructions.

This means, ironically, at first being granted an adulthood passport, which will periodically allow you temporary access to a commodified and commercialised, youthful non-normativity. Although for a few (white, non-disabled, heterosexual, North

American or Western European, middle-class, cisgendered males) this passport may be an entitlement, for many crossing the border zone of youth becomes a necessarily self-disciplining project. This is at best difficult, and, at worst devastating. Furthermore, the requirement of the neoliberal subject to be fluid and flexible enough to jump painlessly between commodified youthful non-normativity and adulthood responsibility is in itself, youthful (Hughes, Russell, and Paterson, 2005; Slater, 2012).

Beware the trip wires of normalcy criss-crossing the border zone of youth – they can be hard to see.

References

Bailey, S. (2011, 10 August). Riots without responsibility, Comment, *The Guardian*. Retrieved from http://www.guardian.co.uk/commentisfree/2011/aug/10/riots-without-responsibility

Baron, S., Riddell, S., & Wilson, A. (1999). The secret of eternal youth: Identity, risk and learning difficulties. *British Journal of Sociology of Education, 20*(4), 483–499. doi:10.1080/0142569999 5227

Bennett, A. (2008). As young as you feel: Youth as a discursive construct. In P. Hodkinson & W. Deicke (Eds.), *Youth cultures: Scenes, subcultures and tribes* (pp. 23–36). Abingdon, United Kingdom: Routledge.

Black Lives Matter. (2015). Retrieved 21 May 2015, from http://blacklivesmatter.com/

Boom, K. (2014, 2 September). The ersatz emancipation of femininity: On being a bulimic, brown lesbian. Retrieved 2 September 2014, from http://www.autostraddle.com/the-ersatz-emancipation-of-femininity-on-being-a-bulimic-brown-lesbian-249792/

Bradley, M. J. (2003). *Yes, your teen is crazy!: Loving your kid without losing your mind*. Madeira Park, Canada: Harbor Press.

Brand, R. (2011, 12 August). Big Brother isn't watching you, *The Guardian*, p. 4. Retrieved from http://www.guardian.co.uk/uk/2011/aug/11/london-riots-davidcameron

Burman, E. (2008). *Developments: Child, image, nation.* Hove, United Kingdom: Routledge.

Cavanagh, A., & Dennis, A. (2012). Framing the riots. *Capital and Class, 36*(3), 375–381. doi: 10.1177/0309816812453599

Clarke, J., Hall, S., Jefferson, T., & Roberts, B. (2006). Subcultures, cultures and class. In S. Hall & T. Jefferson (Eds.), *Resistance through rituals: Youth subcultures in post-war Britain* (2nd ed., pp. 3–59). Abingdon, United Kingdom: Routledge.

Cohen, S. (2002). *Folk devils and moral panics: The creation of the mods and the rockers* (3rd ed.). London, United Kingdom: Routledge.

Corporation Nightclub. (2013). Club nights. Retrieved 9 September 2013, from http://www.corporation.org.uk/nights.php

Crowe, M. (2000). Constructing normality: A discourse analysis of the DSM-IV. *Journal of Psychiatric and Mental Health Nursing, 7*(1), 69–77.

Daily Mail. (2011, 9 August). Rioters may have "lower levels" of brain chemical that keeps impulsive behaviour under control, *Mail Online.* Retrieved from http://www.dailymail.co.uk/ sciencetech/article-2024173/Rioters-lower-levels-brain-chemical-keeps-impulsive-behaviour-control.html

Davis, A. Y. (2003). *Are prisons obselete?* New York, NY: Seven Stories Press.

Davis, L. J. (2010). Constructing normalcy. In L. J. Davis (Ed.), *The disability studies reader* (3rd ed., pp. 3–19). London, United Kingdom: Routledge.

Dorn, N., & South, N. (1999). Youth, the family and the regulation of the "informal". In N. South (Ed.), *Youth crime, deviance and delinquency* (Vol. 1). Aldershot, United Kingdom: Ashgate.

Dyson, E. Z. V. (2013, 20 July). Finally, the conversation about race in America we need, *The Guardian.* Retrieved from http://www.guardian.co.uk/commentisfree/2013/jul/20/conversation-race-america

Elman, J. P. (2014). *Chronic youth: Disability, sexuality, and U.S. media cultures of rehabilitation.* New York, NY; London, United Kingdom: New York University Press.

Embrace Nightclub. (2013). Events Retrieved 9 September 2013, from http://www.embracenightclub.com/index.php?option=com_contentandview=articleandid=9andItemid=4

The (Normal) Non-Normativity of Youth

Enfield, H. (Writer). (1990–1992). *Harry Enfield's Television Programme.* London, United Kingdom: Endemol UK.

Enfield, H. (Writer). (1994–1998). *Harry Enfield and Chums.* London, United Kingdom: Endemol UK.

Filipovic, J. (2008). Offensive feminism: The Conservative gender norms that perpetuate rape culture, and how feminists can fight back. In J. Friedman & J. Valenti (Eds.), *Yes means yes!: Visions of female sexual power and a world without rape* (pp. 13–28). Berkeley, CA: Seal Press.

France, A. (2007). *Understanding youth in late modernity.* Maidenhead, United Kingdom: Open University Press.

Ghosh, P. (2013a, 14 May). Brain scan study to understand workings of teenage mind, *BBC News: Health.* London, United Kingdom: BBC News. Retrieved from http://www.bbc.co.uk/news/health-22510866

Ghosh, P. (2013b). *Brain scan study to understand workings of teenage mind.* London, United Kingdom: BBC News. Retrieved from http://www.bbc.co.uk/news/health-22510866

Giroux, H. (2009). *Youth in a suspect society: Democracy or disposability?* New York, NY: Palgrave Macmillan.

Goodley, D., & Lawthom, R. (Eds.). (2005). *Disability and psychology: Critical introductions and reflections.* Basingstoke, United Kingdom: Palgrave Macmillan.

Hall, G. S. (1904). *Adolescence: Its psychology and its relations to physiology, anthropology, sociology, sex, crime, religion and education* (Vols. 1 and 2). New York, NY: Appleton.

Hall, S., & Jefferson, T. (Eds.). (2006). *Resistance through rituals: Youth subcultures in post-war Britain* (2nd ed.). Abingdon, United Kingdom: Routledge.

Hodkinson, P. (2008). Youth cultures: A critical outline of key debates. In P. Hodkinson & W. Deicke (Eds.), *Youth cultures: Scenes, subcultures and tribes* (pp. 1–22). Abingdon, United Kingdom: Routledge.

Hughes, B., Russell, R., & Paterson, K. (2005). Nothing to be had "off the peg": Consumption, identity and the immobilization of young disabled people. *Disability and Society, 20*(1), 3–17.

Hyde, M. (2013, 19 July). If it's between Bieber and a bombing suspect, who can blame Rolling Stone?, *The Guardian*, p. 36. Retrieved from http://www.guardian.co.uk/commentisfree/ 2013/jul/19/bieber-bombing-suspect-rolling-stone-bore

Jefferson, T. P. (2013, 2 July). I'm afraid to raise a little brown boy. Retrieved from http://www.theyoungmommylife.com/2013/07/02/im-afraid-to-raise-a-little-brown-boy/

Kelly, P. (2003). Growing up as risky business? Risks, surveillance and the institutionalized mistrust of youth. *Journal of Youth Studies, 6*(2), 165–180.

Lesko, N. (1996a). Denaturalizing adolescence: The politics of contemporary representations. *Youth and Society, 28*(2), 139–161.

Lesko, N. (1996b). Past, present, and future conceptions of adolescence. *Educational Theory, 46*(4), 453–472.

Lesko, N. (2002). Making adolescence at the turn of the century: Discourse and the exclusion of girls. *Current Issues in Comparative Education, 2*(2), 182–190.

Lesko, N. (2012). *Act your age: A cultural construction of adolescence* (2nd ed.). New York, NY; London, United Kingdom: Routledge.

McRobbie, A. (1980). Settling accounts with subcultures: A feminist critique. *Screen Education, 34*(Spring), 37–49.

McRobbie, A. (1982). Jackie: An ideology of adolescent femininity. In B. Waites, T. Bennett, & G. Martin (Eds.), *Popular culture, past and present: A reader* (pp. 263–283). London, United Kingdom: Croom Helm.

McRobbie, A. (1990). *Feminism and youth culture.* London, United Kingdom: Routledge.

McRobbie, A. (2000). The culture of working class girls. In A. McRobbie (Ed.), *Feminism and youth culture* (2nd ed., pp. 44–66). London, United Kingdom: Macmillan Press. Retrieved on 5 December 2016 from http://www.gold.ac.uk/media/working-class-girls.pdf

Mills, C. (2014). *Decononising global mental health: The psychiatrization of the majority world.* London, United Kingdom; New York, NY: Routledge.

Ortega, F., & Choudhury, S. (2011). "Wired up differently'": Autism, adolescence and the politics of neurological identities. *Subjectivity, 4*(3), 323–345.

The (Normal) Non-Normativity of Youth

Paronnaud, V., & Satrapi, M. (Writers). (2008). *Persepolis* [Animation]. In X. Rigault & M.-A. Robert (Producer). France, USA: Sony Pictures.

Payne, M. A. (2010). Teen brain science and the contemporary storying of psychological (im)maturity. In H. Blatterer & J. Glahn (Eds.), *Times of our lives: Making sense of growing up and growing old* (pp. 55–68). Oxford, United Kingdom: Inter-disciplinary Press.

Price, M. (2011). *Mad at school: Rhetorics of mental disability and academic life*. Michigan, MI: The University of Michigan Press.

Rattansi, A., & Phoenix, A. (2005). Rethinking youth identities: Modernist and postmodernist frameworks. *Identity, 5*(2), 97–123.

Sheffield Hallam University. (2013). Your learning experience. Retrieved 15 July 2013, from http://www.shu.ac.uk/study/ undergraduate/learning-experience.html

Slater, J. (2012). Youth for sale: Using critical disability perspectives to examine the embodiment of 'youth'. *Societies, 2*(3), 195–209.

Slater, J. (2013a). *Constructions, perceptions and expectations of being young and disabled: A critical disability perspective.* (Doctoral thesis, Manchester Metropolitan University, Manchester, United Kingdom).

Slater, J. (2013b). Playing grown-up: Using critical disability perspectives to rethink youth. In A. Azzopardi (Ed.), *Youth: Responding to lives – an international handbook* (pp. 75–92). Rotterdam, The Netherlands: Sense Publications.

Slater, J. (2013c). Research with dis/abled youth: Taking a critical disability, "critically young" positionality. In K. Runswick-Cole and T. Curran (Eds.), *Disabled children's childhood studies: Critical approaches in a global context* (pp. 180–195). Basingstoke, United Kingdom: Palgrave.

Slater, J. (2015). *Youth and dis/ability: A challenge to Mr Reasonable.* Farnham, United Kingdom: Ashgate.

Smith, M. (2011). Young people and the 2011 "riots" in England – experiences, explanations and implications for youth work. *The encyclopedia of informal education*, http://www.infed.org/ archives/jeffs_and_smith/young_people_youth_work_and_the_20 11_riots_in_england.html

Snowdon, K. (2015, 21 September). Bullingdon Club: Five facts about the super rich elite Oxford University drinking club. *The Huffington*

43

Post, accessed 3 December 2015 at: http://www.huffingtonpost.co.uk/2015/09/21/bullingdon-club-five-things-we know_n_8169064.html

Sparrow, A. (2011, 2 September). Bullingdon Club antics were nothing like the riots, says Cameron, *The Guardian.* Retrieved from http://www.guardian.co.uk/politics/2011/sep/02/bullingdon-club-david-cameron-riots

Tosh, J. (2014). *Perverse psychology: The pathologization of sexual violence and transgenderism.* London, United Kingdom; New York, NY: Routledge.

Watt, N. (2009, 25th August). Cameron the troubled teenager: Leader is latest to admit he drank too much, *The Guardian,* p. 4. Retrieved from http://www.guardian.co.uk/politics/2009/aug/25/davidcameron-williamhague

Watts, I. E., & Erevelles, N. (2004). These deadly times: Reconceptualizing school violence by using critical race theory and disability studies. *American Educational Research Journal, 41*(2), 271–299.

Wyn, J., & White, R. (1997). *Rethinking youth.* London, United Kingdom: Sage.

CHAPTER 2

DECONSTRUCTING THE "NORMAL" STUDENT. A DISCOURSE ANALYSIS OF "PROSPECTIVE STUDENT" MATERIALS ACROSS THREE INSTITUTIONS

Lucia Radcliffe

Summary

This chapter is based on my undergraduate dissertation (2013), which asked how is a "normal" student constructed? This small-scale research project focused on the perceived experience of a prospective student applying to higher education within one city. Discourse analysis was used to highlight and discover what language was used to shape the institutions' expectations of a student. Although it might appear that this study was about normal students, it was in fact about difference and how students are defined and categorised by their individual differences. The findings have been themed around the concepts of futurism, being academic, individual and homogenised constructions of difference. It then proceeded to consider the possible consequences for prospective students when institutional discourses of "normal" and "abnormal" interact using a concept called "spheres of normalcy".

Introduction

This chapter is based on my undergraduate research dissertation, completed in 2013. It was the culmination of a process of healing which began four years previously at the start of my degree, agreeing with hooks (1994, p. 59) who states "I saw in theory then a location for healing". The overarching theme of recruitment and retention in higher education was fuelled by my largely negative higher education experiences and the use of different labels that defined my experiences. I really wanted to utilise these as a tool of critical reflection.

However, I felt that my situational knowledge and, therefore, position as a researcher would have jeopardised the

45

outcomes of any participant focused research (Cohen, Manion, and Morrison, 2011). Thankfully, serendipity led me to discourse analysis which enabled me to continue to focus on the higher education sector, without the need to use participants. As Snyder and Mitchell (2006, p. 201) state "textually based analysis is the only absolute remedy for the exhaustion of people-based research practices".

My original dissertation had a stringent ethics requirement. In order to comply with this I anonymised the institutions analysed. However, due to the non-normative approach of my dissertation, there was little need because participants were not included. On reflection, this is probably why there was some identifying information retained and I decided to leave it anonymised for this chapter in recognition of this struggle.

Contextual Information

Normalton is a northern city in the UK of great contrasts. Some of the poorest council wards sit alongside some of the richest in the country. This is reflected in its higher education provision, which is where the study was focused. The first institution that was used for the study was a further education college "Cobyt"; this provides a number of higher education courses serving 630 students. This provision is based across three campuses within the city in some of the lower socioeconomic areas. The second is a university, "Polus", which is based across two sites and has its roots in being a polytechnic college. It became a university in 1992 and provides higher education to 29,519 students. It has a city centre presence as well as a campus in one of the richest council wards in the country. The third institution, also a university, "Urbix" is based on one campus and provides higher education to 24,765 students. Established in 1905 it is part of the Russell Group of universities which makes it one of the top research universities in the country and it is based in one of the higher socioeconomic areas in the city.

Critical Summary of the Research Plan

The purpose of the study was to use discourse analysis to explore how the three higher education providers in one city constructed the student identity to their prospective students, using true data but anonymised for ethical reasons. These questions were posed:

1. How does the dominant discourse construct a "normal" student?
   a. What language is used to shape the institutions' expectations of a "normal" student?
   b. How is the discourse being maintained?

2. How does the dominant discourse construct an "abnormal" student?
   a. What language is used to shape the institutions' expectations of an "abnormal" student?
   b. How is the discourse being maintained?

3. What are the possible consequences for prospective students when institutional discourses of "normal" and "abnormal" interact?

This study draws on Luna's (2009) use of discourse analysis. Luna (2009) focuses on both language and power relationships to discover the dominant discourse that exists around being a "learning disabled" labelled student at one institution. Incorporating a previous participatory study, Luna (2009) uses documentary, speech and interview analysis. Luna discovers the construction of a negative discourse, which deters students from seeking out support because of the stigma associated with that label and its all-encompassing impact. This was a key text as it reflected the aims and methodology of the study.

Crowe (2000, p. 70) states "texts which align themselves to authoritative discourses are likely to have more authority" and this is also reinforced by Georgakopoulou and Goutsos (1999), who focus on text-based analysis (albeit from a linguistic perspective of discourse analysis). Therefore, focusing on institutional level documentation enabled the collaborative voice of many different authors to be heard, whilst still having the university discourse dominating through the style, branding and editing. It was this voice that was analysed.

Discourse analysis focuses on the language used to construct the realities of these institutions (Mills, 2003, 2004). Unlike other methodologies it enabled the research to get to the heart of the institutions' thinking whilst circumventing the need for direct contact with them. Non-contact was essential for the viability of the analysis, as time was limited and few resources available for direct contact. However, despite sounding ethically dubious, an equivalent participant focused project would be the observation of people within a public space, which would have few ethical restrictions bar anonymity.

Therefore, the final research plan took all of these aspects of discourse analysis and utilised them, taking into account the aims, focus and positionality of the researcher. This approach enabled the researcher to use the situational knowledge (Rose, 1997) of being a prospective student more effectively without jeopardising the results. It also gave a large amount of data and documentation which contain rich discourses, as it is intended to be used at key points along the university admissions process (Lowrie, 2007). As Crowe (2000) stated the validity of a document increases with the number of authors who wrote it. A prospectus is a collaboration of all areas of an institution with many different authors and is the very public face of an institution. Complementing this with other documents that an institution produces for new students would allow the research to discover the overall discourse of the institution.

Unfortunately, although a written prospectus is a uniform aspect of most higher education provision, the lack of uniformity in other areas prevented direct comparison. However, it enabled other conclusions to be made about the lack or existence of expected documentation. Data collection was restricted by the research plan, which was to consider the experiences of a prospective student. Nothing was used that wasn't directly available from new student areas as it was concluded that a prospective student would be limited by the websites' directional cues for prospective students and wouldn't seek out additional policy or documentation.

Using a city where provision was diverse and varied allowed the study of three institutions which resulted in a more coherent and varied analysis. This was also more ethically sound. For example, one of the chosen institutions had little documentation around its higher education provision, which revealed a lot about how it constructs a "normal" student.

In summary, the research plan was to ascertain the dominant discourse of the construction of a student across three institutions in one city. A process of discourse analysis and the lens of normalcy was used (Davis, 2002; Goodley, 2013), situating the researcher as a prospective student to analyse the prospective student materials of each institution.

Literature Review
Whilst attempting to define "normal" for the purpose of this study it was realised how important language is to prospective students and other stakeholders within the study's context. This critical literature review focuses on language and current government policy and ideology to contextualise the findings of the research.

Within disability studies, Davis (2002) explores normalcy and language, arguing that both the disabled/abled binary and correct and incorrect language are social constructs. According to Davis (2002) even the term normalcy has its own rules and "proper" context and use. He argues that the intangible nature of what is considered "normal" makes it problematic to define

49

(Davis, 2002). Although Crowe (2000), Davis (2002) and Madriaga, Hanson, Kay, and Walker (2011) argue that society defines "normality" as the absence of disease, illness or imperfection this can be challenged by language and societal reversal. In the video *Talk* (Disability Rights Commission, 2013) and Green's (2013) article, disability becomes "the normal" and non-disabled people are considered "abnormal". This highlights the inequalities that face disabled people compared to the non-disabled by attempting to portray a fresh perspective and making it easier for them to empathise. This reversal also highlights the social model ideology (Oliver, 1996) that disability and ability only exist within the context of the environmental constraints of a society. As Goodley (2013) aptly argues "normality is a precarious state" and that "normal" people are constantly anxious about remaining normal. This somewhat humorous statement reveals that whoever is considered normal within society has a sense of power, or as Luna (2009) infers, those who don't fit are powerless. Goodley (2013) also argues that the label society assigns you is fluid and can change dependent on time and spatial boundaries.

Language is also important, and as Davis (2002) argues it is paramount to define and shape people's experience within a certain context. If there is an internal desire to be normal, and if the construction of that normality is precarious and somewhat problematic (Goodley, 2013), then there would be a need to seek out a place where the dominant construction of normal fits best within oneself. Through an exclusionary process, Crowe (2000) uses the dominant discourse of mental illness (abnormality) to argue that this will ultimately and conversely construct a "normality". Crowe (2000) argues that the *DSM-IV* is not only used to construct mental illness, but also the opposite and is a type of norming device used by society. Relating this to the research, which hopes to analyse the use of language to ascertain what the normal student is, will therefore, according to Oliver (1996), Crowe (2000), Davis (2002) and Madriaga et al. (2011), reveal the "normal" student that is being recruited, who holds the power within the socially constructed world of the university microcosm. Perhaps, more importantly it will also reveal how the abnormal student is constructed.

Within Queer theory the concept of Heteronormativity is defined as the pervasiveness of practices and language that help to construct society's sexual normality (Sherry, 2004). They argue that the assumption of heterosexuality is a constant and reinforces the notion that homosexuality is abnormal. This assumption is present within all aspects of society on both conscious and unconscious levels. Within that, language is important, as it helps to construct the normal sexual practice as well as turn abnormal practice into deviant behaviour. It can also relate to how the construction of other social norms invades all areas of society's thinking. Relating this to the higher education sector, Madriaga et al. (2011, p. 901) argue that the "pervasiveness of normalcy" encompasses all aspects of the student experience. Anyone who falls outside this will feel excluded by the language, reflected practice and the construction of a reality based on those rules (Luna, 2009; Madriaga et al. 2011). Although Madriaga et al., (2011) focus solely on disability they conclude by calling for "these fixed hierarchies based on normalcy… to be cast aside" (Madriaga et al., 2011, p. 916). These comments justify the expansion of the focus to include all the divisive labels that exist within higher education, rather than perpetuating the segregation by only focusing on one element of discrimination or one minority group.

The current UK government's general ideology centres on the notion of independence from state "dependency" and has resulted in increased privatisation and a free and open market (Department for Business, Innovation and Skills, 2012a;

Seymour, 2012). At the time of writing, the UK government was a Conservative/Liberal Democrat Coalition. Within education the government has introduced free schools and academies, which gives schools the "freedom" to be run outside of local authority control (Department for Education, 2013). Paradoxically, the government has also introduced an "academically rigid curriculum" focused on "traditional educational values" (Richardson, 2010). Despite an apparent push towards independence, the government is still controlling educational policy and ideology.

This paradox can also be seen in the higher education sector. In 2012, the government introduced a free and open market through the implementation of uncapped fees (Department for Business, Innovation and Skills, 2012b). This made monetary value the new focus of higher education, instead of the previous indicators of competition and academic ability (Meek, 2000). As Lowrie (2007) elaborates, money is a catalyst that drives the objectification of a degree and the institutions as a brand to be bought and sold. What is key, however, is the source of this funding. In 2012 when uncapped fees were introduced (Department for Business, Innovation and Skills, 2012b) the government cut the teaching grants directly to the institutions (Thompson and Bekhradnia, 2010). This shifted the main source of funding for the institutions on to students (Department for Business, Innovation and Skills, 2012a). This in turn made it essential for institutions to recruit and retain students in order to maintain the level of funding needed to continue providing education (Department for Business, Innovation and Skills, 2012b). However, as the government continues to provide financial support for students (GOV.UK, 2013) it could be argued that they still fund this sector, but in a more fragmented and second-hand way.

This would suggest that the government and higher education institutions are acting as gatekeepers. Corra and Willer (2002, p. 180) state that "a gatekeeper controls access to 'benefits' valued by others as their clients". Within the higher education sector the institutions would be situated in this role, as they act as a gatekeeper to the student and graduate identity. Although it might appear that the institutions "own" the "product", Corra and Willer (2002) go on to argue that there is a certain degree of externality to the gatekeeper role, which when relating this to education, happens in two ways. Firstly the student retains the benefits of education when they graduate, as education is more of a transfer of knowledge than the transaction of a product (Lowrie, 2007), and secondly the government's role and influence reduces the institution's "ownership". The government's position situates them as another gatekeeper to the student identity, as they financially control both the institutions and the majority of students entering higher education (GOV.UK, 2013), despite the appearance of state independence.

At this level then we see the web of complex identities and power relationships that make up the higher education sector. The institutions and the government act (sometimes in conflict with each other) as gatekeepers (Corra and Willer, 2002) to the benefits of being a student and having "that" graduate identity. This appears to place students within a consumerist role, actively involved in holding institutions to account by the choices they make. In reality, however, due to the government's financial influence, students are pseudo consumers, which helps to create a new student identity (Meek, 2000).

This means that it is even more important that higher education institutions are responsive to the needs of their consumers and market themselves appropriately (Lowrie, 2007). According to Fazackerley (2013), students have increased access to institutions' statistical information on aspects of teaching, learning and the future prospects of their students (career focused) which provides them with the power to choose an institution based on many factors, and not just the educational aspects of the institution. This is reflected by an NUS report (2008) into the reasons why students go to university which lists "improving my chances of getting a job" (53%) and "to improve my earning potential" (44%) (NUS, 2008, p. 3) as key factors alongside "to gain qualifications" (68%) (NUS, 2008, p. 3). This duality of roles, and its power was already having an influence on student choice before fees were uncapped, which will now in turn influence how institutions market themselves to these students (Lowrie, 2007; Department for Business, Innovation and Skills, 2012b).

Summary of Findings
The data collected from Cobyt (a further education college) was from its website for prospective higher education students (C1). For Polus (a "post 1992" university) its full-time, undergraduate prospectus 2014 (P1) and an online entry requirements page (P2) were used. For Urbix, (a Russell Group University) its full-time, undergraduate prospectus 2014 (U1) and online admissions policy (U2) were used. A summary of each institution's student construction was written which focused on the tense used, differences, key themes and anything else of relevance. This material was used in the following data analysis.

How the Dominant Discourse Constructs "Normal" and "Abnormal" students at Cobyt
Its "normal" student appeared to be a full-time, further education student, aged 16–19 as the data gathered on higher education was limited and stark. It was framed as a last resort and was focused on the better future of being at university. However, the study then took a step back and analysed foundation degrees, which were the main courses provided by

Cobyt, as it enabled an explanation of its negative discourse. The degrees were introduced in 2001 by a Labour government in an attempt to strengthen vocational education (Pratt, 2000). College-based provision is a key part of the widening participation agenda, which in turn is part of the government's rhetoric (Department for Business, Innovation and Skills, 2012a). Foundation degrees were subsidised, fees are about half of a "traditional" degree and the course is two years long (Pratt, 2000). They were a financially stable source of income for further education colleges until 2012, when the Conservative Coalition government introduced variable fees (Department for Business, Innovation and Skills, 2012a). This changed the main source of funding from a direct government source to students (Department for Business, Innovation and Skills, 2012b), which relates to effective recruitment and retention by institutions. This would then increase costs, and could have destabilised Cobyt's provision. In addition, as Cobyt was partnered with a university to award degrees, it doesn't have the independent power to control their provision (Exley, 2011). The traditional discourse of education implemented by the government (Richardson, 2010), and the mandatory education age being raised to 18 years from 2015 (Coughlan, 2013), has resulted in Cobyt shifting its focus on to this area, with the introduction of a new curriculum for 16–19 year olds to "improve their prospects during tough economic times".

The Dominant Discourse at Polus and Urbix Constructed a "Normal" Student Through the Word "You"

The primary and predominant language used in the literature supplied for new students at Polus and Urbix surrounded the words "you" and "we". Whilst "we" consistently referred to the institution, "you" was used across all three institutions to refer to prospective students. However, the way in which "you" was used changed the meanings of the word and in turn changed

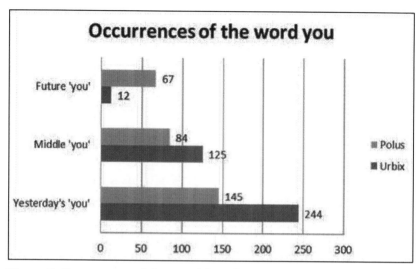

Figure 1: Occurrences of the word "you" in Polus and Urbix.

how "you" was used to construct very different "normal" students at each institution.

At Polus, an uncertain future tense "you" was used. It was also emotive and appealing directly to the individual student. "If you", "you maybe" and "we want you to enjoy your time here" are key examples of this. Despite the word "you" being singular, the phrase "most students" is a reflection of how "you" was actually being used. Although it appears to be personal and fostering a sense of community and belonging, it was actually constructing a pluralisation of the word and should perhaps have read as "you all". This also led to the homogenised construction of a student identity. This exclusive homogeneity separated and "othered" students who didn't fit (Swain, French, Barnes, and Thomas, 2004). Only disabled and mature students were overtly mentioned with the data used, whereas other minority groups were hidden. "You" was referring to the "normal" student and one that was "the same as everyone else".

Deconstructing the "Normal" Student

The assumption of normalcy (Madriaga et al., 2011) made it easier to narrow down the definition of a student that Polus used from clues in the documentation. Primarily the normal student was future focused, whose sole aim was to get "that job". They were moving to Normalton for the first time and wanted to live in halls. They were sociable people (so much so that they didn't exist as individuals) and wanted "the university experience". They had little experience of what university was, so needed terms explaining to them. They were using university as a transitional space from a past of deficit to a future of prosperity and were aware of the temporary nature of university. Learning was only important if it was deemed relevant to the future, specifically job prospects. Differences were seen as a bad thing, but were tolerated if relevant to learning and dealt with separately.

In complete contrast to Polus, Urbix used "you" in a more personalised and fixed way. It referred to "you" in the immediate future tense "whatever 'you' study" being a key example of this. "Your future" wasn't mentioned until page 24, in direct contrast to Polus which used the future as a key theme. "You" was still pluralised; however, it felt much more personalised and "you ... be part of" demonstrated the personalisation of "you" in the community context. The teaching environment was also personalised at Urbix, as there was the opportunity to shape your own curriculum. The title of the whole prospectus was "make a change". This phrase appeared to be situated at the university, and although it was unclear how, it was clear that it was urging the "you" found in the prospectus to do so. It was, at least in part, a reference to a personalised learning experience where "you" were in control. Although it might have appeared that the power was left to the student to construct their own experience, and that this was seen positively, the underlying message of exclusivity reveals something different. Urbix constructed its prospectus using a three-way split. The first introduced Urbix and had a positive, personalised and inclusionary focus. However, the final section after the course lists set out Urbix's exclusionary criteria. Like Polus, Urbix separated "different to the norm" students but in a starker way. Within section one the student construction was slightly homogenised. "You started at school or college" implied the expectation of a standardised schooling experience and within the "exclusive" section this was confirmed with the provision of special allowances for "different" students. This "you" was easier to see, but harder to define because it focused on individualised identities and "making a change".

The Future Focused Construction of a "Normal" Student at Polus

Polus's student was constructed in a future focused discourse. The marketing campaign also reflected this. However, reversing the focus on to yesterday's "you" revealed the underlying message: where "you" came from didn't matter to Polus, as what was more important was what "you" can become. The language used in the admissions criteria was heavily focused on explaining basic terminology, and with no access to formal policy reinforced the idea that yesterday's "you" had no direct experience of university and needed to make this positive step towards the future. However, "middle you" was forgotten. Cooper (2013) argued that disabled children are always focused on their futures and denied the opportunity to be children. This focus is centred on rehabilitative services' attempts to "cure" disabled children, for a better future. Clegg (2010) argues that universities are also being used as a norming device for a better future. This results in a lack of thought into the present, and perceives the past to be a problem. It also assumes a hegemonic utopian vision of employment, which Clegg (2010, p. 347) states causes a "reductionist discourse of employability". Everything was related to getting "that job", even leisure time was devoted to CV building.

To some extent the government discourse influences this trend towards future thinking. As Clegg (2010) states the word future is even included in the title of the 2004 policy. Government policy is also focused on the future prospects of graduates, singularly focused on careers and jobs (Department for Business, Innovation and Skills, 2012a). The NUS report (2008) also argues that this is one of the main reasons that students go to university; Polus could have been simply responding to the impact of government discourse. However, it was still a systemic approach to norming students into their future selves.

The Academically Focused Construction of a "Normal" Student at Urbix

Urbix's construction of a student was predominantly focused on academic qualities and the "middle you" which was mentioned 125 times (Figure 1). It appeared that its aim was to create an individualised and "independent student". However, this was in the context of a strict and exclusive admissions policy, linking background to future potential. Where "you" originated was key, and this was expected to be a standard "school or college" experience. The "Applying" page even detailed which "traditional" academic courses to take post 16. The emphasis on "a traditional" education revealed more about what a normal student wasn't than was.

It might appear that current government rhetoric (Department for Business, Innovation and Skills, 2012a) is having an impact on Urbix's traditional and academic approach. However, as Urbix has a long history of academically focused learning, it's likely the reverse is more accurate. The government's education reforms focus on the benefits of a traditional, academic education (BBC News, 2013; Richardson, 2010; Paton, 2013) which aligns itself to Urbix's construction of a student. As the government funds this sector this will only reinforce Urbix's construction of the education it provides because both the government and the institution act as gatekeepers (Corra and Willer, 2002) to the student identity. If they are ideologically intertwined then this eases Urbix's burden of justification of their provision for the purpose of gaining continued funding and other support from the government.

The Individually Focused Construction of an "Abnormal" Student at Polus

The analysis of Polus revealed its construction of difference. Any student differences which weren't considered relevant were completely hidden and not acknowledged at all. The differences that were mentioned only functioned to separate these identities from the main student "one". Disability is constructed as a deficit and only mentioned in a "health context" or as a need for "special requirements" in accommodation, placing them as separate from "most students". Polus reinforces this attitude by detailing how "you" could have volunteered for disabled people as a separate group from adults and children. The construction of a disabled student was the same as the medical model discourse (Oliver, 1996), whereby disabled people are seen as passive, are individualised and their disability seen as a deficit. The only other "different" student mentioned was a mature student. "Becoming a mature student" was also distinct from a "normal" student experience and they were viewed through an equally passive and deficit lens, as they were seen to be in need of support to decide which course was suitable and "flexible entry requirements" suggested a deficit with their previous life experience. Transferring this attitude across all minority groups that haven't been mentioned, Polus's construction of a normal student was so rigid that it simply didn't allow for any difference. These students were still being admitted, but if it wasn't deemed "relevant" to the institution then it was a completely separate identity, and if it was deemed relevant, then it was only allowed "to be" in certain contexts. The student identity ("you") was the predominant identity, being referenced 296 times through P1 (Figure 1).

The Homogeneously Focused Construction of an "Abnormal" Student at Urbix

Urbix's prospectus was heavily focused on a student's background and it is this that formed the basis of their construction of an abnormal student. Key to this was the paragraph about "widening participation". Unlike the rest of the prospectus "you" was not used, which could be interpreted in a number of ways. If "you" was seen as the standard, then its absence revealed that this type of student fell outside of the norm. This was further reinforced in other areas, relating lower socio-economic groups with a challenging education and the need to accommodate this. Additionally it could also be interpreted that the intended audience was the "you" student and was a subtle way of promoting equality alongside statements such as "the widest range of educational, social and cultural backgrounds" that affirmed inclusivity.

As Urbix's prospectus was literally split between the inclusive front and the exclusive admission sections it could be concluded that these "othered" student groups existed separately. However, analysis of the language used to construct different groups of students revealed an internal homogenisation marked by the different approaches used for each group. Within the admissions pages the distinction was made between those who have had a "normal" school experience, a challenging one, those who are disabled or have a specific learning difficulty or those who are classed as mature. It was assumed that these groups will have had a different education to each other, with little recognition or allowance of individual differences within that group. To demonstrate, disabled students were only considered as having support needs, which were separate from the admissions process, and no consideration was made of their potentially different or disrupted education, whereas it was assumed that all mature students will be in need of flexible entry. The word reasonable was used in relation to disabled students (the same language as the Equality Act 2010 (Department for Culture, Media and Sport, 2013)); it could be to conform with the law or even for other reasons. However, as Madriaga et al. (2011) state this can also homogenise and reduce the disabled students' experiences and needs, and doesn't account for differences or intersectionality (Sherry, 2004). The lack of tentative language reinforced the notion that all minority or different students were "the same" within their own group, in the same way that the "you" student was categorised and stereotyped at Polus.

What were the Possible Consequences for Prospective Students When Institutional Discourses of "Normal" and "Abnormal" Interact?

Polus and Urbix both had a strong (although different) student identity. At Polus this was centred on a future focused student whereas Urbix focused on the academic qualities of their student. The dominant discourse was apparent upon analysis of prospective student documents. However, what was interesting was how these have been constructed using contrasting and opposite approaches to achieve the same outcome. Polus had more control over its student identity and Urbix had more control over its "abnormal" identity. Both institutions homogenised this construction and reduced it into stereotypical traits they expect of that group. If "normal" is highlighted as the preferred option, people will be drawn to that (Crowe, 2000) and as Luna (2009) concludes, this is sometimes through non-disclosure. The strong construction of "abnormal" as a separate and othered identity in a deficit framework will have the same effect of norming students (Madriaga et al., 2011; Crowe, 2000).

This small-scale study is reinforced by previous studies (Crowe, 2000; Luna, 2009; Madriaga et al., 2011) and the widening participation agenda's conclusion about the position and construction of normal was preferred.

Davis (2002) makes reference to the bell curve (or the normal curve). This statistical tool is used to display the normal distribution of data. This is the inspiration for the visual representation of the results because it clearly demonstrates where and how normality compares with each institution. This section theorises the results using Figure 2 and Figure 3 (overleaf) to help explain this new concept.

Normal is a Self-Contained and Separate Identity
"Normal" is a clearly defined and separate identity at both institutions. However, the fixed nature of this definition resulted in the fluid movement in and out of being considered normal (Goodley, 2013). Although it was easier to leave the "sphere" it was also possible (but harder) to enter it by the amount of conformity that the student had with the normal identity (Goodley, 2013; P1; U1). Although Urbix's definition of normal was a lot more individualised than Polus's, it had been shaped by the existence of other identities that acted as exclusionary criteria to the normal identity.

"The Gaps"
As a result of the homogenisation of identities at both institutions there were those students who didn't fit within any of the "spheres", which resulted in them falling into "the gaps" (Sherry, 2004; P1; U1). Within institutions focused on the categorisation of students, those without a clear label can be further isolated, marginalised and denied an identity (Sherry, 2004). Polus doesn't mention or even see its external identity as relevant within the institution. Urbix highlights the non-conforming "othered" identity and the inflexible nature of these othered identities.

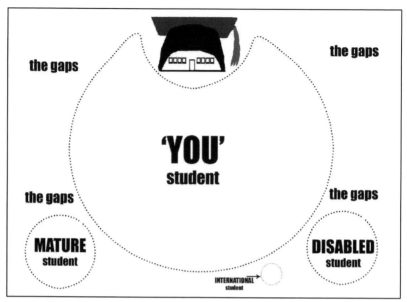

Figure 2: How Polus constructs its student identity.

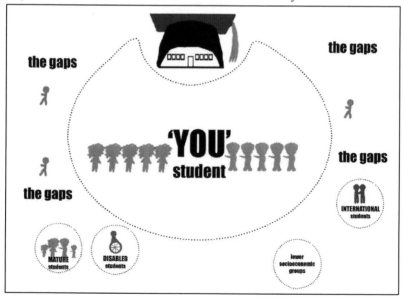

Figure 3: How Urbix constructs its student identity.

Intersectionality
Those students who fit within more than one sphere were also left confused and within "the gaps" at these institutions (P1, U1). As the "spheres" didn't interact with each other and have clear defining characteristics there wasn't the flexibility to recognise the existence of more than one characteristic within a student (P1, U1). Both Urbix and Polus treated disabled students and mature students were even further categorised by an impairment label (Sherry, 2004; P1).

Value of a Label
The position and dimension of the "sphere" in relation to the institution analysed represents the perceived value the institution placed on the label. Its size denotes its visibility within the documents. The word "you", given its context in all of the prospectuses represents the "normal" student. The abnormal labels have been marginalised, reduced and devalued by the way the institutions use them (Luna, 2009).

Risk
The Higher Education Funding Council for England (HEFCE) recognises that the recruitment and retention of disabled and other "non-normative" students incurs a higher cost through financial support for institutions (HEFCE, 2015). Although in a purely economic context there may appear to be a financial incentive in recruiting these students, this is balanced by the implied higher risk. Therefore being labelled as different, for the student, the institution and the HEFCE is seen in a deficit framework. This reinforces the need to be seen as "normal" and that "normal" is not only preferred, but essential for success. The students who fit within the gaps of both "normal" and "different" pose the greatest risk, as they don't attract extra funding but may still need more support.

Conclusion

It is somewhat difficult to summarise the findings of this analysis into one neat paragraph, mainly because they were not neat or ordered, but were as individual and nuanced as the institution being studied. However, as to whether it was possible to determine the "normal" or "abnormal" student through the use of their language, then yes, it was. Each institution had a very clear dominant student identity that was subtly defined throughout the documents used. Although these were distinctly different, they still had the underlying aim of controlling who does or doesn't enter the institution to study there. The prospective student documents acted as a gatekeeper to the institution, in much the same way that other institutions and agencies use this method to control the dominant ideology (Corra and Willer, 2002). The main way this was achieved was with the word "you". Universally this was constructed as the "normal", and across the two bigger institutions it was used 677 times (Figure 1). The manipulation of the word revealed how each institution constructed the dominant student. "You" was pluralised and tensed (past, present and future) appropriately for each setting, which considering the small size of the word gave it an incredible amount of power.

Despite the "limited, specific and partial knowledge" (Rose, 1997, p. 307) that this small-scale study produced it is methodologically valid and therefore a valuable contribution to knowledge. It is hoped that the methodological framework utilised by this research can act as a springboard for future studies aiming to discover more about the construction of student identities.

References

BBC News. (2013). Gove stresses "facts" in school curriculum revamp. Retrieved from: http://www.bbc.co.uk/news/ education-12227491

Clegg, S. (2010). Time future – the dominant discourse of higher education. *Time and Society, 19*(3), 345–364. Retrieved from: http://tas.sagepub.com

Cohen, L., Manion, L., & Morrison, K. (2011). *Research methods in education* (7th ed.). Abingdon, United Kingdom: Routledge.

Cooper, H. (2013, April). *No time to lose: Childhood time following the diagnosis of an impairment in babyhood.* Paper presented at the Disability Research Forum, Sheffield Hallam University.

Corra, M., & Willer, D. (2002). The gatekeeper. *Sociological Theory, 20*(2), 180–207. Retrieved from http://onlinelibrary. wiley.com

Coughlan, S. (2013). *Raising leaving age in 1970s "improved children's GCSEs".* Retrieved from http://www.bbc.co.uk/news/ education-21033278

Crowe, M. (2000). Constructing normality: A discourse analysis of the DSM-IV, *Journal of Psychiatric and Mental Health Nursing, 7*(1), 69–77. Retrieved from http://onlinelibrary.wiley.com

Davis, L. (2002). *Bending over backwards: Disability, dismodernism and other difficult positions.* New York, NY: New York University Press.

Department for Business, Innovation and Skills. (2012a). *Making the higher education system more efficient and diverse (policy).* Retrieved from https://www.gov.uk/government/policies/making-the-higher-education-system-more-efficient-and-diverse.

Department for Business, Innovation and Skills. (2012b). *Making the higher education system more efficient and diverse (detail).* Retrieved from https://www.gov.uk/government/policies/making-the-higher-education-system-more-efficient-and-diverse/supporting-pages/creating-a-new-funding-system-for-higher-education

Department for Culture, Media and Sport. (2013). *Equality Act 2010: Guidance.* Retrieved from https://www.gov.uk/equality-act-2010-guidance

Department for Education. (2013). *Increasing the number of academies and free schools to create a better and more diverse school system (policy).* Retrieved from https://www.gov.uk/government/policies/

increasing-the-number-of-academies-and-free-schools-to-create-a-
better-and-more-diverse-school-system

Disability Rights Commission. (2013). *Talk (part 1 of 2)*. Retrieved from
http://www.youtube.com/watch?v=FZfOVNwjFU0

Exley, S. (2011, August 5). Colleges take step towards full degree-
awarding powers. *Times Higher Education*. Retrieved from
http://www.timeshighereducation.co.uk/news/colleges-take-
step-towards-full-degree-awarding-powers/417054.article

Fazackerley, A. (2013, 11 March). Students not told which universities
are struggling. *The Guardian*. Retrieved from http://www.
guardian.co.uk/education/2013/mar/11/universities-falling-
applications-ucas-protecting

Georgakopoulou, A., & Goutsos, D. (1999). *Discourse analysis: An
introduction*. Edinburgh, United Kingdom: Edinburgh University
Press.

Goodley, D. (2013, March). *The psychopathology of the normals: Why non-
disabled people are so messed up around disability*. Lecture presented at
Sheffield University, Sheffield, United Kingdom.

GOV.UK. (2013). *Student finance*. Retrieved from https://www.
gov.uk/student-finance/overview

Green, J. (2013, 17 May). Disability at university: See the world through
my eyes. *The Guardian*. Retrieved from http://www.
guardian.co.uk/education/2013/apr/17/disability-at-university-
see-the-world-through-my-eyes

HEFCE. (2015). *How we fund student access and success*. Retrieved from
http://www.hefce.ac.uk/sas/funding/

hooks, b. (1994). *Teaching to transgress*. Abingdon, United Kingdom:
Routledge.

Lowrie, A. (2007). Branding higher education: Equivalence and
difference in developing identity. *Journal of Business Research, 9*(60),
990–999.

Luna, C. (2009). "But how can those students make it here?": Examining
the institutional discourse about what it means to be "LD" at an Ivy
League university. *International Journal of Inclusive Education, 13*(2),
157–178.

Madriaga, M., Hanson, K., Kay, H., & Walker, A. (2011). Marking-out normalcy and disability in higher education. *British Journal of Sociology of Education, 32*(6), 901–920.

Meek, V. (2000). Diversity and marketisation of higher education: Incompatible concepts?. *Higher Education Policy, 13*(1), 23–39.

Mills, S. (2003). *Michel Foucault.* Abingdon, United Kingdom: Routledge.

Mills, S. (2004). *Discourse.* (2nd ed.). Abingdon, United Kingdom: Routledge.

NUS. (2008). *Student experience report.* Retrieved from http://www. nus.org.uk/PageFiles/4017/NUS_StudentExperienceReport.pdf

Oliver, M. (1996). Defining impairment and disability: Issues at stake. In C. Barnes & G. Mercer (Eds.), *Exploring the divide* (pp. 29–54). Leeds, United Kingdom: The Disability Press.

Paton, G. (2013, 10 May). Spelling and grammar test for all 11-year-olds to tackle poor literacy. *The Telegraph.* Retrieved from http://www.telegraph.co.uk/education/educationnews/10049372 /Spelling-and-grammar-test-for-all-11-year-olds-to-tackle-poor-literacy.html

Pratt, J. (2000, 3 March). The uncertain future of foundation degrees. *Times Higher Education.* Retrieved from http://www. timeshighereducation.co.uk/150498.article

Richardson, H. (2010). *Gove puts focus on traditional school values.* Retrieved from http://www.bbc.co.uk/news/education-118 22208

Rose, G. (1997). Situating knowledges: Positionality, reflexivities and other tactics. *Progress in Human Geography, 21*(3), 305–320.

Seymour, R. (2012, 29 March). A short history of privatisation in the UK: 1979–2012. *The Guardian.* Retrieved from http://www. guardian.co.uk/commentisfree/2012/mar/29/short-history-of-privatisation

Sherry, M. (2004). Overlaps and contradictions between queer theory and disability studies. *Disability and Society, 19*(7), 769–783.

Snyder, S., & Mitchell, D. (2006). *Cultural locations of disability.* Chicago, IL: University of Chicago Press.

Swain, J., French, S., Barnes, C., & Thomas, C. (2004). *Disabling barriers – enabling environments.* (2nd ed.). London, United Kingdom: Sage.

Thompson, J., & Bekhradnia, B. (2010). *The government's proposals for higher education funding and student finance – an analysis.* Retrieved from http://www.hepi.ac.uk/455-1875/The-government%27s-proposals-for-higher-education-funding-and-student-finance-%E2%80%93-an-analysis.html

CHAPTER 3

IS THIS INCLUSION? TEACHERS RESISTING NORMALCY WITHIN THE CLASSROOM

Sue Chantler

Summary
This chapter was written to reflect the education system and policies in place in England during 2012 and 2013. In June 2014 the Children and Families Act (Department for Education and Department of Health, 2014a) was approved by Parliament and the new SEND (Special Education Needs and Disability) Code of Practice (DfE and DoH, 2014b) was launched. The chapter explores the potential that teachers have to resist the process of normalisation within the education system in England in the context of the development of inclusion for children and young people labelled as having SEND. Education policies introduced in England by both the New Labour government between 1997 and 2010, and the Coalition Conservative/Liberal Democrat government since 2010 have created significant tensions for those working in schools, as well as for the children who attend those schools and their families. Ball (2013) argues that teachers have much to contribute to the development of education policy but that their voices are increasingly removed from this process. The chapter examines the interaction between inclusive and performative policies and their impact on the work of teachers, and how teachers make sense of their practice in schools in the English education system today. It concludes with reflection on how they might be *able* and *enabled* to resist the process of normalcy which is a fundamental part of the performative policy agenda.

Introduction
In this chapter I explore the potential that teachers have to resist normalcy within the education system in England in the context of the development of inclusion for children (for brevity I use this term to include young people as well) labelled as having SEND.

71

Education policies introduced in England by both the New Labour government between 1997 and 2010, and the Coalition Conservative/Liberal Democrat government since 2010 have created significant tensions for those working in schools, as well as for the children who attend those schools and for their families. As a teacher and then as an academic who led postgraduate courses for teachers working with children labelled with autism, I was constantly aware of the tensions that teachers experience in their practice between the expectations of working inclusively, as well as meeting performative targets. I believe that teachers have much to contribute to the development of education policy but that their voices are increasingly removed from this process (Ball, 2013). Whilst the focus of this chapter is the perspectives of teachers, I recognise that all those involved in the education system have much to contribute to this debate. I do not, by focusing on teachers, privilege their voices over those of others. The chapter was written to reflect the education system and policies in place in England during 2012 and 2013. In June 2014 the Children and Families Act (DfE and DoH, 2014a) was approved by Parliament and the new SEND (Special Education Needs and Disability) Code of Practice (DfE and DoH, 2014b) was launched.

I examine in this chapter the interaction between inclusive and performative policies and their impact on the work of teachers, and consider how teachers make sense of their practice in schools in the English education system today. I conclude with reflection on how they might be *able* and *enabled* to resist the process of normalcy which is a fundamental part of the performative policy agenda. To illustrate my arguments I draw on the results of a research study which explored the perspectives of a group of primary school teachers, working in schools in England, on educational inclusion for children labelled with autism (Chantler, 2013).

Is This Inclusion?

Performative, Normalising and Inclusive?

Whilst it is common to refer to those who are "disabled", it is not so common for people who identify as "able" to be so labelled (Goodley, 2011). Such persons are the "taken for granted", the dominant majority, who assume an identity of "normal" and, as the dominant group in society, label only those deemed to be "abnormal". This process is described as the process of "othering" distinct beings, where those who do not conform to some "norm" of society are labelled as "not normal" whether in relation to gender identity, sexuality, race, culture or intellectual or physical impairment. Normalisation pervades all aspects of society in the UK, with a drive to achieve at the very least "normal" in whatever sphere of development or endeavour is addressed. This process is represented in the English education system by the notion of mainstream education (schools which are attended by non-disabled children as well as by some children labelled as having SEND) and special education (schools which are designated solely for children labelled as having SEND), where mainstream could be seen to be synonymous with "normal" and special is synonymous with the "non-normal".

Normalcy is evident in the education system in England where a constant drive in both primary and secondary schools has been to create a school population where all students are expected to strive towards a "normal" level of passing a standardised assessment (Benjamin, 2002). However, as Benjamin observes, many students will not pass standardised assessments at the "normal" level because such tests assess skills and abilities which are beyond their range of ability. Such standardised assessments are exclusive in that they exclude some students from the assessment process. The "problem" of such students is one to which I return later in the chapter.

It is within this process of normalisation that educational inclusion currently and uncomfortably sits. In the context of this chapter, government policy, when using the term inclusion, refers to the practice of educating students labelled as having SEND in mainstream schools. The English education system falls far short of being "inclusive" for this group of children and can instead be described as implementing a process of integration, where students are present in mainstream school but unable to fully participate because the mainstream has remained effectively unchanged (Hodkinson, 2012). Here inclusion is something that is done to a group of students, those labelled as having SEND, as opposed to a process which works to change the education system, such that it is rendered accessible and equitable for all students, whatever their learning style and ability. The continued use of the term "mainstream" when referring to schools is in itself an exclusionary practice implying that there is also a "non-mainstream". Titchkosky (2011) argues that the concept of inclusion (into the "mainstream") can only exist in opposition to the concept of exclusion (from the "mainstream").

In addition to inclusive education policy, there has been the drive under both New Labour and the Coalition government towards what Goodley (2011) describes as the neoliberalism of the English education system. Performativity permeates the current English education system and is a key feature of the neoliberal marketisation of education. Teachers in the English education system find their practice driven by processes which include judgement of schools and teachers through pupil performance, as measured by standardised assessments such as the Standard Assessment Tasks taken at the age of 11 and General Certificate in Secondary Education taken at 16. This results in competition between schools based on performance-related outcomes (Ball, 2013) and works in opposition to the development of an inclusive system (Atkinson, 2004). It is within the context of an education system driven by performative policy that I examine how teachers might act to resist normalcy and better enable that system to become more equitable and accessible for all children.

What is the Problem?

The policy and practice of educational inclusion are based on the social model of disability (Oliver, 1996), which locates the disablement of the individual with the exclusionary barriers constructed by society. However, the current system of identifying special educational need and disability is based on the individual model of disability, which serves to marginalise and exclude children labelled as having SEND. There is a strong argument that inclusive educational policy falls far short of creating equitable and accessible education for all children when implemented in practice (Armstrong, 2011; Hodkinson, 2012). In an education context the identification of groups of students through such labels as "special educational need" or "autistic" is illustrative of a discourse of power in education, where a dominant majority, which includes psychologists, the medical profession, and teachers, is able to represent a minority as deviant in some way from what is considered to be "normal" (Armstrong, 2002). The "problem" is understood to be the labelled individual and his or her pattern of development which differs from the "norm" (Titchkosky, 2011). Titchkosky (2011, pp. 12-13) argues that current notions of access and inclusion within social institutions, for example schools, are predicated on the notion of the disabled individual as the "problem": "*What* the problem is, then, is disability as an individual matter. Disability is the location of trouble since it results in the difficulty of having one's needs met, as well as potentially causing academic problems and barriers to learning."

This conceptualisation persists in practice within the English education system with the identification of "special educational need", "disability" and "specialist supports and resources" for the individual child. At the same time educational policy regarding inclusive education requires schools to identify and remove barriers to access and learning for children (DfES, 2004) based on at least a partial acknowledgement of the social model of disability.

Educational inclusion as it is currently practised is a process which is based on the identification and labelling of "individual pathology" and as a result the education system continues to be exclusionary and problematic for many pupils labelled as having SEND. Titchkosky (2011, p. 39) extends this argument when she writes that: "Those who 'we' can't, won't, or don't imagine as potential participants are those who remain excludable ... In this way, assertions of inclusion help to normalise conceptions of those who are *essentially excludable.*"

For the education system to become equitable and accessible for all children, those children must cease to be positioned as "the problem", and the system itself problematised. Educational inclusion should be conceptualised as more about an acceptance and embracing of diversity within society and of developing an educational system that is not built to "include" children but which is built with all children and their rights to education in mind. In the next section I consider some of the challenges there may be to conceptualising and constructing such an education system.

Imagined Possibilities
Throughout the chapter I shall be drawing on the data from a research study that I undertook with a group of eight primary school teachers. The aim of the study was to gather the perspectives of teachers about the factors which affect the process of educational inclusion for children labelled with autism. I recorded the conversations of the teachers as they worked together as a group, as well as collecting their individual reflections written as a weekly diary. At the time of the research

they were all working in local authority maintained primary schools. Two, David and Liz, worked in a special school and the remaining six, Ros, Wendy, Lynn, Karen, Dee and Pat, in mainstream settings. Each had an interest in, and some experience of, working with children labelled with autism. I use pseudonyms throughout for these teachers so that their identities are protected.

For Armstrong (2011, p. 8) inclusive education "implies a transformation in the social, cultural, curricular and pedagogic life of the school, as well as its physical organisation" and is situated in the belief that all members of a community have an equal entitlement and access to it. This is reflected by one teacher from the study, Pat, who commented that: "Inclusion is not just about geography! Children need to be able to access the entire curriculum within mainstream school (at their own level) without being withdrawn from class, to be truly included."

David, who had worked in both mainstream and in special schools, felt there was a mismatch between the learning requirements of the students in his class and the curriculum he was expected to deliver: "In mainstream schooling I had the issue over delivering what is best for children or delivering what will bring best academic results. The pressures put on schools to perform to certain criteria often had a negative effect on the pupils ... particularly those who were lower abilities."

For Karen the current education system works against developing inclusive schools: "The school system itself creates barriers for the child with autism. They are placed in situations which can often set them up for failure."

Here the child labelled autistic is the child who does not fit into the normate model of a pupil within this normalising system and is in danger of failing.

It may be that within the limitations of the notion of an unchanging mainstream there are limits to "imagined possibilities" as well. The bureaucratic structures of the current school system can inhibit the way in which teachers are able to conceptualise changes to their practice (Broderick et al., 2011). Perhaps, for some teachers, they are so immersed in the segregated school system and associated practices that they are unable to conceive of a "social model of education" (Apple, 1982, cited in Goodley, 2011, p. 151). To imagine new possibilities for inclusive education Cochran-Smith and Dudley-Marling (2012) argue that perhaps teachers and academics need to work together to co-construct these new possibilities. It is only through being able to interrogate the theory behind educational change that teachers will be able to have an impact on educational change beyond the surface features of education (Timperley and Parr, 2005). In order for our schools and educational system to become fully inclusive it would seem therefore that there needs to be a radical restructuring so that all learners achieve equality of access and entitlement. Such developments will depend on teachers being enabled to both initiate and promote change through their practice.

Teachers as Change Agents
Nind writes that "... inclusion is an issue primarily for teachers – and that, perhaps, it is them we need to hear more from" (2005, p. 273) maintaining that inclusion is an issue of pedagogy as well as an issue of human rights. She continues her argument by reflecting on the role of teachers as "change agents – as enactors of inclusive policy" (2005, p. 273). She cites O'Hanlon as arguing that "there is no professional change without personal change" (p. 273) and that educational change happens often because teachers make it happen. This resonates with the perspectives of Armstrong and Moore (2004) who, in the context of working with teachers in a professional development capacity, perceive teachers to be agents of change as they explore and evaluate their practice. The implication here is that teachers initiate the changes

to their practice, locating teachers in a position of power over that change, in contrast to a situation where teachers are expected to respond to change imposed through external policy development. The performative agenda however serves to prevent teachers from acting innovatively and as possible agents of change, through inspection processes in which teachers are judged against a limited set of standards (Atkinson, 2004). Fullan (2006) argues that in order for educational change to be sustainable teachers need to be able not just to respond to and implement externally imposed changes to their practice but also to initiate that change, to act as change agents.

In the following section I reflect on the conflicting tensions brought about by the impact of both performative and inclusive policies and examine what this means for teachers, and how this might impact on their ability not just to respond to, but to initiate change.

A Confusing Policy Landscape: Performativity and Normalcy
Goodley (2011, p. 146) refers to the "neoliberalism" of education, arguing that in neoliberal conceptions of education and childhood there is a "cultural imperative to fit in, under a rubric of normality, to strive to be normal". In this way the process of assessment against the national curriculum and the associated competitive league tables of school performativity perpetuate a model of education which problematises the children whom it is unable to "normalise". This process works against an inclusive agenda as Benjamin (2002) argues. This in turn could lead to teachers feeling that they have failed, or even being judged by others to have failed, if they are unable to make the performance of some children against SATs "normal" (Howard, 2000).

Rix (2011) argues that the processes of performativity and choice in education have forced schools to compete through focusing narrowly on pupil performance outcomes assessed through SATs and GCSEs. This could in turn impact on the behaviour of schools towards students who seem unlikely to meet the required standards in these tests as a result of intellectual capacity, motivation or behaviour and attitude to school (Ball, 2013). Allan (cited in Rix, 2011) suggests that the accountability regimes which have come about as a result of the increased marketisation of education have resulted in inclusion outcomes based on "presence" of students rather than full participation.

Armstrong (2011) considers the educational policy landscape to be confusing and it could be argued that educational policy which relates to educational inclusion is ambiguous and will not enable real change to the current segregated system. Armstrong asserts that there is a mismatch in the UK between "the apparent intentions of one set of policies and what actually happens in practice" (2011, p. 7). The process of "inclusion" continues to be compromised by the performative agenda of testing and league table comparisons.

An Increasingly Fragmented System
The policy reforms outlined in The Children and Families Act (DfE and DoH, 2014a) signal a continuing commitment to the development of greater variety and choice in educational provision as outlined in the White Paper *The Importance of Teaching* (DfE, 2010). Under both New Labour and the Coalition government there has been a rise in the number of schools with academy status and of free schools. Academies are publicly funded independent schools run by a trust. They follow the same rules for admission, exclusion and special educational needs as other state schools but do not have to follow the national curriculum. Free schools are funded by the government but are not run by the local council. They can set their own terms and conditions of employment for staff and do not have to follow the national curriculum. Within special education there is an increase in the number of voluntary sector schools claiming to

offer specialist support to particular pupil groups, for example those labelled as having autism, an example of schools positioning themselves within the education marketplace (Rix, 2011), a process which can further increase segregation of students between mainstream and special education.

The Children and Families Act does not offer an unconditional commitment to inclusive education, rather a commitment reflected in other aspects of the Coalition government's education policy to further fragmentation of the education system (DfE, 2010). In such a policy landscape the possibility of an inclusive education system appears to diminish as does the potential for teachers to develop a more inclusive professional identity. It is within this confusing and contradictory policy landscape that teachers enact their daily practice. Educational policy can have a significant impact on the development of a teacher's professional identity and how teachers might act as agents of change within their professional communities. If, as Nind (2005) argues, teachers can act both as change agents and as enactors of policy, it is pertinent now to reflect on how performative policies might affect the potential for a teacher to pursue the development of inclusive practice.

Teachers' Perspectives of Their Work

Ball (2013) argues that in 2012 teaching was rated by the Health and Safety Executive as one of the three occupations in Britain reporting the highest incidence of stress and depression. He also cites a study for UNICEF by Ipsos MORI and Nairn which placed the UK at the bottom of the child well-being league table among developed countries (Ball, 2013). If, as is argued in *An Education Declaration to Rebuild America* (Education Opportunities Network cited in Ball, 2013, p. 33), "The working conditions of teachers are the learning conditions of students", then it is of critical importance that the work of teachers and their perspectives of, and attitude to, that work are taken into account in policy development.

The combination of performative and inclusive educational policies results in teachers being required to extend their practice with a more diverse student group at the same time as being asked to meet ever more demanding assessment targets. Ball argues that changes to educational policy will affect "what it means to teach and what it means to be a teacher" (2003, p. 218). Teacher identity and attitude are inextricably related. Where a teacher's identity is determined by assessment results, then inclusive practice is unlikely to be prioritised due to how the teacher perceives what is important in their work.

Nias argues that, for teachers, their personal and professional identities are often so closely interwoven that the classroom is a place for the development of self-esteem and fulfilment, but also a site of their vulnerability: "The emotional reactions of individual teachers to their work are intimately connected to the view that they have of themselves and others ... So, the unique sense of self which every teacher has is socially grounded" (Nias, 1996, p. 294). Following this argument, the work that teachers see themselves as doing, their pre-conceptions of their role, of the pupils with whom they will work and the school settings in which they practise, reflect their sense of professional identity which, in turn, is affected by their emotional response to their work.

Identity and Teaching

A teacher's professional identity will affect how that teacher perceives and acts out his or her role within a school. Most of what we know about ourselves we know by reflecting upon our actions and their contexts, as well as upon how others perceive or respond to our actions (Crossley, 2005). In this sense then our identity is in part formed through a mirroring of who we are through the responses of those around us to our actions. For Crossley an individual's identity is affected by the context in which they work and the judgements of those around them: "... we continue to internalize the perspectives of both specific significant and generalized others, judging, assessing and making sense of ourselves from their point of view" (2005, p. 135).

For a teacher this may be in the form of mentor peers, respected colleagues, senior colleagues, outside agencies, families and students. All of these influences, it could be argued, inform the development of a teacher's professional identity.

In this way, where teacher performance is judged by outcomes in terms of pupil performance on SATs, a teacher may understand that his or her professional identity is as a teacher who achieves such targets and may consider that children who are labelled as having SEND within the class will impede this achievement. For this teacher, the professional identity of "teacher who achieves test results" is challenged by the process of inclusion. So some teachers may not develop a professional identity which allows them to perceive of themselves working inclusively with classes of children who have diverse learning styles and abilities. Rather, their professional identities may be located firmly within the notion of "mainstream teacher" as the teacher whose purpose, or "meaning" (Howard, 2000), is to achieve good SATs results. For such teachers the idea of inclusive practice can be seen as a threat to that identity, resulting in resistance to such change in practice. It could be argued that the role of "teacher" is being normalised through the processes of performativity.

A Question of Attitude
Teachers, as members of a diverse society, each develop their own personal and professional value systems. Their perspectives on issues such as disablement, inclusion and exclusion are

shaped by their own experiences. As Hart (2004, citing Quine) argues, some deeply held beliefs and attitudes are very resistant to change. This could suggest that many teachers whose deeply held beliefs run contrary to an inclusive education system may be very resistant to change which promotes inclusive practice. For Ainscow, Booth, and Dyson (2004) it is these deeply held beliefs that teacher educators and education policy makers should be interested in for the successful implementation of educational change.

For the teachers in my study, teacher attitude can act to facilitate a child, as well as to have the opposite impact, as Pat observes: "It seems to me that staff attitudes in school can have the greatest impact on whether inclusion is successful or not." She continues by reflecting that professional identity, for some teachers, is threatened by the notion of inclusion and that such teachers do not believe working with children with the label of autism (or those labelled as having SEND) to be part of their professional role:

> I have noted that some staff have attitudes that can cause barriers to inclusion and learning of these children. Some staff have a low tolerance of behaviours and find it hard to adapt their teaching methods so that the children feel more comfortable and safe. They think that 1-to-1 support should be full time, almost, so they don't have to do anything.

In contrast Wendy commented that: "As a SENCo and a teacher removing barriers is really part of everyday practice. It is about identifying problems and trying to implement solutions."

Rieser (2011) has argued that part of the development of inclusive education is to include wider learning opportunities about disablement and inclusion in the school curriculum, as well as in wider society. Sikes, Lawson, and Parker (2007, p. 358) argue that the perspectives of teachers who are charged with implementing inclusive practice are "of paramount significance in that they shape the "inclusion experience" of the community in which they work". They continue, citing Deleuze and Guattari (1987/2004), in reflecting that: "... socially just pedagogies can only evolve and be becoming in so far as they are grounded in personal experience, questioning, action and interpersonal relationships".

Whilst schools continue to be evaluated through emphasis on performance on assessment-based league tables, then perhaps teachers will feel some confusion about how "inclusive" their practice is meant to be. In the following section I consider ways that teachers are *able* and can be *enabled* to act as agents of change and so resist the encroachment of normalcy within the education system.

Teachers Resisting Narratives of Normalcy: Sustainable Educational Change
Education policy change is commented upon frequently in the media, making political headlines, and is considered a problematic arena, as Hargreaves (2002) and Timperley and Parr (2005) argue. One key problematic aspect of such change is that even where change is initiated and welcomed it is frequently not *sustained*. In the context of the sustainability of educational change, Fullan (2006, p. 114) defines sustainability as "the capacity of a system to engage in the complexities of continuous improvement consistent with deep values of human purpose".

Hargreaves (2002) argues that in order to be capable of sustainable educational change and progress, educational systems must become professionally diverse environments which enable the process of creative and adaptable professional learning. In contrast, he positions educational change initiatives based on "rational, standardised scientific efficiency" (for example a performative agenda based on attempts to normalise student performance and teacher behaviour) to be "the enemy of healthy and creative diversity" (Hargreaves, 2002, p. 191). He argues that such standardised reform endangers those members of the system who are the weakest, for example those students who are labelled as having SEND. For Hargreaves, an approach to teaching which enables sustainable change to take place is an approach which includes:

> ... not just knowing what, but knowing why (deep understanding), knowing how (application) and knowing who (building social networks and social capital) (OECD, 2001) ... Merely maintaining practices that raise test scores or produce easily measurable results does not sustain these deeper aspects of teaching and learning. (Hargreaves, 2002, p. 192)

In this way the production of a normalised "teacher" workforce will work against the development and sustainability of inclusive practice.

Teachers, as the implementers of educational change, cannot sustain change initiatives without being willing (and being enabled) to engage with and understand the theoretical underpinnings of such change. In addition, change initiators must appreciate that teachers perceive teaching not as a mechanistic formulaic activity but as a craft, one in which they invest their emotions and their self-esteem, and from which their identities stem. Timperley and Parr (2005) argue that communities of teachers working together can provide a forum in which the knowledge and understanding to develop new skills can be achieved. They also comment that "The acquisition of skills and knowledge are motivated by what is valued" (2005, p. 247). Change will only be sustainable when initiators and implementers of educational policy "both critique the other's theories and have their own theories critiqued" (Timperley and Parr, 2005, p. 248). In the context of educational inclusion this would mean that teachers should be engaged as active agents in the development of inclusive educational policy. In order for this to be effective, teachers need to be enabled to understand the theoretical basis of educational change and to be able to initiate change themselves.

Educational policy is additionally affected by the political climate in which that policy is developed (Ball, 2003), and teachers need also to understand the political context of educational reform. Ball (2013) states that both New Labour and the Coalition government, as well as the preceding Conservative governments between 1979 and 1997, have developed education policy which acts to remove local authorities and teacher associations and unions from the policy process rather than having them as part of the development of policy. He argues that for an inclusive education system to develop, it is necessary to "reconnect education to democracy and work towards an educative relationship between schools and their communities" (2013, p. 4). De Lissovoy (cited in Ball, 2013, p. 4) maintains that "we should recognize the centrality of education to larger projects of democracy and community building".

Teachers are able to act politically as individuals who vote, as well as collectively as members of teacher unions. They have the potential to affect the process of educational inclusion, within the classroom, their school, the wider community of schools and through their professional bodies and trade unions. This potential to act as agents of change is limited by the professional strait-jacketing of performative policy and practice, but it is not eradicated. In the context of education for children labelled as having SEND, the process of normalisation could be challenged and inclusive practice can be extended by the individual and collective actions of teachers within their professional communities, despite the impact of performative policy. The role of professional development, in particular that which includes reflection on practice within a community of teachers working alongside academics, has been the focus for much educational enquiry (Ainscow, Booth, and Dyson, 2004; Armstrong and Moore, 2004; Dadds, 2005; Sikes, Lawson, and Parker, 2007). The impact of such professional development on the potential for teachers not just to enact but initiate educational change is explored in the following section.

Professional Development Through Educational Enquiry
The success of professional development is felt by some researchers to be dependent on the personal attitude of teachers (Nias, 1996; Sikes, Lawson, and Parker, 2007). In the context of professional development Cochran-Smith and Dudley-Marling (2012, p. 242) understand teachers to be: "… knowers, learners, and generators of knowledge, rather than simply the objects of others' research or the consumers/implementers of knowledge generated outside of the contexts of practice for use inside them".

For Cochran-Smith and Dudley-Marling, teacher education and professional development should be enquiry led, and should avoid a search for universally appropriate "best practices" (p. 242), reflecting Biesta's rejection of a search for "what works" in all contexts (2007, p. 1).

Dadds (2005, p. 31) comments that teacher knowledge about practice in the classroom is central to educational research which "burrows into the ethical heart of teaching and learning". She argues for the importance and value of the reflexive subjective voice in educational research as do Sikes, Lawson, and Parker (2007). These researchers emphasise the role of what Dadds describes as meaningful professional and academic conversations. These conversations may be in the form of seminars or conferences and these "conversation research communities" (Elliott cited in Dadds, 2005, p. 37) play an essential role in educational research. Dadds continues by arguing that when educational policy change fails to take into account "practitioners' situational judgement", that policy change will be difficult to implement and maintain. She reflects on the professional "crises of confidence" (2005, p. 38) experienced by teachers when their knowledge base is devalued in educational reform.

In the view of the teachers in my research study, professional development opportunities which enable them to learn about the learning and thinking style associated with the label of autism, were central to the development of inclusive pedagogies. Karen reflected that: "To allow all children no matter what their needs to reach their full potential, real organised training in a range of approaches and strategies is needed ..."

The opportunity to share examples of practice was valued by Wendy: "There is a need too for good practice to be shared and from my own experience there is a knowledge gap, even with recently trained colleagues ..."

Ballard (cited in Broderick et al., 2011, p. 838) argues that, in order for inclusive practice to develop, graduate teachers as they enter the teaching profession should:

> ... understand how they might create classrooms and schools that address issues of respect, fairness and equity. As part of this endeavour they will need to understand the historical, socio-cultural and ideological contexts that create discriminatory and oppressive practices in education ...

They continue by arguing that student teachers should have knowledge and understanding of the dominant discourses in inclusive education and the theoretical knowledge to be able to interrogate the implication of such discourses for practice.

Ainscow, Booth, and Dyson (2004) argue that the most effective forum for developing teachers' knowledge about inclusive practice is for academics to work with practising teachers, using their existing teaching activity as the focus for their professional development. The same authors argue (2006) that this form of professional development can be effective provided that teachers are enabled to reflect on and critique the values that underpin the competing performative and inclusive agendas in education. This would include reflection on the impact of the social construction of disablement and of the process of normalisation which permeates the education system. This aspect of teacher professional development is a central part of the move towards developing an education system that is equipped to work with a diverse range of pupil learning styles.

Conclusion

Currently in the development of inclusive education, teachers are able to make changes at the classroom level with the children with whom they work, at the school level through processes of school policy and practice development, and within groups of their peers through professional development opportunities and professional networks. It could be argued that the potential for teachers to act as agents of change more widely is limited by government policy through the performative agenda, which encourages conformity through processes of performance management. Changes at a level beyond this require teachers to act politically through their union or professional body, by offering a critique of government policy through the process of consultation on new policy proposals. The ground for this level of action needs to be prepared by teachers having access to the theoretical basis upon which educational policy is developed, and through being enabled to debate this theory in the context of reflection on their practice. This would include being enabled to critique and challenge the social construction of disablement and the process of normalcy which pervades the education system. This is where academics and teachers could work together as Ainscow, Booth, and Dyson (2004) and Armstrong and Moore

(2004) suggest. It is through a combination of teachers and their practice knowledge, and academics and their access to wider research-based knowledge and understanding, that real contribution to debate about educational policy could be effected.

The area of educational inclusion is in a constant state of flux, as are other areas of educational policy development, placed as it is at the heart of political debate. Teachers find themselves working in a normalising education system, affected by existing political developments, and pulled between the competing agendas of performativity and inclusion. Teachers, as individual members of society, will have diverse views on disablement and inclusive education. For some the notion of an accessible and inclusive education system is an issue of social justice, whilst for others the priority is an education system which promotes academic success above all else. For some the social construction of disablement will guide their approach to practice, whilst for others disablement continues to be an "individual tragedy". Existing education policy reflects this tension in attitude to, and conceptualisation of, disablement and acts to limit the development of an equitable and accessible education system, and the actions of the teachers within that system (Ball, 2013). Teachers work within an education system imbued with normalcy and it can be argued that the work of schools and teachers is normalised along with the performance of the children in those schools.

The potential for teachers to act as agents of change is currently limited by the practice and policy landscape within which they work. Perhaps this limit to "imagining the possibilities" of an inclusive education system could in part be addressed by teachers being enabled to critique and challenge the narrative of normalcy which permeates the education system, and to disseminate their perspectives through "conversation research communities" (Dadds, 2005), working together with academics to co-construct or re-imagine a model of an accessible and equitable education system for the future.

References

Ainscow, M., Booth, T., & Dyson, A., (2004). Understanding and developing inclusive practices in schools: A collaborative action research network. *International Journal of Inclusive Education, 8*(2), 125–139.

Ainscow, M., Booth, T., & Dyson, A. (2006). *Improving schools, developing inclusion*. Abingdon, United Kingdom: Routledge.

Armstrong, F. (2002). The historical development of special education: Humanitarian rationality or 'wild profusion of entangled events'? *History of Education: Journal of the History of Education Society, 31*(5), 437–456.

Armstrong, F. (2011). Inclusive education: School cultures, teaching and learning. In: G. Richards & F. Armstrong (Eds.), *Teaching and learning in inclusive classrooms: Key issues for new teachers* (pp. 7–18). Abingdon, United Kingdom: Routledge.

Armstrong, F., & Moore, M. (2004). Action research: Developing inclusive practice and transforming cultures. In F. Armstrong & M. Moore (Eds.), *Action research in inclusive education: Changing places, changing practice, changing minds* (pp. 1–16). London, United Kingdom: RoutledgeFalmer.

Atkinson, E. (2004). Thinking outside the box: An exercise in heresy. *Qualitative Inquiry, 10*(1), 111–129.

Ball, S. J. (2003). The teacher's soul and the terrors of performativity. *Journal of Education Policy, 18*(2), 215–228.

Ball, S. J. (2013). *Education, justice and democracy*. Retrieved from http://classonline.org.uk/docs/2013_Policy_Paper_ Education, _justice_and_democracy_

Benjamin, S. (2002). "Valuing diversity": A cliché for the 21st century? *International Journal of Inclusive Education, 6*(4), 309–323 http://dx.doi.org/10.1080/13603110210145949

Is This Inclusion?

Biesta, G. (2007). Why "what works" won't work: Evidence-based practice and the democratic deficit in educational research. *Educational Theory*, *57*(1), 1–22.

Broderick, A. A., Hawkins, G., Henze, S., Mirasol-Spath, C., Pollack-Berkovits, R., Prozzo Clune, H., Skovera, E., & Steel, C. (2011). Teacher counternarratives: Transgressing and 'restorying' disability in education. *International Journal of Inclusive Education*, *16*(8), 825–842.

Chantler, S. A. (2013). *"Is this inclusive?": Teachers' perspectives on inclusion for children labelled with autism.* Unpublished thesis, Sheffield Hallam University, Sheffield, United Kingdom.

Cochran-Smith, M., & Dudley-Marling, C. (2012). Diversity in teacher education and special education: The issues that divide. *Journal of Teacher Education*. *63*(4), 237–244.

Crossley, N. (2005). *Key concepts in critical social theory.* London, United Kingdom: Sage Publications.

Dadds, M. (2005). Taking curiosity seriously: The role of awe and Wanda in research-based professionalism. In K. Sheehy, M. Nind, J. Rix, & K. Simmons (Eds.), *Ethics and research in inclusive education values into practice* (pp. 28–42). Abingdon, United Kingdom: RoutledgeFalmer.

Department for Education and Science. (2004). *Removing barriers to achievement.* Retrieved from https://www.education.gov.uk/publications

Department for Education. (2010). *The importance of teaching: Schools White Paper.* Retrieved from http://www.education.gov.uk/schools/toolsandinitiatives/schoolswhitepaper

Department for Education (DfE) and Department of Health (DoH). (2014a). *Children and Families Act 2014.* Norwich: TSO (The Stationery Office). Retrieved from https://www.legislation.gov.uk/ukpga/2014/6/pdfs/ukpga_20140006

Department for Education (DfE) and Department of Health (DoH). (2014b). *Special educational needs and disability code of practice: 0 to 25 years.* DfE-00205-2013. Retrieved from https://www.gov.uk/government/publications/send-code-of-practice-0-25

Fullan, M. (2006). The future of educational change: System thinkers in action. *Journal of Educational Change, 7*, 113–122.

Goodley, D. (2011). *Disability studies: An interdisciplinary introduction.* London, UK: Sage Publications.

Hargreaves, A. (2002). Sustainability of educational change: The role of social geographies. *Journal of Educational Change, 3,* 189–214.

Hart, K. (2004). *Postmodernism: A beginner's guide.* Oxford, United Kingdom: Oneworld Publications.

Hodkinson, A. (2012). Illusionary inclusion – what went wrong with New Labour's landmark educational policy? *British Journal of Special Education, 39(1),* 4–11.

Howard, J. A. (2000). Social psychology of identities. *Annual Review of Sociology, 26,* 367–393.

Nias, J. (1996). Thinking about feeling: The emotions in teaching. *Cambridge Journal of Education, 26(3),* 293–307.

Nind, M. (2005). Inclusive education: Discourse and action: A thematic review *British Educational Research Journal, 31(2),* 269–275.

Oliver, M. (1996). Defining impairment and disability: Issues at stake. In C. Barnes & G. Mercer (Eds.), *Exploring the divide* (pp. 29–54). Leeds, United Kingdom: Leeds Disability Press.

Rieser, R. (2011). Disability, human rights and inclusive education and why inclusive education is the only educational philosophy that makes sense in today's world. In G. Richards & F. Armstrong (Eds.), *Teaching and learning in inclusive classrooms: Key issues for new teachers* (pp. 156–169). Abingdon, United Kingdom: Routledge.

Rix, J. (2011). Repositioning of special schools within a specialist, personalised educational marketplace – the need for a representative principle. *International Journal of Inclusive Education, 15(2),* 263–279.

Sikes, P., Lawson, H., & Parker, M. (2007). "Voices on": Teachers and teaching assistants talk about inclusion. *International Journal of Inclusive Education, 11(3),* 355–370.

Timperley, H. S., & Parr, J. M. (2005). Theory competition and the process of change. *Journal of Educational Change, 6,* 227–251.

Titchkosky, T. (2011). *The question of access: Disability, space, meaning.* London, United Kingdom: University of Toronto Press.

CHAPTER 4

THE "URGE TO KNOW" NORMAL: THEORISING HOW IMPAIRMENT LABELS FUNCTION

Rebecca Mallett and Katherine Runswick-Cole

Summary

We explore the cultural work carried out by impairment labels and consider what is at stake when they are deployed in response to the "urge to know" what's "wrong" with a person "with an impairment". We take an eclectic approach by delving into this "urge to know" as it manifests itself in personal encounters, scholarly practice and popular culture. We do this to demonstrate the ubiquity of the phenomenon, and therefore to underline the importance of radically theorising the functioning of impairment labels. We also aim to demarcate the socio-cultural functioning of impairment labels as an important issue to be considered in terms of a label's ability to impact the lives of disabled people as an instrument of psycho-emotional oppression (Reeve, 2002).

Using Foucault (1977, 1984), we further outline our purpose to examine a label's ability to function like an author's name. From here we examine an area of scholarly practice which focuses on "correctly" revealing the impairments of authors and literary characters, in order to ensure "correct" interpretations. We then discuss how impairment labels work to explain and account for "difference". In order to explore *what* is being explained, we move to interrogate a moment in popular culture which offers a glimpse into the work done by the explanations offered. Finally, we discuss how impairment labels enable the danger of difference to be neutralised by the demarcation of a "new" normal for the abnormal. Along the way, we acknowledge the political significance of choosing to reveal "disability" in otherwise hidden places and suggest that bio-graphic availability (the availability of information, often written, detailing the current state of bio-medical knowledge about that category of "abnormal") is key to understanding both the socio-cultural functioning of impairment and its potential consequences.

Introduction: Establishing the "Urge to Know" Via an Impairment Label

> At a conference, a colleague and I gave a presentation on care in which I mentioned that I was the parent of a disabled child. Over lunch, a woman I didn't know approached me and briefly said she was interested in the presentation and then asked "What is your son's problem?" I replied: "He doesn't have a problem, he is disabled." She countered, "Yes, but what is his disability?". I said I'd prefer not to say. (Author's Personal Encounter)

The vignette above illustrates what, for many disabled people, their friends and their families, is an everyday part of life, the casual request for an impairment label. Snyder and Mitchell (2006, cited in Mallett and Runswick-Cole, 2014, p. 123) have also discussed how "disability scholars and activists frequently encounter journalists who seem to believe that gaining access to one's disability label somehow delivers the truth of one's social identity". Our interest here is in *how* such knowledge is, more often than not, asked for and desired in the form of an impairment label. In the story above, knowing that the child was disabled was deemed *not enough* information; despite a clear attempt to rebuff further questioning on the topic of impairment, the "urge to know" compelled the stranger to persist in her line of questioning. The denial of information in the form of a label is often considered unreasonable, unnecessary and rude. "What's the problem with just telling me what the problem is?" could be the next question on the stranger's mind, if not her lips. It is in the "unreasonableness" of the denial that we glimpse the cultural acceptance of the "urge to know".

In this chapter, we seek to explore the cultural work carried out by impairment labels and consider what is at stake when they are deployed. While we acknowledge the central role of medical science in the creation and maintenance of such labels, we have chosen a rather more eclectic approach by delving into the "urge to know" as it manifests itself in personal encounters, scholarly practice and popular culture. We do this to demonstrate the ubiquity of the phenomenon, and therefore to underline the importance of radically theorising the socio-cultural functioning of impairment labels. We argue that this is important because of the impact it can have on the lives of disabled people and their families and allies. We suggest that the "urge to know" operates as a form of less favourable treatment of disabled people and is an example of psycho-emotional disablism placing limits on what "labelled" people "*can do*" and "can be" (Thomas, 2007, p. 72).

Using Foucault (1977, 1984), we position the impairment label as a similar entity to that of the "author" in order to examine a label's ability to function like an author's name. From here we continue our eclectic investigation, by examining an area of scholarly practice which focuses on "correctly" revealing the impairments of authors and literary characters, in order to ensure "correct" interpretations. Here we position the "urge to know" as an urge to "correctly" explain and discuss how impairment labels work to account for "difference". In order to explore what is being explained, we move to interrogate a moment in popular culture which further reveals this "urge to know" but also offers a glimpse into the work done by the explanations offered. Here, we discuss how impairment labels enable the perceived "danger" of difference to be neutralised by the demarcation of a "new" normal for the abnormal. Along the way, we acknowledge the political significance of choosing to reveal impairment in otherwise hidden places and suggest that bio-graphic availability is a key aspect in understanding the discursive functioning of impairment.

Theorising Normalcy and the Mundane

Impairment Labels and the Author-Function

> To understand the book, a little must be known about its author.
> (Anon, *c*.1924, p. 5 – "Introduction" to Harriet Beecher Stowe's
> [1852] *Uncle Tom's Cabin*)

By beginning this section with an anonymous quotation of indeterminate date (*c*.1924) we begin with a quotation which is capable of unsettling many attempts at interpretation: the significance, tone, intention and profundity of this remark are hard to assess for the usual authorial indicator is missing. That the quotation was deemed worthy enough to be included in a commercially produced copy of an American "classic" (*Uncle Tom's Cabin* by Harriet Beecher Stowe) hints at its legitimacy; however, its significance lies for us in its failure to signal its own origins.

As Foucault (1977, 1984) discussed, the lack of an author's name does not simply correspond to the inability to identify the exact historical person responsible for the production of the work, it also corresponds to a lack of, amongst other things, a punctual explanation, a unifying principle, a neutralising force and/or a source of expression. Without a "name" the work has no readily apparent origin and therefore its existence becomes difficult to assess and legitimise as valid.

By way of a response to Derrida and Barthes, who were occupied with the so-called "death of the author", Foucault (1977, p. 121) argues that rather than merely reiterate the empty slogan and maintain that the author is irrelevant:

> we should re-examine the empty space left by the author's disappearance; we should attentively observe, along its gaps and fault lines, its new demarcations, and the reapportionment of this void; we should await the fluid functions released by this disappearance. In this context we can briefly consider the problems that arise in the use of an author's name.

98

The "Urge to Know" Normal

The focus and aim of this chapter draws much from Foucault. By focusing on an entity, similar to that of the "author" (the impairment label), we are able to explore its ability to function like an author's name and to consider the problems that arise from its (dis)appearance and use. While we uphold the classic "social model" distinction between "impairment" and "disability" (Mallett and Runswick-Cole, 2014), we maintain that impairment (or, more precisely, the labels which seek to name impaired states) should be understood *bioculturally* rather than as existing biologically, before and untouched by the social and cultural contexts within which they are experienced (Davis, 2008, 2010; Mallett and Runswick-Cole, 2012, 2014, forthcoming). This mirrors Foucault's (1984, p. 119) insistence that authors are not entities that precede the work but rather "a certain functional principle by which, in our culture, one limits, excludes, and chooses". This comparison enables us to suggest that impairment labels have become an accepted part of our routine and scholarly attempts to limit, exclude and construct difference. Indeed, as Foucault (1984, p. 119) comments, "the author" (for us the impairment label) "is therefore the ideological figure by which one marks the manner in which we fear the proliferation of meaning". We begin our journey at a point where a certain sort of literary endeavour meets impairment.

File Under Impaired: The Urge to "Discover" Impairment
In *Enforcing Normalcy*, Lennard Davis (1995, p. 6) asks whether:

> people realise that when they encountered the work of Rosa Luxemburg (who limped), Antonio Gramsci (a crippled, dwarfed hunchback), John Milton (blind), Alexander Pope (dwarfed hunchback), George Gordon Byron (club foot), José Luis Borges, James Joyce and James Thurber (all blind), Harriet Martineau (deaf), Toulouse-Lautrec (spinal deformity), Frida

99

Kahlo (osteomyelitis), Virginia Woolf (lupus), they were meeting people with disabilities?

The presumed answer to all is a definitive "no" and the implication of Davis's remark is that, for disability to become a significant issue, the "dominant" culture needs to realise it is not a marginalised "minority" issue; that disability is, indeed, everywhere. Part of this public-outreach project involves uncovering disability in hitherto unacknowledged places – historical or contemporary. This "uncovering" is done, in part, by seeking out authors who were/are impaired and is a practice which brings together two seemingly neutral categories: the "author" and the "impairment label". Rather than exploring the difference an "impaired authorship" makes to the (often-historical) literary text, our aim is to ask what does the urge to do so reveal about current scholarly practices around, and personal encounters with, impairment. We begin by exploring current scholarly practices, and in particular examine the area of "literature and medicine".

As Mallett and Runswick-Cole (2014) discuss, "literature and medicine" is a sub-discipline of medical humanities (Jones, 2013) which introduced the study of literature into US medical schools. As a teaching discipline, it aims to help physicians develop skills and methods in the human dimensions of medical practice (Charon et al., 1995) such as understanding "pain and suffering" and interpreting "narrative" in clinical settings (Charon, 2000). This interest has been combined with archival research and sees some scholars seeking to label authors and literary characters with contemporary medical diagnoses (Mallett and Runswick-Cole, 2014). It is argued that the "means the doctor uses to interpret accurately what the patient tells are not unlike the means a reader uses to understand the words of a writer" (Charon, 2000, p. 24) and therefore it is not a great leap to attempt accurate diagnostic interpretation of the medical conditions of historical literary authors and characters. From there, the literary work is often re-read in the light of this new knowledge. In other words, a strand of scholarly practice in this area reveals an "urge to know" the impairment status of the author or character in order to better understand the text.

A good example of a historical author upon which attempts to diagnose have been made is Dr Samuel Johnson, who has garnered a great deal of attention. Murray (2003, p. 272) claims "over 80 physicians" have written about Johnson and it is worth noting, as summarised by Murray, the expanse of diagnoses he has inspired:

> There are excellent accounts of the scrofula (the King's Evil) he suffered as a child, unsuccessfully treated by the Royal Touch of Queen Anne; the recurring depression that plagued him like "a black dog of melancholy"; his tics and gesticulations; the stroke that left him aphasic but able to write; his death in 1784; and his necropsy. (Murray, 1979, cited in Mallett and Runswick-Cole, 2014, p. 124)

The remainder of Murray's article is given to a consideration of a diagnosis of Tourette's Syndrome. Other conditions attributed to Dr Johnson include poor eyesight, gout, sarcoma of the testicles, right heart failure with cor pulmonale and hypertension (McHenry, 1967; Murray, 2003).

Interestingly, despite the extent of writings on him, Murray (2003, p. 368) comments that "Johnson had many illnesses, but was probably no more unhealthy than most of his generation", suggesting that interest in Johnson is not a function of his medical peculiarity, although he appears an abundant source, but more a function of "biographic" availability. To give some indication of this, Johnson was not only the subject of Boswell's intensively researched *Life of Johnson* but also appears in the personal journals of Thomas Campbell, the portraits of Sir Joshua

Reynolds (both cited in Deutsch, 2002), and has been the subject of many subsequent considerations such as Thomas Carlyle's *On Heroes, Hero-Worship and the Heroic in History* (1903) and Richard Holmes's *Dr. Johnson and Mr. Savage* (cited in Deutsch, 2002). This notion of *biographic availability* is something we will return to shortly.

An allied interest of "literature and medicine" is in diagnosing literary characters, an example of which appeared in the *British Medical Journal*. Bashir et al. (2004, p. 1435) assert that Tolkien's character Gollum is "certainly disturbed" but, they ask, "is he physically or mentally ill?". The character, from *The Hobbit* (1937) and the three-volume *The Lord of the Rings* (1954–1955), receives formal diagnosis in the conclusion:

> Gollum displays pervasive maladaptive behaviour that has been present since childhood [...] He fulfils seven of the nine criteria for schizoid personality disorder. (Bashir et al., 2004 cited in Mallett and Runswick-Cole, 2014, p. 124)

Another example is Ostrowski's (1998) article, which attempts to diagnose a character from Nathaniel Hawthorne's 1836 short story *The Minister's Black Veil* (1955). The story tells of the Reverend Mr Parson Hooper who arrives, one day, at the Sunday service wearing a black veil. The congregation is unnerved by his appearance and becomes more so as he preaches a sermon about secret sins. Hooper continues to wear the veil, even in death, despite the townspeople's increasing discomfort with this practice. Ostrowski (1998, p. 197) asserts that Parson Hooper does not, as most interpretations contend, wear a veil as a "heroic act of self-sacrifice" or due to an inability to "negotiate the demands of adult sexuality". Instead, Ostrowski (1998, p. 198) suggests, it is because he: "suffers from a physical (and moral) infirmity that is quite literally visible on his face and that he wishes to hide from the community of Milford: Hooper's face is scarred by the ravages of syphilis". Part of the evidence offered for this diagnosis is given by way of a comparison between Hooper's behaviour and the "known" symptoms of the disease (such as a slow, stooping gait and potential possession of a skin rash or pock marks on the face resulting in the use of a veil) as well as the coherences with other works in the Hawthorne canon which consider the body as a site for punishment due to moral failing (Ostrowski, 1998).

Likewise, Frith (2003) suggests that the fictional character Sherlock Holmes may have had a form of autism and Bermis, Harton, Brunet, and Schmitt (2003) contend that Achilles, in Homer's epic poem, *The Iliad*, suffers recurrent recollections which cause very agitated sleep; a situation they describe as "post-traumatic reactions" or, to use the diagnostic label, post-traumatic stress disorder (PTSD). Although such writing is not formally within "literature and medicine", it can be seen to be following the traditions of the sub-discipline by engaging in the retrospective diagnosis of literary/historical characters.

An interesting inversion to this approach is the urge to negate the widely accepted literary representation of "hunchback" of another historical and literary figure, Richard III. Oestreich-Hart (2000, p. 244) comments that "while Shakespeare may have created Richard as a hunchback villain, based on the Tudor-spawned histories with which he was familiar", some scholars argue that the "real" Richard III was in fact "not a hunchback, but was tolerably fair of form, feature, and character" (Oestreich-Hart, 2000, p. 243). Such scholars included the physician Rhodes (1977, p. 1650) who sets out his intentions thus:

> to follow Shakespeare in building up an image of what might have been the medical diagnosis in Richard's case, then compare that with the facts about the man as they seem to be known, and so develop a hypothesis to describe what may have happened to

him at birth or in utero which may have affected his later appearance.

Rhodes (1977, p. 1651) deduces that "from portraits and other evidence it now seems certain that Richard did not have a hunchback," concluding that the king probably had no great bodily abnormality and was slight of build with a normal though "unusual raised shoulder, or that he had a minor degree of Sprengel's deformity" (Rhodes, 1977, p. 1652). A position repeated in 2009 by Tulloch who goes on to link the portrayal as a hunchback to attempts to tarnish Richard III's reputation for political reasons.

What is interesting about this urge to negate such a widely accepted portrayal is, rather than literature being interrogated for diagnostic clues, literature is charged, by medical practitioners, with working to obscure medical "truth". However, in this case, the tussle over the medical "truth" of Richard's hunchback has recently seen archaeological intervention by the discovery of the remains of Richard III in September 2012. At the time, it was widely reported that the adult male skeleton's spine shows signs of "deformity"; this has since been formally diagnosed and reported in the *Lancet* as scoliosis (Appleby et al., 2014).

What this final example demonstrates clearly is the urge to bring the discourses of "modern" diagnosis to bear on historical and/or literary figures. Scholars are interested in revealing the "truth" and there is a strong sense that an accurate interpretation rests on an accurate medical diagnosis. Rather than this being a concern of a specific corner of academia, we argue that it is simply an extreme example of the "urge to know" and that "discovering the details of impairment" is a significant way in which the uncertainty of difference is routinely negotiated. Before moving on we want to acknowledge the political significance of some of this work.

Reclamations: A Political Act of Revelation?

As touched on above, there *is* a political impetus to revealing impairment/disability in places it has yet to be noticed, whether that be in literary authors, characters or historical figures. For us, whether it is *impairment* or *disability* being noticed makes a significant difference to the political potential of that act of revelation.

In his book *Autism and Creativity* (2004), Fitzgerald claims an array of historical figures, such as George Orwell, Isaac Newton, Albert Einstein and Andy Warhol as "autistic subjects". Brown (2010) adds Hans Christian Andersen, Lewis Carroll, Herman Melville and Emily Dickinson to the list of "authors with autism" in her book *Writers on the Spectrum: How Autism and Asperger Syndrome Have Influenced Literary Writing*. Similarly, Adelman and Adelman (1987) cite Hans Christian Andersen along with Charles Darwin, Winston Churchill and Leonardo da Vinci as people who have been posthumously labelled with "learning disabilities". All these moves could be termed "celebratory interpretations" (Lewis 2006, p. 27) and they also, like the moves Davis (1995) makes, can be seen as a political act to reveal impairment in places it has yet to be acknowledged. As Brown (2010, p. 11) states:

> I want to celebrate the good news that many of the world's most important writers – those who have made original, brilliant, daring contributions to literary achievement – were able to do so, in part, because of their place on the autistic spectrum.

However, after reviewing the available evidence for Albert Einstein having "learning disabilities", Thomas (2000) concludes that despite there being little evidence to support these claims, their continued repetition could be explained by a desire to believe that "even geniuses can suffer from learning disabilities"

(Adelman and Adelman, 1987, cited in Thomas, 2000, p. 157). It is here we glimpse the motivation for such revelations.

Mallett (2007) has suggested that the act of uncovering and reclaiming literary authors can be said to have five important purposes:

(a) challenging the idea that all literary and cultural works have been exclusively produced by non-disabled people;

(b) amending the historical record by reinstating "disability" eclipsed or erased by the mechanisms of success;

(c) challenging the designation of the literary and cultural archive as a repository full of *only* devalued and negative images;

(d) challenging the idea of disabled people as "completely" and "uniformly" oppressed by cultural production processes;

(e) disputing the idea that "disability" issues have no import in literature and/or literary studies.

However, she does this while making a distinction between "impaired" and "disabled" authors. Mallett (2007) explains that she makes this linguistic move because "impaired" does not *immediately* implicate a contemporary political dimension in quite the same way that the word "disabled" does and which the historical author cannot be said (without due substantiation) to possess. This is a "conceptual gap" also highlighted by Davis (1995, p. 10) when he remarks "[a]s soon as we use the term "disabled" we add a political element: suddenly there is a disabler and a disabled".

For us, this is an important distinction and we do not intend to marginalise or play down reclamations which are politically motivated by a desire to reveal the hidden history of disability, where disability is understood as the experience of societal prejudice and oppression. In terms of literary and cultural criticism, it is important that disability be placed alongside race, sexuality and gender as significant perspectives to bring to an author's work. In terms of wider impacts, such reclaiming also has a part to play in offering alternative resources for positive disabled identities. These, in turn, can lead to increased individual and collective self-esteem (Borsay, 2002). For example, Crow (2000) has demonstrated how the image of Helen Keller as a little deaf blind "miracle child", eclipses the life of a woman who was a writer and radical activist, a suffragette and a Socialist. Crow (2000) ends by speaking about how resistance is built up by the passing on of history and how, for her, researching Helen Keller became a reclaiming of her story as part of disability history.

We argue that while these reclamations have an important role to play, they should be seen as making politically *strategic* moves rather than "revealing" the "truth" about literary works or of the past. This refocuses our concern on reclamation exercises which involve the designation of a "correct" "impairment label". Foucault (1977, p. 123) comments in relation to an author's name: "its status and its manner of reception are regulated by the culture in which it circulates". Similarly, Davis (2010, p. 228) has commented that "no diagnosis is actually unproblematic or freed from social and cultural issues". Consequently, it is *how* the "impairment label" functions within the act of reclamation which is of concern to us. For example, our interest would be in how the "correct" label of "autistic" goes on to function as a "punctual explanation" and, even, as a "source of expression" (Foucault, 1977, p. 1984) for figures such as George Orwell, Isaac Newton, Albert Einstein and Andy Warhol.

The ease and voracity with which authors and historical figures are reclaimed as having certain impairments indicates, once more, the unquestioned presence, and the cultural acceptance, of the use of impairment labels. In the next section we discuss the socio-cultural work such labels do when they are deployed by considering a moment of reality make-over TV in which, we argue, it is possible to glimpse what is really at stake in such seemingly mundane and unproblematised interactions with difference.

For More Information: The Urge to "Know" Impairment Categories

In January 2010, Channel 4 broadcast an episode of the reality make-over programme *How to Look Good Naked*[2] in which the host, Gok Wan, meets a "single-mum Tracy Warren [...] who has been using a wheelchair since 2007". It was the first in a trilogy of episodes to be subtitled ... *with a difference*, each focusing on a person with a physical impairment. Twenty minutes into this first episode, just before an advertising break, a Gok Wan voice-over informs the viewers: "For more information on any of the disabilities featured in the show go to www.channel4.com/ naked" (*How to Look Good Naked ... with a Difference*, 2010).

In a programme navigating the treacherous waters of disability and reality make-over entertainment, this moment reveals a fracture in the logic of the show and once again reveals the important part played by the "urge to know". The programme's self-confessed remit, as outlined on the website, was as follows: Gok Wan presents the inspirational fashion series that shows women how to look fantastic with their clothes on or off no matter what their body shape – and all without a surgeon's

---

[2] The format of this TV series is a familiar one. Each episode focuses on an individual, usually a female, and explores how "drab" and "dull" they look and dress. They are then led through a series of "challenges" which boosts their self-esteem while increasing their knowledge of contemporary fashion trends. The finale in each episode of *How to Look Good Naked* is often a fashion show in a shopping centre on a rainy day during which the individual "struts their stuff" wearing very little and thus declares – look how good I look (nearly) naked!

scalpel in sight ... (*How to Look Good Naked ... with a Difference*, 2010).

If we consider the implied content of the *"more information"* being offered we can deduce that it will be biomedical knowledge intended to explain the featured disabled person's body or behaviour – a far cry from the claim to not care about "body shape" or "surgeon's corrective scalpel". The significance of offering such knowledge reveals a perceived need for it to be available, a perceived urge to "know" more, revealing an admission that what was presented in the programme was not enough and lacked the basic details: an echo of the personal encounter with which we began.

If we consider the intended use of the *"more information"* in *How to Look Good Naked*, we can further speculate that such biomedical knowledge could be read by viewers hoping to learn something about themselves, family members, friends or work colleagues. When discussing Obsessive Compulsive Disorder (OCD), Davis (2008, p. 229) has highlighted how the "stream of information about the disease entity swirls through the media, self-help books, memoirs, and word of mouth" resulting in the possibilities that "individuals, family and friends can 'know' these symptoms, find them in a friend or relative, 'understand' what needs to be done, and place the simplified streamlined disease entity within a confident and knowing treatment regime". In other words, Gok Wan's offer of *"more information"* can be said to be about more than supplying medical facts or pandering to idle curiosity. We suggest here that the specificities of impairment labels are revealed as a way to indirectly interact with difference and, in doing so, neutralise its danger by gaining knowledge over it.

Foucault's (1977, p. 123) insight was to treat the presence of an author's name as "functional in that it serves as a means of classification". We argue that impairment labels function in a similar way because they offer a way to make sense of what is before us. As Davis (2010, p. 229) has stated, the "implication of the word 'diagnosis' is that we can know a disease apart from other diseases or apart from anything". Impairment labels enable us to name a discrete categorisation of human "being" and through doing so, come to "know" it. In the next section we ask: if author's names/impairment labels provide a classification function, could it be that their attraction – why we seem to have an "urge to know" through them – lies in how they organise infinite possibilities into clear, easily handled units?

Essential Tourist Information: Bio-Graphic Availability of the "Normal Abnormal"

The crucial point we want to make here is that impairment labels are not just helping to classify and explain diversions from "normal", but by marshalling the vastness of humanity into discrete "categories of existence" (Davis, 2008), those "categories" go on to provide new sets of norms for what it means to be within the specified sub-category. In other words, medical diagnostic categories provide, and are used as, essential tourist information for those travelling to or through the land of impairment.

Sometimes travellers in this land are interested in first-hand accounts and local knowledge, evidenced, for example, by the voracious publication and consumption of autistic narratives in recent years (see Jessica Kingsley publications for examples). However, it is the authoritative authorial voice of the travel writer that reveals the "truth" about the tourist location and, in the land of impairment, the most valued tourist information draws its authority from medicine. The "truth" about the impairment category is determined by the most legitimate and accurate travel writer – the biomedical "author". To a large extent, even first-hand accounts rely on the pre-described features of the diagnostic destination offered by medical science.

Consequently, the extent to which a category is able to provide tourist information depends on its *bio-graphic availability* – the availability of information, often written, detailing the current state of bio-medical knowledge about that category of "abnormal".

Available information on what is "normal" to find within a particularly category of "abnormal" often includes potential lifespan, possible behavioural traits and probable co-morbidity factors. The internet is one place which allows unfettered public access to such tourist information. For example, the online user-led encyclopaedia, Wikipedia, had the following information on Down Syndrome:

> Individuals with Down syndrome may have some or all of the following physical characteristics: microgenia (abnormally small chin), oblique eye fissures with epicanthic skin folds on the inner corner of the eyes (formerly known as a mongoloid fold), muscle hypotonia (poor muscle tone), a flat nasal bridge, a single palmar fold, a protruding tongue (due to small oral cavity, and an enlarged tongue near the tonsils) or macroglossia, a short neck, white spots on the iris known as Brushfield spots, excessive joint laxity including atlanto-axial instability, congenital heart defects, excessive space between large toe and second toe, a single flexion furrow of the fifth finger, and a higher number of ulnar loop dermatoglyphs and short fingers. (Wikipedia, 2010)

It is here we again understand why "literature and medicine" seeks to diagnose authors and why Gok Wan sought to reassure his viewers with the promise of *"more information"*: like the name of an author on the cover of a book, an impairment label acts as a punctual explanation, a unifying principle and a neutralising force by *normalising the abnormal* (Foucault, 1977, p. 1984). Freely available descriptions such as this take away the danger posed by the myriad of possibilities presented by the unknown and the "abnormal" (here, Down Syndrome) by presenting and imposing a knowable, unified and neutralised order. And, crucially, it suggests that the only way we have to deal with the abnormal is to create alternative normals, or "normal abnormals". So, rather than a narrow focus on the abnormal, we are arguing that it is these "alternative normals" which medicine is busy creating. The *Diagnostic and Statistical Manual of Mental Disorders (DSM)*, published by the American Psychiatric Association, is an example of an "official" compendium which offers a common classification system and standard criteria for the diagnosis of mental disorders, or in other words, offers standardised categories and criteria for the "normal abnormals".

However, elsewhere on the Wikipedia page it states: "Many of the common physical features of Down Syndrome may also appear in people with a standard set of chromosomes" (Wikipedia, 2010). Far from being punctual, unifying and neutralising, we argue, impairment labels enact a mass and compelling deception for, ultimately, they cannot do what they promise to do: they cannot, once and for all, nullify difference.

Falling Through the Cracks: When "Normal Abnormal" Isn't Enough

When discussing the impact of a diagnosis of autism on families, Hodge (2005, p. 345) has commented:

> In three cases I have been researching in depth, the diagnosis of ASD [autistic spectrum disorder] has had a largely devastating impact on the parents, disempowering them by causing them to question their ability to interact with and provide for their child without specialist training, even though they were doing an excellent job up to the time of diagnosis. The term "Autistic Spectrum Disorder" causes them to rethink completely their child's potential future, making them fearful of what lies ahead. Through talking with others and through their reading, the parents become unsure of how their child will be in the future; one family who had a very cooperative young son began to

become highly anxious that he would, in the future, develop severely non-cooperative behaviours like children they read about in textbooks.

It becomes clear here that being told your child is not "normal" is quickly followed by anxiety over whether your child will match the "normality" of the abnormal, as told to you by the array of tourist information offered by professionals, other families, textbooks and, as we saw earlier, the internet. Impairment labels may provide relief by imposing a knowable and neutralised order, but such a relief is often short-lived as one realises that the multitude of possibilities remain.

We know that parents of disabled children and practitioners often want to know impairment labels, not least because, in the UK, these are often tied to resource allocation, but, as we are demonstrating, the difficulty with impairment labels is that they satisfy the "urge to know" only partially and only temporarily. Impairment labels may seem to offer the hope of certainty but, we argue, as Davis (2010) does, that this certainty is misleading.

In a research interview with a mother, Natalie, of a child labelled with Down Syndrome, one of the authors asked Natalie what she would change if she had a magic wand. Natalie replied "Am I allowed to say Nadia [her daughter]?" She paused and added:

> If I said I didn't want her to have Down's Syndrome [*sic*] I don't know what that would mean. Our family, my relationship with my partner, my children, we are all defined by having a disabled child. Can I wave the magic wand so that Nadia has a normal version of Down's Syndrome?

In asking for her daughter to have a "normal version" of Down Syndrome, Natalie was reflecting on her feeling that her daughter was not following a typical developmental pathway for a child with Down Syndrome: she was on the "severe" rather than the "moderate to mild" side of learning disability, she was not a particularly "happy, smiley and affectionate child", in fact Nadia "doesn't like to be touched". For Nadia, then, the diagnosis of Down Syndrome was a form of unreliable tourist information. The certainty of a label which promised a "normal" version of "abnormality" is fractured by a child who fails to match up to the normal version of the abnormal: an atypical child with Down Syndrome. At the time of the interview, however, not surprisingly and understandably, Natalie's faith in impairment labels was not shaken, as she wondered if her daughter might also have "autism" – therefore seeking to neutralise the dangers of the abnormal Down Syndrome by introducing another "category of existence" and hoping the overlap would provide the punctual explanation and unified order. If that was successful, she would finally "know" her daughter and be able to explain her to others. We are starting to see here, what is at stake when we interact with difference through labels of impairment.

What is at Stake in "Knowing" Through Labels of Impairment?
There has been much written in recent years about the place of "impairment" in Disability Studies, especially if we think in terms of the debates between those loyal to a materialist social model and those asking for biological concerns not to be forgotten. We will not dwell on these fraught and complex discussions; suffice it to say that it is this realm of theory in which we are interested.

Shakespeare (2006, p. 40) admits that "attention to labelling and discourse is important" but adds "there is a danger of ignoring the problematic reality of biological limitation". By paying attention to the discursive functioning of impairment we do not seek to deny impairment effects or advocate a naive celebratory perspective on difference. On the contrary, by insisting on paying attention to the biocultural nature of impairment we are refusing to reify the false dichotomies between biology/culture, physical/mental, material/ symbolic. We seek to address the problematic reality of a proliferation in the "biologisation of difference" (Shakespeare, 2006, p. 41) which directly impacts upon how biological difference is encountered and experienced. In the cases we have discussed, the "biologisation of difference" is rewriting literary texts, historical lives and, in the cases Hodge describes, it is rewriting children.

While Davis (2010) and Parker (2010) tussle over the role of certainty in the diagnostic process, we would argue that impairment labels do function via a promise to explain, unify and neutralise uncertainty. We tend to be a little nearer Davis's conceptualisation but even if, as Parker (2010, p. 291) states, "diagnostic categories in psychological medicine, like those in physical medicine, are provisional, probabilistic and often uncertain", that does not preclude them from *culturally* functioning via certainty.

Davis (2008, pp. 12–13) has argued that "the danger of a clinical perspective is that it tends to define the disease entity in universal terms, such that a patient with a particular disease will have these particular symptoms and outcomes in all situations at all times". We argue here, it is precisely when the ambiguities of the diagnostic process are forgotten and the use of the resulting impairment labels is unquestioned, that those labels function as essentialising, all-encompassing bio-medical "truth". This, in turn, enables routine and everyday assumptions of not only what it means to be "normal" but also of what it means to be "normally abnormal". These assumptions give us a false sense of certainty over difference, provide arbitrary measures for legitimisation and prevent the full acceptance of humanity.

Conclusion

We have argued that there is an urge to "know impairment", and that by "knowing" impairment we seek to gain control, replace uncertainty with certainty, and receive comfort (however misleading or temporary this may be) in discovering the "normal" version of the abnormal. Finally, we argue that the consequences of the urge to know impairment, especially those which effect psycho-emotional disablism, are not merely "private troubles" for individuals or families but are crucially significant for disabled people and those interconnected with them.

References

Adelman, K. A., & Adelman, H. S. (1987). Rodin, Patton, Edison, Wilson, Einstein: Were they really learning disabled? *Journal of Learning Disabilities, 20,* 270–278.

Appleby, J., Mitchell, P. D., Robinson, C., Brough, A., Rutty, G., Harris, R. A., Thompson, D., & Morgan, B. (2014). The scoliosis of Richard III, last Plantagenet King of England: Diagnosis and clinical significance. *Lancet, 383*(9932), 1944.

Bashir, N., Ahmed, N., Singh, A., Tang, Y. Z., Young, M., Abba, A., & Sampson, E. L. (2004). A precious case from Middle Earth. *British Medical Journal, 329,* 1435–1436.

Bermis, P., Harton, L., Brunet, A., & Schmitt, L. (2003). Early historical literature for post-traumatic stress symptomatology. *Stress and Health, 19,* 17–26.

Borsay, A. (2002). History, power and identity. In C. Barnes, M. Oliver, & L. Barton (Eds.), *Disability studies today* (pp. 98–119). Cambridge, United Kingdom: Polity.

Brown, J. (2010). *Writers on the spectrum: How autism and Asperger syndrome have influenced literary writing.* London, United Kingdom: Jessica Kingsley Publishers.

Carlyle, T. (1903). *On heroes, hero-worship and the heroic in history.* New York, NY: Scribner.

Charon, R. (2000). Literature and medicine: Origins and destinies. *Academic Medicine, 75*(1), 23–27.

Charon, R., Banks, T. J., Connelly, J. E., Hawkins, A. H., Hunter, K. M., Jones, A. H., Montello, M., & Poirer, S. (1995). Literature and medicine: Contributions to clinical practice. *Annals of Internal Medicine, 122*(128), 599–606.

Crow, L. (2000). Helen Keller: Rethinking the problematic icon. *Disability and Society, 15*(6), 845–859.

Davis, L. J. (1995). *Enforcing normalcy: Disability, deafness and the body.* London, United Kingdom and New York, NY: Verso.

Davis, L. J. (2008). *Obsession: A history.* Chicago, IL: University of Chicago Press.

Davis, L. J. (2010). The bioethics of diagnosis: A biocultural critique of certainty. *Journal of Bioethical Inquiry, 7*(2), 227–235.

Deutsch, H. (2002). Exemplary aberration: Samuel Johnson and the English canon. In S. Snyder, B. J. Brueggemann, & R. G. Thomson (Eds.), *Disability studies: Enabling the humanities* (pp. 197–210). New York, NY: The Modern Language Association of America.

Fitzgerald, M. (2004). *Autism and creativity: Is there a link between autism in men and exceptional ability?* Hove, United Kingdom: Brumner-Routledge.

Foucault, M. (1977) [1969]. What is an author? In D. F. Bouchard (Ed.), *Michel Foucault: Language, counter-memory, practice: Selected essays and interview* (pp. 113–138). Oxford, United Kingdom: Blackwell. Trans: D. F. Bouchard & S. Simon.

Foucault, M. (1984) [1969]. What is an author? In P. Rabinow (Ed.), *The Foucault reader: An introduction to Foucault's thought* (pp. 101–120). London, United Kingdom: Penguin.

Frith, U. (2003). *Autism: Explaining the enigma.* Oxford, United Kingdom: Blackwell.

Hawthorne, N. (1955) [1836]. The Minister's Black Veil. In N. Arvin (Ed.), *Hawthorne's short stories* (pp. 9–23). New York, NY: Vintage.

Hodge, N. (2005). Reflections on diagnosing autism spectrum disorders. *Disability and Society, 20*(3), 345–349.

How to Look Good Naked … with a Difference (2010). Channel 4 [online] Last accessed 23 January 2010. Retrieved from: http://www.channel4.com/programmes/how-to-look-good-naked

How to Look Good Naked … with a Difference (2010, 19 January) [TV broadcast]. London, UK: Channel 4.

Jones, A. H. (2013). Why teach literature and medicine? Answers from three decades. *Journal of Medical Humanities, 34*(4), 415–428.

Lewis, B. (2006). *Moving beyond Prozac, DSM, and the new psychiatry*. Ann Arbor, MI: University of Michigan Press.

Mallett, R. (2007). *Critical correctness: Exploring the capacities of contemporary disability-criticism* (unpublished doctoral dissertation). Sheffield, United Kingdom: University of Sheffield.

Mallett, R., & Runswick-Cole, K. (2012). Commodifying autism: The cultural contexts of "disability" in the academy. In D. Goodley, B. Hughes, & L. Davis. (Eds.), *Disability and social theory: New developments and directions* (pp. 33–51). London, United Kingdom: Palgrave Macmillan.

Mallett, R., & Runswick-Cole, K. (2014). *Approaching disability: Critical issues and perspectives*. Abingdon, United Kingdom: Routledge.

Mallett, R., & Runswick-Cole, K. (2016). The commodification of autism: What's at stake? in K. Runswick-Cole, S. Timimi, & R. Mallett (Eds.), *Rethinking autism*. London, United Kingdom: Jessica Kingsley Publishers.

Murray, T. J. (2003). Samuel Johnson: His ills, his pills and his physician friends. *Clinical Medicine 3*(4), 368–372.

McHenry, L. C. (1967). Samuel Johnson's tics and gesticulations. *Journal of the History of Medicine and Allied Sciences, 22*(2), 152–168.

Oestreich-Hart, D. J. (2000). "Therefore, since I cannot prove a lover". *Studies in English Literature 40*(2), 241–260.

Ostrowski, C. (1998). The Minister's "grievous affliction": Diagnosing Hawthorne's Parson Hooper. *Literature and Medicine 17*(2), 197–211.

Parker, M. (2010). Diagnosis, power and certainty: Response to Davis. *Journal of Bioethical Inquiry, 7*(3), 291–297.

Reeve, D. (2002). Negotiating psycho-emotional dimensions of disability and their influence on identity construction. *Disability and Society, 17*(5), 493–508.

Rhodes, P. (1977). Physical deformity of Richard III. *British Medical Journal, 2*, 1650–1652.

Shakespeare, T. (2006). *Disability rights and wrongs*. Abingdon, United Kingdom: Routledge.

Stowe, H. B. (*c.*1924) [1852]. *Uncle Tom's Cabin*. London, United Kingdom: Odhams Press.

Thomas, C. (2007). *Female forms: Experiencing and understanding disability*. Buckingham, United Kingdom: Open University Press.

Thomas, M. (2000). Albert Einstein and LD: An evaluation of the evidence. *Journal of Learning Disabilities, 33*(2), 149–157.

Tolkien, J. R. R. (1937). *The Hobbit: Or there and back again*. London, United Kingdom: George Allen and Unwin.

Tolkien, J. R. R. (1954a). *The Fellowship of the Ring: Being the first part of The Lord of the Rings*. London, United Kingdom: George Allen and Unwin.

Tolkien, J. R. R. (1954b). *The Two Towers: Being the second part of The Lord of the Rings*. London, United Kingdom: George Allen and Unwin.

Tolkien, J. R. R. (1955). *The Return of the King: Being the third part of The Lord of the Rings*. London, United Kingdom: George Allen and Unwin.

Tulloch, I. (2009). Richard III: A study in medical misrepresentation. *Journal of the Royal Society of Medicine, 102*(8), 315–323.

Wikipedia. (2010). *Down Syndrome*. [online] Last accessed 2 September 2010. Retrieved from: http://en.wikipedia.org/wiki/Down_syndrome

CHAPTER 5

PASSING OR TRESPASSING? UNSEEN DISABILITY, CONTAINMENT AND THE POLITICS OF "FEELING LIKE A FRAUD" IN A NEOLIBERAL BUREAUCRACY

Harriet Cooper

Summary

How do we do identity politics when this feels like doing "identity fraud"? Although critical theory has long been interested in identity as an unstable category (see for example, Butler, 1993), in this chapter, I hope to make a new intervention in the debate by drawing on my own experiences of passing as non-disabled and "feeling like a fraud". Claiming a named political and social identity, and enacting that identity, can be a very troubled and troubling affair for the subject who "passes" as one of the dominant group. In this chapter, I adapt the psychoanalyst Bion's (1962, 1963) model of containment in the mother-baby dyad to examine the emotional labour of managing an invisible disability in a social context. Later in the chapter, I seek to politicise what seems to be a personal problem. I politicise the personal both by exploring the demands of official paperwork through the prism of a Foucauldian demand for self-government (Rose, 1999) and "legibility" (Siebers, 2004, p. 4), and by considering how terms such as "fraudulence" and "work" are ideologically loaded in a neoliberal economy of meaning.

Introduction

How do we do identity politics when this feels like doing "identity fraud"? Although critical theory has long been interested in identity as an unstable category (see for example, Butler, 1993), in this chapter, I hope to make a new intervention in the debate by drawing on my own experiences of passing as non-disabled and "feeling like a fraud". Claiming a named political and social identity, and enacting that identity, can be a very troubled and troubling affair for the subject who "passes" as one of the dominant group. Having said this, it is worth noting that, in the work of Jacques Lacan (which, for want of words, I will not explore further in this chapter), the very idea of claiming an identity might be associated with fraudulence, because identity is built on a primary misrecognition of the self (Lacan, 2006 [1949]).

I begin by situating my own work in the context of recent critical debates in the field. I then discuss my personal experience of passing, adapting the psychoanalyst Bion's (1962, 1963) model of containment in the mother-baby dyad to examine the emotional labour of managing an invisible disability in a social context. Bion's concept becomes a key trope in my argument as I move into a discussion of my own fear that I might in some way be "a fraud", which is activated by the process of having to categorise myself in various ways on official forms. In the second half of the chapter, I seek to politicise what seems to be a personal problem. I politicise the personal both by exploring the demands of official paperwork through the prism of a Foucauldian demand for self-government (Rose, 1999) and "legibility" (Siebers, 2004, p. 4), and by considering how terms such as "fraudulence" and "work" are ideologically loaded in a neoliberal economy of meaning. At this point, I discuss the media construction of passing subjects in what is pejoratively termed "benefits culture". I conclude by reflecting on the acts of "containment" undertaken (sometimes unconsciously) by passing subjects on behalf of society, examining a potentially problematic parallel between psychical and political containment.

Passing: Contours of the Debate
In this chapter I draw on Leary's definition of passing as "a cultural performance whereby one member of a defined social group masquerades as another" in order to enjoy the privileges

afforded to the dominant group" (1999, p. 85; Leary quotes from Crutchfield, 1997, p. 1). Passing is, as Leary's definition suggests, an experience that has historically been associated with a range of identity categories, including race, gender and sexual orientation. For want of words, I shall mainly discuss theorists here who consider disability passing. I use the term "the passing subject" in the chapter, and in so doing I am conscious that I am universalising, since passing is not a single, monolithic experience. This term is chosen in the spirit of "a *strategic* use of positivist essentialism in a scrupulously visible political interest" (Spivak, 1987, p. 205) – also known as "strategic essentialism" – since I am analysing passing as a political experience. The chapter is auto-ethnographic, and whilst I do not claim to be able to speak for anyone else, I contend that it is by juxtaposing my discussion of personal experience alongside an analysis of the discursive construction of "fraud" that the argument gathers momentum and broad social relevance.

It has been observed by Lingsom that the potential to pass leaves the individual with "[d]ilemmas of concealment and disclosure", which are in themselves "impairment effects" (2008, p. 2). This chapter focuses on these "dilemmas" in terms of the ways in which, over time, they structure the experience of the one who passes. I suggest that in some cases – especially in the case of one who has been passing for as long as she can remember – the term "dilemma" needs to be modified, as it implies conscious decision-making, whereas passing may happen as part of a relatively subconscious process. This is by no means to say that it does not involve much taken-for-granted extra labour on the part of the passer. I use the trope of "containment" in this chapter (Bion, 1962, 1963) to figure the way in which the passer "manages" her disability, and others' awareness of it, in a range of different ways which require emotional labour on her part, but which may be invisible to others. I will argue that the work of passing is a work of containing something inside oneself – a containment both of aspects of the self, and of aspects of the non-disabled other. For the one who passes, the stuff that one ends up containing – and concealing – can feel toxic. Its toxicity, which will be conceptualised in terms of unwarranted feelings of fraudulence, is made worse by the fact that the extra labour of passing usually goes unexamined by the passing subject (indeed, this is part of what I intend by "containment").

For Samuels, passing "provides both a certain level of privilege and a profound sense of misrecognition and internal dissonance" (2003, p. 239). What does it mean, and how does it feel, to live with "internal dissonance" over a long period, and especially to experience it as an "unthought known" (Bollas, 1987, p. 4)? I draw on personal experience to explore this dissonance in terms of feeling like a fraud: for me, neither the label "disabled" nor that of "non-disabled" feels accurate, and the impossibility of occupying either position comfortably ricochets through the fabric of my psyche, expressing itself in some intriguing ways, as we shall see. Sedgwick argues that homosexual disclosure is fraught with "double binds" which problematise both the act of coming out and that of remaining in the closet (2008, p. 70). Although cultural phobias about disability differ from those surrounding homosexuality, the concept of the double bind is illuminating in relation to disability passing too; it echoes throughout this chapter.

Another significant concept in the literature on disability passing is that of Siebers' "disability masquerade" (2004, p. 9). The masquerade, which may involve exaggerating impairment or strategically deploying aids such as a walking stick, a wheelchair or a white cane, partially liberates the passing subject from the "[d]ilemmas of concealment and disclosure" identified by Lingsom, because it ensures that disability is *simply seen*. The passing subject makes use of a "semiotics" of disability in order

123

to avoid the work of explaining (Siebers, 2004, p. 13). Indeed, we might understand explaining disability as, in itself, a labour of containment because it involves judging the right moment to broach the subject, and knowing how to manage the other's feelings in relation to their discovery that disability is present. In the masquerade, the showing of disability replaces telling. In an ocularcentric culture (see Jay, 1993), telling is – I contend – less closely associated with authenticity than showing is; it is what is done in the absence of visual evidence, and it is linguistically connected with the fictional, in terms like "telling tales". However, even if the disability masquerade resolves the problem of passing in a *social* sense, I suggest that it does not resolve the dissonance of the passing subject's experience of self, since feelings of fraudulence are at stake. Having explored some of the contours of the debate on disability passing, I now turn to my own experience of passing as non-disabled. I consider my own labours of containment and my sense of "feeling like a fraud".

Containing "Abnormal" Inside Myself

I usually pass as someone who doesn't have hemiplegia (a mild form of cerebral palsy that affects the left side of my body). I also usually pass as someone who doesn't have anxious thoughts. I have come to understand the second type of passing, and the shame associated with a sense of the illegitimacy of certain kinds of anxiety, as contingent upon the first experience of shame about the inability to pass, wholly and completely, as non-disabled. I will explain what I mean by this in the course of this section and the next.

In the conference paper which was to develop into this chapter, I examined the relationship between the two types of passing in psychosocial terms, exploring my internalisation of certain social norms around disability, which led me, as a child, to feel that containing and concealing my hemiplegia (and later my anxiety) was best (see also Cooper, 2015). I drew on Bion's conceptualisation of the relationship between primary caregiver and baby in terms of container and contained to do this (Bion, 1962, 1963; see also Cooper, 2015). In Bion's model, the pre-verbal infant expels unbearable sensations through the psychoanalytic mechanism of "'projective identification'" (Klein, 1980 [1946], p. 8). The parent or caregiver, acting as container, takes in (introjects) the baby's pain (which, since it is wordless, cannot be divided up into the psychic and the physical), digests it and then returns it to the infant in a form which can be tolerated (Bion, 1963, p. 31; see also Klein, 1980 [1946] on introjection). Via this process, the infant develops psychic maturity. The reader will note that this is a normative model, and, as such, has been critiqued by critical disability studies and critical psychology (see for example Burman, 2008; Goodley, 2011). I agree that we need such a critique, but I also contend that Bion's model is helpful for developing a politically inflected psychosocial understanding of passing, as I hope to show in this chapter (see also Cooper, 2015).

What happens if the process of containment is disrupted because the parents are themselves handling the diagnosis of a baby's impairment, and are coming to terms with the social meanings of disability, whilst simultaneously seeking to protect their baby from the negativity of these? A great deal of emotional labour is performed by the parents of disabled children (see Runswick-Cole, 2013). These parents suddenly find themselves handling not only their baby's projections, but those of society in relation to disability, as they attempt to shield their baby from the effects of such projections. The diagnosis of impairment in babyhood in a society that sees disability as a tragedy (Oliver, 1983), is thus a complex experience for the parents, with an even more complicated legacy for the child. It is not surprising if the child who is able to pass grows up feeling as though passing is a good thing, which makes everything easier for everyone. I was a loved child. I was a privileged child. I know these things more fully now than I have ever known them, and I am deeply grateful to my parents. For me the purpose of drawing on the personal in disability studies is not to individualise, nor to place blame at the door of particular individuals, but so that connections can be made between the experience of a family and the society in which that family finds itself, and above all so that the relationship between disability and shame can be disentangled.

As a child, I quickly learnt that impairment was a queer, awkward thing that I should ideally keep under the skin because everything in the social world seemed to run more smoothly when I did. In parallel, I learnt to keep prickly, unmanageable, overwhelming feelings under the skin (Cooper, 2015). I kept what threatened to overwhelm me and others on the inside, deeply buried. The problem was that these overwhelming feelings could not – it seemed – be kept under the skin forever, and they kept returning as anxious thoughts. Indeed, such thoughts repeat the dynamics that I have rehearsed throughout my life with hemiplegia: to the outside world they are invisible, and I tend to keep them to myself out of shame, even though to speak of them would often be helpful. This is an example of the "[d]ilemmas of concealment and disclosure" which Lingsom associates with the experience of passing.

The act of coming out, and of laying claim to particular impairment labels, is fraught with ambivalence for me. Mallett and Runswick-Cole identify the "urge to know impairment" as a coercive part of mainstream discourse on disability, which seeks to categorise impairments within a spectrum of the "'normally abnormal'" (2016, p. 123). Yet the use of labels is also part of an act of "disability telling" in the absence of being able to "show": the label functions as a means of authenticating – of making real – an impairment or symptom that is, to all intents and purposes, invisible (and so might be "made up"). My hemiplegia is just visible when people look for it, but if, in public spaces, I ask for help with things (carrying a tray, for example), I have to explain that I have an impairment. This in itself requires emotional labour, because one never knows how the other will respond, and there is often a need to "contain" the other's difficult feelings in particular ways. In a similar way, I keep my anxiety well hidden most of the time, but to do this successfully also requires work on my part (also a labour of containment). For the remainder of this chapter I focus on my own (conscious and unconscious) "dilemmas of concealment and disclosure" in the specific context of bio-political visibility, reflecting on how these relate to my sense that somewhere, deep down, I must be "a fraud". Alongside this, I consider the framing of "fraudulence" in neoliberal discourses of disability, and I see what happens when I put these two things – a discussion of personal experience and a discussion of politics – into dialogue with one another.

Harriet, the Fraud?

One of the things I struggle with at the moment – at a time when my anxiety is much more manageable than it used to be, and so I am able to attend to the finer details of its nature – is filling in official forms. I find myself wanting to amend forms, to add my own discursive spiel, explaining that I am somewhere between tick-box A and tick-box B. I do not just mean that I find myself between the category "disabled" and "non-disabled" although this might be understood as the original issue; I mean that categorising myself in any way, using the terms given to me by officialdom, seems to me impossibly difficult. I cannot seem to believe that no one cares about the detail of what the exact "truth" is – that they really just want to be able to file me away in the right drawer. I am sure that when, on the various occasions that I have compulsively added description where there was no official space for it, I have made the day of the bureaucrat who is in receipt of my form very wearisome. Was I trying to give the bureaucrat a sense of my day-to-day experience that I am somehow "damned if I do and damned if I don't" by making the day of that anonymous person as frustrating as mine? Filling in forms is supposed to be that thing you can do quickly, *get done*, so you can move on to the more interesting things in life. For me, form-filling is full of the labour of checking, and the anxiety of not feeling authorised to know which box to put myself in. I am governed by a sense of dread that if I am enjoying the interesting things, I must have got there fraudulently, by not checking carefully *where I placed myself* on the form. This seems to mirror my early experience of physiotherapy, where I was forced to focus on *how I was placing my feet on the ground*. There would be plenty of scope for a Lacanian analysis of these issues, since they relate to questions of (self)signification and authority; however, for want of words this will have to wait for a future piece of writing.

In conversations, I feel that I would really rather just "come out" and say, "I have hemiplegia", but I know that the Other hasn't yet noticed, and so to come out would disrupt the conventions of small talk. So I exist in a liminal state between disabled and non-disabled, longing to actually "be" one or the other, rather than feeling that I just "seem to be". In the same way, to "come out" with a discursive spiel on a form that requires that either the "yes" box or the "no" box be ticked, is to violate the principles of what is bureaucratically and bio-politically sayable (Foucault, 1981 [1978]). We think of "coming out" as the liberatory passage into being able to occupy one's "true" identity openly, indeed it seems to be an activity that liberalism invites us all to embrace, because *everyone* is welcome in the "cuddly" world of "diversity" (see Ahmed, 2012, p. 71). However, sometimes "coming out with it" can be splurging compulsively at the side of a multiple choice questionnaire in such a way as to confuse the computers that read it. This kind of coming out only makes everyone embarrassed. I am supplying too much information. In the impossible quest to give the Other the "right amount of information", I shuttle between a sense of having concealed and a sense of having exaggerated. In the world of the disability-explanation, both feel like misrepresentations of me. In the world of the official form, both options feel fraudulent.

The tick-boxes of this world offend me precisely because they imply that there *is* a right amount of (neatly containable) information; the challenge they pose – mockingly, it seems to me – is to locate, to light upon, that "right amount", a task which is apparently second nature for most people. What a certain irrational part of me struggles to understand is that the tick-boxes are not interested in knowing what is inside my soul in a moral sense. For those of us who have internalised a Panoptic gaze, this can be hard to believe (Foucault, 1991 [1977]). The boxes want me to govern myself (Rose, 1999), of course, so that I become a governable bio-political subject (Foucault, 1981 [1978]). But in this way, the tick-boxes leave me with the burden of containing something impossible, something which moves in two directions at once inside me and threatens to pull me apart. The tick-boxes want me to contain my own information, to package it up and place it nicely on the form, making it manageable for the Other.

Box-ticking is scary because it is a requirement to "tell" in the absence of being able to "show". The form is a stand-in for the body that might, or might not, be able to "show". With an impairment that barely shows, and that is not a huge hindrance in itself, there is always that sense that I should probably just "get on with things" and not make a fuss about being different. But am I then concealing something, in certain scenarios? My diagnosis with hemiplegia came shortly before my first birthday, taking place after an earlier medical encounter in which there had been a failure to diagnose it: the signs of it were simply not visible enough. As a neurological condition, hemiplegia only becomes readable on the body gradually, in response to a lack of use of the limbs and a consequent wasting of the unused muscles. The "telling" of diagnosis concretised something which hardly showed, with very particular effects for me, which I have discussed at greater length elsewhere (see Cooper, 2015). Although diagnosis can be felt as an act that legitimises a particular embodied experience (see for example Madden and Sim, 2006), for the child who does not perceive her body as disabled, it can have a profound impact on her relationship with herself (see Cooper, 2015).

Having explored my own, misplaced sense of "feeling like a fraud", I now intend to explore these ideas further in terms of contemporary political discourses which connect disability with fraudulence. What if we were to displace "fraudulence" from the situations in which it might have begun to seem "at home", and to re-orientate ourselves in relation to its meaning – to frame this in Ahmed's terms (2006, p. 9)? Indeed, in a recent lecture which I heard shortly before this chapter went to press, Ahmed (2015) highlighted the way in which the dominant culture constructs certain kinds of passing subjects as fraudulent. She spoke of the labour of passing in the following terms:

> [y]ou have to demonstrate that you are not passing for what you are not (that you are what you claim you are) in order to take up residence within a nation or to receive any benefits. The effort to establish that you are not a fraud has life consequences: a system becomes a hammer directed against those who are perpetually being rendered dubious because of their origins, because their bodies, their story, their papers, are not in the right place. To be judged as passing is to inherit a demand to establish one's legitimacy to those who decide the criteria for legitimacy. We sense what we know: this system is wearing, it works by being wearing. (Ahmed, 2015)

As Ahmed points out, whereas some of us are judged to belong simply by virtue of what we inherit, others are judged to be only passing as belonging. The effort to prove our belonging when it does not simply "show up" is laborious – it is, in Ahmed's terms, "wearing". But what if we were to look elsewhere for "dubious[ness]", to reframe this category and the terms according to which we are placed in it? What if we were to find fraudulence in a different place, in the definitions of work we are given, in the construction of official forms which require us to place ourselves in binary opposition to one another? It is to these questions that I now turn, in an attempt to bring politics to bear on personal experience.

Disabled Enough? Thinking Fraudulent Thoughts About the Meaning of "Work"

I have never filled in a form to apply for Employment and Support Allowance (the UK benefit for those with a disability or illness which prevents them from working). I am not disabled enough to be entitled to this benefit, which makes me feel something of a fraud – or at least an imposter – in writing this chapter (but we are all only temporarily able-bodied: see Marks, 1999, p. 18). Yet I want to turn the tables on my feelings of fraudulence – which I have analysed in terms of feeling that I do not belong safely in any identity category – by denaturalising the connections that get made in contemporary British culture between disability and fraudulence. I shall begin by deconstructing my own statement about being "disabled enough" in order to reflect on how our conceptual framework for thinking about "work" has been hijacked by neoliberal ideology. My easy use of the term "disabled enough" tells us that the "common sense" position in contemporary British discourse is that people who can work, should work. Steven Graby (2015) offers an excellent analysis of the way in which this position, if undeconstructed, generates certain tensions and contradictions for the project of disability activism: by adhering to it, we become unable to detach a notion of disability pride and dignity from an investment in work.

My use of the phrase "disabled enough" also tells us that, to use Ahmed's terms, the idea of fraud seems to "get stuck to" the idea of disability (2010, p. 69): the "enough" reveals a logic of adequacy and proof that "gets attached to" disability (2010, p. 192). Disability is always already a site of suspicion, a site of an innocent/guilty binary, by virtue of the fact that its very existence threatens to unveil the problems which inhere in an ideology of self-sufficiency (Cooper, 2010; Graby, 2015; Taylor, 2004; Taylor, 2008). The concept of work, moreover, is necessarily fully invested with the fantasy of self-sufficiency and in the disavowal of our (frightening) interconnectedness and our (even more frightening) dependency on a planet of rapidly depleting resources. In her illuminating critique of the concept of work, Taylor has argued that Western society has a "very limited idea of what being useful to society is" (2004, para. 27); I would suggest that (paid) work as a category is no longer necessarily bound up with a notion of social usefulness at all, although it masquerades as being so. We need only think about the kinds of work being done in the financial sector, which precipitated the global financial crisis of 2007–2008, to feel that work is no longer primarily about ensuring that everyone in the world can put food on their table in the long term but rather about individuals being self-sufficient in the short term (that is, about turning a profit, which will in turn sustain the illusion of self-sufficiency up to a point).

In such a system – I contend – fraudulence "gets attached to" anyone who shatters this illusion. A recent comparison of speeches given by Conservative and Labour ministers on the subject of benefits in a given time-frame showed that the former had deployed the word "dependency" many more times than the latter, alongside words such as "addiction" and "entrenched" (Walker, 2013, para. 4). In neoliberal rhetoric, then, dependency becomes, in itself, the real fraud. As Lister points out, in an article which maps the changing linguistic terrain of "benefits" discourse, the term "social security" is now outmoded (2013, para. 3). Whereas "the language of welfare is divisive", Lister argues, "[t]he language of social security has the power to unite us by reminding us that it offers a shared mechanism for safeguarding the economic security of us all, as well as the means through which the more fortunate can express social solidarity with the less fortunate" (para. 7). Inherent in the concept of "social security" is the idea of participation in a society of interdependent people. By contrast, the excessive emphasis on "benefits" in contemporary political discourse plays on the connections between this term with its specific pecuniary meaning and the more general meaning of the noun and verb "benefit", with its connotations of profit and advantage.

In etymological terms, a benefit is simply a good deed ("benefit, *n.*", *OED Online*, 2014): it is not something we give-in-return-for-nothing, as government rhetoric constructs it, but simply something we give. In a capitalist order where exchange value reigns supreme, the asymmetrical logic of the gift appears as an anomaly (Hyde, 2006, xvi; see also Cooper, 2015; Derrida, 1992; Diprose, 2002; Graby 2015). Whether or not the "real" gift is impossible as Derrida argues (1992), capital de-legitimises the idea of the gift, which comes to be associated in the context of benefits not with magnanimity on the part of the giver, but with gullibility, with a failure to think strategically about the so-called "needs of the economy". In this formulation, the economy is anthropomorphised as a being with "needs". As Phillips and Taylor note, in the contemporary world, we are incredulous about the notion that as human beings we might actually be given to being kind and are instead "convinced that self-interest is our ruling principle" (2009, p. 7). This conceptualisation of ourselves is, they suggest, a relatively new phenomenon in human history (2009, pp. 5-6), but it certainly seems to serve neoliberal ideology well. Indeed, under capitalism, the gift is transformed into the "handout", a term in which all hint of good feeling and emotional connection has been removed. Feeling is replaced by the clinical emptiness of a bureaucracy that must do what is prudent according to the demands of the free market, but never what is kind or good – a bureaucracy that must disassociate itself from whatever is not given *in exchange* for that which is valuable to the market. The "handout" is a gift that is given not by a whole person with a head and a heart, but by a synecdoche of a person (the hand). This discussion exposes one of the major contradictions at the heart of capitalist ideology, that is, the investment in an ideal of self-sufficiency alongside a (veiled) reliance on a system of exchange, that is, of interdependence (see Cooper, 2010). The transaction functions in society as a way of distancing us from our knowledge of our interconnectedness, as Lewis Hyde has suggested (2006, pp. 62–64). In Hyde's analysis of the difference between the gift and the commodity, "a bond precedes or is created by donation" whereas "it is absent, suspended, or severed in commodity exchange" (2006, p. 64).

As mentioned, the existence of disability is problematic for the dominant order in that it highlights the illusionary nature of self-sufficiency (Cooper, 2010; Taylor, 2004; Taylor 2008). Disability can lead us to reflect on alternative models of living that are based around acceptance, rather than disavowal of, interdependence as our basic state (Cooper, 2010; Mairs, 1996; Taylor, 2004; Taylor, 2008). More radically, the idea of not being able to work (in the conventional forms that work takes) poses fundamental questions about what it means to work, to contribute, to be useful, as well as – to put it in terms of the reification that capitalism would rather we did not see – about what it means to have a use value and an exchange value (see Taylor, 2004). This might lead us to assert our "[r]ight [n]ot to [w]ork" (Taylor, 2004), which we might conceptualise in terms of a rejection of the commodification that accompanies our entry into the labour "market" and a refusal to accept a fraudulent definition of "work". To invoke Žižek's model of "[t]he ideological 'quilt'" (2008, p. 95), neoliberalism quilts the signifier "work" in such a way as to mask the fact that within this ideology, this signifier is permitted, without appearance of contradiction, to denote activities that are destructive of economic security, social cohesion and scarce planetary resources. It is simultaneously disqualified from being ascribed to genuinely useful activities such as giving one's time to important, socially useful causes (on the usefulness of protest, see Taylor, 2004), or indeed the act of making space in one's life to think, which might well be the most useful activity of all, but is made to appear useless by the fact that almost no one will pay you to do it. Of course, activities such as thinking and protesting have the potential to destabilise the status quo: it is hardly surprising that they are not seen as work.

My purpose here has been to de-familiarise the concept of "fraudulence" and to understand how and why it "gets attached to" certain people and things (Ahmed, 2010, p. 192), and not others, in contemporary discourse. Under neoliberalism there is an equivalence between "benefit claimant" and "fraud" because the figure of the claimant represents the universality of dependency, which must be disavowed. Similarly, "disability" and "fraudulence" come to be equated with each other via the disruption posed by disability to the fabric of meritocratic liberal individualism. Yet, insomuch as the dominant order has to acknowledge – however reluctantly – the existence of disability, the idea of invisible disability is a greater threat. It is perhaps even more "fraudulent" than visible disability because of the challenge it poses to a brittle binary of disabled/non-disabled, which is relied upon as a means of measuring and mapping deservingness in an advanced capitalist bureaucracy. The bureaucratic need for *"biocertification"* as a means of authorising entitlement casts the burden of proof on to the passing subject, whose passing then becomes a subject of suspicion (Samuels, 2014, p. 122; Ahmed, 2015). Samuels documents the dominance of a position which equates disability with visibility in her analysis of posts on a vigilante website which exposes individuals who are presumed to be using disabled parking permits illegally (2014, pp. 133–140). What is read as fraudulence could instead be understood as a failure to communicate or perform using the dominant cultural "semiotics" of disability (Siebers, 2004, p. 13). However, if the dominant order demands the deployment of a coherent system of signs to denote disability, it thereby disqualifies unseen disability as not "enough". Is it making a demand for exaggeration?

Introjecting Fraudulence: Psychical and Political Containment
Concealment and exaggeration are, I argue, both ways of containing an unruly experience of disability in ways that make it simultaneously acceptable and unacceptable to the dominant order. For those of us with an unseen disability, box-ticking can feel like being forced to represent oneself using one or other strategy; it is an experience of being surveilled by the Other's suspicious yet unfinding gaze. If the dominant order genuinely wants me to be able to express myself in a way which is neither concealing nor exaggerating, why doesn't it dispense with boxes? My truth cannot be codified in the terms of a box-ticking exercise. The act that Samuels calls *"biocertification"* (2014, p. 122) requires that disability, or able-bodiedness, be proven according to a codified – but ultimately constructed – binary. A system which apparently deplores untruth pressurises the subject into

taking up a position of "untruth" by disallowing an ambiguous, indeterminate, fluctuating or liminal subject position. Even though it feels as though what is desired by the system here is truth, what is actually desired is (in a very Foucauldian sense) only legibility. This untruth, legibility, is the truth of a system that is reliant on the classification of disability (see Mallett and Runswick-Cole, 2016).

The recent changes in the administration of benefits in the UK, associated with the government's cuts to welfare provision, have made it more difficult for disabled people who are unable to work to claim a living allowance (Graby, 2015). Graby observes that one of the changes, the introduction of the Work Capability Assessment, "replaced a 'criterion-based' system with a 'norm-referenced' system of decision-making about eligibility for the benefit" (2015, p. 134; see also Franklin, 2013). In effect this means that some of those who, under a criterion-based scheme, would qualify for help, will simply not receive help because of the finite amount of funding available and the target system deployed by those implementing the changes (Franklin, 2013; see also Graby, 2015). Very often, those whose disabilities are not easily legible – those who pass, or those whose disabilities do not have a media profile – are likely to be the ones who have to struggle for recognition within such a system (see Mallett and Runswick-Cole, 2016; Viney, 2014). Instead of being "contained" by a caring system – to invoke Bion again – such individuals are often left to undertake the psychic work of containing their own impairments in such a way as to ensure that they fit with a notion of the "'normally abnormal'" (Mallett and Runswick-Cole, 2016, p. 115). I use the term containment here to indicate my sense that for the liminal subject, the work of completing forms is an experience of being left with something "leftover", a remainder of the self, an abject part that cannot be assimilated into the required format, because it is not "'normally abnormal'". This part must be re-introjected (to draw on Klein's (1980 [1946]) terminology), contained by the disabled subject rather than by the form. It then *feels* as though it is a fraudulent part, but this is only because the form refuses to see it for itself. The form is experienced by the passing subject as a request that she contain something inside herself that she needs to have seen. The injustice of an impoverished (in all senses) social security system is, in part, its inability to contain (in a Bionian sense) the information we need to give it, so that our experience of being in the world can be recognised. There is, of course, a direct relationship between the financial impoverishment of the system and its impoverished capacity to contain and securely hold those who need it, but the former can also be seen as arising out of an ideological need to wilfully overlook those whose subjectivity poses a challenge to the fantasy of self-sufficiency and to the fraudulence of capitalistic definitions of "work".

There is, moreover, a need not only to *overlook* disabled and passing subjectivity with the dangers it presents to the integrity of *"[t]he ideological 'quilt'"* (Žižek, 2008, p. 95), but also to *project* fraudulence into it, in a fraudulent displacement of signifiers. For those of us who have grown up containing a sense of our failure to belong properly to either identity category, and have contained both our own shame about this and the emotions of the Other in relation to the discovery of our impairment, it is only too easy to become the object of dominant cultural projections of fraudulence. For those who pass and who also need state support to live, it is surely a frighteningly small step from an internal world dominated by feelings of fraudulence to a fear that one is, in fact, a "benefit scrounger", since one's social experience of disability is one of having to tell – which can be met by disbelief – rather than being able to show, which is a self-verifying act in an ocularcentric culture (see Jay, 1993). Shame about not-belonging – a form of internalised oppression – can render us docile and governable (Foucault, 1991 [1977]), ready to be exploited by the dominant order for excelling at the work of psychical containment. If we are not careful, this will turn us into agents of political containment. By this, I mean that the work of psychical containment might, in this context, be bound up with the maintenance of the political status quo. I know that in my case, my endless brooding about how to fill in forms "properly" – how to satisfy my compulsion to have my truth understood and accepted (which, in my fantasy would permanently expel my sense of being a fraud), whilst also obeying the Other's law of legibility – feels as though it takes up a lot of space inside me. Containing it expends energy that could be used for political work and activism. Containing it is – or should be understood as – a form of work.

The psychic containment I have undertaken in relation to my impairment might be understood as a perversion of the container-contained relationship which leads, for Bion, to both the capacity, and space, for thought (1962, 1963). Instead, space has been taken up inside me by my "dilemmas of concealment and disclosure". The work of seeking out a non-existent space where I do not "feel like a fraud" is a never-ending task, since that space will never exist within a dominant order which demands legibility over experiential truth. This order asks that experiential truth be contained within the self as a feeling of fraudulence, returning the failure to resolve truth into a given cultural category to the subject, over and over again, as though it were something personal. Yet, as I have been arguing, this individualising move transforms "fraudulence" into a category of the personal, rather than casting it as a relational or social concept. Although my ideas in this chapter will need to be developed further in future writing, I have tentatively suggested here that one of the ways we can address this issue is by re-framing "fraudulence". By examining how the terms "fraudulence", "work", "dependency" and "benefits" are "quilted" together in a particular way under neoliberalism, those of us who struggle with the ambivalent work of passing may afford ourselves some space to attach new meanings to the feelings of "fraudulence" in our own internal worlds.

Acknowledgements

I am grateful to the conference participants at the *Theorising Normalcy and the Mundane Conference* in 2013 for their comments on my paper, which was a very early version of this chapter. I would also like to thank Nick Hocking, Sophie Jones, and members of my family for their feedback, as well as the editors and the anonymous reviewers of the chapter.

References

Ahmed, S. (2006). *Queer phenomenology: Orientations, objects, others.* Durham, NC; London, United Kingdom: Duke University Press.

Ahmed, S. (2010). *The promise of happiness.* Durham, NC; London, United Kingdom: Duke University Press.

Ahmed, S. (2012). *On being included: Racism and diversity in institutional life.* Durham, NC; London, United Kingdom: Duke University Press.

Ahmed, S. (2015). Some striking feature: Whiteness and institutional passing. Keynote Lecture at *Disrupting visibility: The politics of passing,* 12 June, Goldsmiths College, University of London, United Kingdom. Retrieved from http://feminist killjoys.com/

"benefit, n.". *OED Online* (2014). Retrieved from http://www.oed.com/search?searchType=dictionary&q=benefit&_searchBtn=Search

Bion, W. R. (1962). *Learning from experience.* London, United Kingdom: Tavistock.

Bion, W. R. (1963). *Elements of psycho-analysis.* London, United Kingdom: Heinemann.

Bollas, C. (1987). *The Shadow of the object: Psychoanalysis of the unthought known.* London, United Kingdom: Free Association Books.

Burman, E. (2008). *Deconstructing developmental psychology.* (2nd ed.). Hove, United Kingdom: Routledge.

Butler, J. (1993). *Bodies that matter: On the discursive limits of "sex"*. New York, NY; London, United Kingdom: Routledge.

Cooper, H. (2010). *The ideal of self-sufficiency and the physically disabled subject in contemporary Anglo-American culture*. (Unpublished master's dissertation). Birkbeck, University of London: London, United Kingdom.

Cooper, H. (2015). *Making the disabled child: Critical disability studies at the intersection of cultural representation and lived experience*. (Unpublished doctoral thesis). Birkbeck, University of London: London, United Kingdom.

Crutchfield, S. (1997). *Color-blindness as "passing" fancy: Race and blindness in American cinema*. Unpublished manuscript [Referred to in Leary, 1999; not available for consultation].

Derrida, J. (1992). *Given time: 1. Counterfeit money*. Trans. by P. Kamuf. Chicago, IL; London, United Kingdom: University of Chicago Press.

Diprose, R. (2002). *Corporeal generosity: On giving with Nietzsche, Merleau-Ponty, and Levinas*. Albany, NY: State University of New York.

Foucault, M. (1981 [1978]). *The history of sexuality, volume 1: An introduction*. Trans. by R. Hurley. Harmondsworth, United Kingdom: Pelican Books.

Foucault, M. (1991 [1977]). *Discipline and punish: The birth of the prison*. Trans. by A. Sheridan. London, United Kingdom: Penguin.

Franklin, K. (2013). *Investigating the real reason for the misery of "fit for work" assessments*. Sheffield, United Kingdom: The Centre for Welfare Reform.

Goodley, D. (2011). *Disability studies: An interdisciplinary introduction*. London, United Kingdom: Sage.

Graby, S. (2015). Access to work or liberation from work? Disabled people, autonomy and post-work politics. *Canadian Journal of Disability Studies, 4*(2), 132–160.

Hyde, L. (2006). *The gift: How the creative spirit transforms the world*. Edinburgh, United Kingdom: Canongate Books.

Jay, M. (1993). *Downcast eyes: The denigration of vision in twentieth-century French thought*. Berkeley, CA: University of California Press.

Klein, M. (1980 [1946]). Notes on some schizoid mechanisms. In R. Money-Kyrle (General Ed.), *Envy and gratitude and other works*

1946–1963 by Melanie Klein (pp. 1–24). (2nd impression). London, United Kingdom: The Hogarth Press and the Institute of Psychoanalysis.

Lacan, J. (2006 [1949]). The mirror stage as formative of the I function as revealed in psychoanalytic experience. In J. Lacan, *Écrits* (pp. 75–81. Trans. by B. Fink in collaboration with H. Fink & R. Grigg. New York, NY; London, United Kingdom: Norton.

Leary, K. (1999). Passing, posing and "keeping it real". *Constellations: An International Journal of Critical and Democratic Theory*, 6(1), 85–96.

Lingsom, S. (2008). Invisible impairments: Dilemmas of concealment and disclosure. *Scandinavian Journal of Disability Research*, 10(1), 2–16.

Lister, R. (2013, 1 April). How the language of welfare poisoned our social security. *The Guardian*. Retrieved from http://www.theguardian.com/commentisfree/2013/apr/01/language-welfare-social-security

Madden, S., & Sim, J. (2006). Creating meaning in fibromyalgia syndrome. *Social Science and Medicine*, 63, 2962–2973.

Mairs, N. (1996). *Waist-high in the world: A life among the non-disabled*. Boston, MA: Beacon Press.

Mallett, R., & Runswick-Cole, K. (2016). The "urge to know" normal: Theorising how impairments labels function. In R. Mallett, C. A. Ogden, & J. Slater, *Theorising Normalcy and the Mundane: Precarious Positions* (pp. 95–119). Chester, United Kingdom: University of Chester Press.

Marks, D. (1999). *Disability: Controversial debates and psychosocial perspectives*. Abingdon, United Kingdom: Routledge.

Oliver, M. (1983). *Social work with disabled people*. London, United Kingdom: Macmillan.

Phillips, A., & Taylor, B. (2009). *On kindness*. New York, NY: Farrar, Straus and Giroux.

Rose, N. (1999). *Governing the soul: The shaping of the private self*. (2nd ed.). London, United Kingdom: Free Association Books.

Runswick-Cole, K. (2013). "Wearing it all with a smile": Emotional labour in the lives of mothers and disabled children. In T. Curran & K. Runswick-Cole (Eds.), *Disabled children's childhood studies: Critical approaches in a global context* (pp. 105–118). Basingstoke, United Kingdom: Palgrave Macmillan.

Passing or Trespassing?

Samuels, E. (2003). My body, my closet: Invisible disability and the limits of coming-out discourse. *GLQ: A Journal of Lesbian and Gay Studies, 9*(1–2), 233–255.

Samuels, E. (2014). *Fantasies of identification: Disability, gender, race.* New York, NY; London, United Kingdom: New York University Press.

Sedgwick, E. K. (2008). *Epistemology of the closet.* (Updated ed.). Berkeley, CA: University of California Press.

Siebers, T. (2004). Disability as masquerade. *Literature and Medicine, 23*(1), 1–22.

Spivak, G. C. (1987). Subaltern studies: Deconstructing historiography. In *In other worlds: Essays in cultural politics* (pp. 197–221). New York, NY: Methuen. (Reprinted from *Subaltern studies IV: Writings on South Asian history and society,* pp. 330–363, by Ranajit Guha (Ed.), 1985, Delhi, India: Oxford University Press).

Taylor, A. (Director). (2008). *Examined life* [Motion Picture]. Canada: Sphinx Productions.

Taylor, S. (2004). The right not to work: Power and disability. *Monthly Review: An Independent Socialist Magazine, 55*(10). Retrieved from http://monthlyreview.org/2004/03/01/the-right-not-to-work-power-and-disability/

Viney, M. (2014, 5 November). Work Programme adviser: "Almost every day, one of my clients mentioned feeling suicidal". *The Guardian.* Retrieved from http://www.theguardian.com/society/2014/nov/05/work-programme-adviser-box-ticking-sanctioning-sick-people

Walker, P. (2013, 5 April). Government using increasingly loaded language in welfare debate. *The Guardian.* Retrieved from http://www.theguardian.com/society/2013/apr/05/government-loaded-language-welfare

Žižek, S. (2008). *The sublime object of ideology.* (New ed.). London: United Kingdom: Verso.

CHAPTER 6

ARMLESS DREAMS OR CARNAL PRACTICES?: TRANSABLEISM AND THE LEGITIMISATION OF THE IDEAL BODY

Cassandra A. Ogden

Summary

A transable individual is a term used to describe a person who is born without impairment but their actual bodily reality remains incongruent with their sense of identity. A transable individual therefore seeks to obtain or feign an impairment to realign their sense of identity with their body. There have been attempts by neurobiology, psychology and psychiatry to obtain a medicalised definition of this phenomenon (Body Integrity Identity Disorder, "BIID") but there has been no agreed aetiology and therefore the *Diagnostic and Statistical Manual for Mental Disorder* – Fifth Edition (*DSM-5*) (American Psychiatric Association (APA), 2013) fails to include this label within the latest edition. The lay reaction and responses to transableism often demonstrate disgust, confusion and anger (Baril, 2015; Davis, 2014) in contrast to the general public's acceptance of people's engagement with aesthetic, elective cosmetic surgery. This could be seen to highlight how neoliberal ideals of self-sufficient, aesthetically pleasing, independent subjects that are economically useful are exalted in contemporary society. Through an in-depth exploration of the various contradictions in science, biomedicine and lay perceptions in thinking about the contested label of "BIID", it is shown how transable individuals serve to trouble the ideas of stability, unity and containment. This chapter adopts a sociological perspective and argues that a postconventionalist approach needs to be adopted before one dismisses the possibility of offering some transable individuals the option of "impairment enhancement" surgery. Nevertheless transableism also disturbs the binary explanations of disability/ability as a tool to understand the various positions in relation to arguments for and against these procedures. Transable people's experiences appear so perplexing and far from "normality" that they can only be understood by re-imagining essentialist views of the body, to allow for acceptance of anomalous embodiment.

Introduction

By turning on the television you can immerse yourself in the range of documentaries, sitcoms, advertisements, soap operas and reality programmes that tell us that our bodies are important and that we should care about them. These range from programmes that give advice about how to ensure a "healthy" body to those that fetishise the body "peculiar" (see the ongoing Channel 4 documentary *Bodyshock*), those that give tips about how to "correctly" apply makeup and how to ensure correct clothing choices, and insiders' stories about cosmetic surgery. Whatever the position of the programme maker it appears that the public like nothing more than to talk about bodies: whether they are condemning someone about caring too much about their body, or persecuting those who are "letting themselves go".

The purpose of this chapter is to explore society's contradictory messages about the body and to trouble the often dichotomised debate that centres around whether certain elective surgery on the body is better understood as a rational, autonomous, empowering choice or whether people's decisions to have surgery are due to wider social/cultural/political pressures and contexts. The context of this debate, however, will not focus primarily on the normative uses of surgery (deemed cosmetic and otherwise) but will trouble these discourses of normalcy through the exploration of transableism (or Body Integrity Identity Disorder ("BIID")). The refusal by medical practitioners to perform surgical procedures for transable people and the condemnation from the general public, contrasts with the rise of people engaging with intrusive surgery for cosmetic purposes and its general acceptance and normalisation.

Similarly, the engagement with intrusive surgical procedures or other forms of therapy (which bear similar levels of risk) are very common for people with recognised illness, disease and health problems. This creates an interesting paradox that not only tells us much about healthism (societal obsession with maintaining a healthy diet, body and lifestyle and its increasing permeation into all aspects of everyday life), consumer capitalism, ableism and the cost of achieving the desirable body, but also highlights the public and professionals' attitudes and assumptions towards disabled people in the twenty-first century. There will be instances in this chapter whereby a focus is placed on transable individuals who need a more permanent form of impairment to help resolve the incongruence between their bodies and identities (as opposed to "acting out" their impaired identity) and this will demonstrate how transableism challenges people's perceptions of "normalised aesthetic standards" and "useful" bodies. The chapter nevertheless acknowledges that the need for permanent impairment does not represent the needs of all those identifying as transable and in turn explores the social and cultural milieu that serves to construct the assumptions made about transable people and also highlights many of the discriminatory and confused attitudes towards this diverse group.

The author utilises a sociological analysis throughout the chapter which demands a critical exploration of the various contexts in which transableism is understood. This requires a discussion of medicalised (often pathologising) discourses which attempt to "rationalise" and medicalise transable individuals' needs and to interrogate the contradictions inherent in these arguments. The term "impairment" will be utilised to refer to a physical difference of the body (following the distinction between impairment and disability as outlined in the work of

146

Oliver, 1990) which may be acted out, needed or obtained by transable individuals.

What is Transableism and "Body Integrity Identity Disorder"?
Transableism is a term coined by O'Connor in 2009 to describe individuals who are born without impaired bodies and need to acquire impairment to allow their bodily appearance to match their identity (Stevens, 2011). Some transable individuals seek out surgery to help permanently transform their bodies, or more commonly, might live their lives as though they have an impairment (e.g. by using a wheelchair). Baril (2015) discusses the importance of the word "transability" which offers a less stigmatising understanding than medical terms (such as "BIID") and avoids perceiving transability as "perverse or irrational" (p. 32). With this in mind, the term transableism is employed throughout as the preferred way to describe the community and when the term "Body Integrity Identity Disorder" is employed, it will be referred to in inverted commas to demonstrate the contested nature, utility and problems associated with the term. This chapter outlines the history of the understanding of transability within biomedicine and enables the reader to understand, in part, how reactions to transability are formulated through a range of medicalising discourses.

Very little research has been done with or about transable people with Swindell and Lawrence (2009) observing that since the first case study describing such desires in 1957, there was no mention of these phenomena again until 1977. The literature that does exist regarding transableism, has in the main come from professionals that serve to pathologise and dichotomise the experiences of this community. It is nevertheless necessary to understand the context of this work to enable a critical discussion (and better understanding) of the ways in which transableism crips ideas of bodily normalcy and "rationalising" medical discourses. In Money,[3] Jobaris and Furth's 1977 report (cited in Swindell and Lawrence, 2009) the term apotemnophilia was coined (amongst many other terms for paraphilias) to describe a person with an intense need to have their own healthy limb amputated and specifically held sexual fantasies about this. Baril (2015) notes that the understanding of transableism as a paraphilia serves to exclude individuals whose need for transition is not sexual and can lead to the stigmatising of transableism. The term "Body Integrity Identity Disorder" ("BIID") did not exist until 2005 when First published research based on 52 semi-structured interviews with people having similar "desires" (phrasing utilised in First's work). First's (2005) renaming/rejection of apotemnophilia is regarded as important as it firstly acknowledges that a person's need to become disabled is not based entirely on sexual desire. Although First (2005) acknowledged that sexual desire might feature in the need for surgery, primarily the need to modify bodies is on the basis of a mismatched identity. Secondly in creating this term, some research suggests transable experiences are legitimised further as they exist as more than a subset of a paraphilic disorder (see Davis's work (2012b), which highlights how the term "BIID" has become the preferred term for researchers and some from the transable community). Despite this there are still many authors who prefer the term "apotemnophilia" although this paraphilic hypothesis has not been confirmed and has stigmatising effects. Thirdly the creation of a medical term (such as BIID) signals an attempt to validate the transable experience which otherwise

---

[3] Money is a medical psychologist and sexologist who has been heavily criticised for his work on so-called "atypical" sexual practices and embodiment. His work here is utilised only as a means to identify the biomedical understandings of "apotemnophilia".

remains a cultural group not recognised by the medical profession (an idea critically explored throughout this chapter).

The label of "BIID" for some (both amongst transable people and healthcare professionals) has acknowledged that transable individuals do not suffer from a sexual fetishism or a kind of body dysmorphic disorder (e.g. developing a preoccupation with one or more perceived bodily flaws which has caused "clinically significant distress or impairment in social [or] occupational ... functioning" (APA, 2013a, p. 242)), but suffer from a lack of congruence "between [the person's] bodily identity and their actual anatomy" (Phillips et al., 2010, p. 583). Despite the existence of the label of "BIID", there is still much debate about whether the need for amputation or the need to "pass" as disabled can be explained via a psychological/psychiatric or neurological perspective (Sedda and Bottini, 2014). Sedda and Bottini's review of the available studies shows there is no conclusive evidence of either a neurologic or psychological/psychiatric aetiology for "BIID" and therefore the "clinical robustness" (2014, p. 1263) of the term (and other labels explored including apotemnophilia and xenomelia) remains contested.

The advantage of using the term transability over "BIID" includes firstly the fact that this moves the power away from the medical professions to transable people, and secondly helps make "an apparent lingual comparison to the word "transgender" as both words can signify (but is not exclusively describing) people transitioning from one state of embodiment to another" (Stevens, 2011, n.p.). Davis (2012b) also highlights how the term transableism better "encompasses the full range of impairment desires including paraplegia, quadriplegia, blindness, deafness and so on, as well as the desire for amputation" (Davis, 2012b, p. 600). With research such as Sedda and Bottini's (2014) also noting the diagnostic ambiguity in labelling such needs within medical circles, "transableism" appears to help create an inclusive, umbrella term which includes all individuals within this diverse community with their different impairment needs. Baril's use of transability is guided by "personal activism" (2015, p. 32) and to utilise a term that enables the centrality of individuals' experiences (as opposed to the hijacking of their medicalised identity by biomedicine).

Davis's (2012b) research into the (now shut down) online community for transable individuals (Transabled.org) also highlighted a range of useful lay terms, used to describe the individuals' relationships with and experiences of being transable. "Wannabes" are people who have a strong need for physical impairment, "pretenders" are those who act as though they have a physical impairment and "devotees" are those who hold "fetishistic sexual attractions towards those with physical impairment" (Davis, 2012b, p. 600). This latter category could be said to challenge in particular the problematic label of "apotemnophilia" and further helps differentiate transableism from fetishistic desire. The creation of such terms by transable people is not always, however, a rejection of "BIID". Indeed Davis's work highlights the frequency of discussions featured on Transabled.org that actively appeal for the term's inclusion into the *DSM-5*. It is to this topic that the chapter will now turn to help further problematise and question the power of medical labelling.

The Diagnostic and Statistical Manual for Mental Disorders (*DSM-5*) and "BIID": A Form of Legitimacy?

There has been considerable pressure and support to include "BIID" into the *DSM-5* by transable individuals themselves (Davis, 2012b) as well (as you might expect), by medical professionals who developed a criterion for its diagnosis which it submitted to the *DSM-5* task force (Baubet et al., 2007). Before the *DSM-5* publication, however, there was much discussion surrounding whether it should be included/ excluded and whether there was enough data to "support the existence" of "BIID" (Baubet et al., 2007; Bayne and Levy, 2005; First and Fisher, 2012). In contrast, other transable people found "BIID" a problematic term which served to pathologise the transable identity (Stevens, 2011). The *DSM-5* (APA, 2013), however, does not include "BIID" although not due to pressure from transable individuals who would prefer to not be pathologised, but because the term "BIID" had not obtained diagnostic validity and further research needs to be done to achieve this. "BIID" is not even included in section III (which is entitled *Emerging Measures and Models* and includes diagnostic categories that require further research). This would have acknowledged the need to collect further empirical evidence for the purpose of validating a reliable diagnosis and to help determine a "clinical need" for the term "BIID".

The apparent split of opinion regarding whether "BIID" is a useful/dangerous label amongst transable individuals under-lines a wider debate regarding the usefulness of psychiatric labels. In Davis's prosumption study (2012b) she describes how the term transable acts as a de-medicalised counter to "BIID" and is particularly effective in highlighting the transable experiences of cultural/social contexts in the case of transable people who do not require surgery. Such a perspective brings to mind the critics of the *DSM* who are concerned with how it pathologises individual behaviour and increases the likelihood of being prescribed unnecessary and possibly harmful treatment (Goodley, 2014). The inclusion of "BIID" into such manuals may increase the likelihood of transable people becoming the focus of medical attention and analysis.

There is evidence to show, however, that some transable individuals feel that full integration of "BIID" into *DSM-5* could have helped legitimise their experiences and in addition their own identities (Davis, 2012b). Davis quotes a blogger from the now shut down Transabled.org website:

> Having "BIID" documented would ... ensure us a certain level of legitimacy. Too many people are saying we're "just sick". Being able to point to the *DSM* and say "yes, we are, but it is not just a fancy, a fantasy, or an invention, it is a REAL condition" would be very helpful. (2012a, p. 613)

This quote lies in contrast to other research with transable people (Baril, 2015; Stevens, 2011) who sometimes situate the attempts by medical professionals to construct a medicalised term for transableism, as potentially problematic for transable individuals. However, even within this work there is a belief that "BIID" is an improved label to others which once described transable people. Stevens's (2011) work illustrates clearly the moral denigration of transable individuals through the term "apotemnophilia" which identified the need for an impaired body as being driven solely by sexual desire. Davis's (2014) work, in keeping with this, also shows how many transable individuals have been accused of being "sexually perverted" by the lay public which could be understood as a throwback of the label of "apotemnophilia". This understanding of transableism demonstrates how labels placed on individuals or a group of individuals can create the pathologising of a given group.

Adversely "BIID" moves away from defining transableism as a paraphilic disorder which perhaps explains why some (such as Davis's respondent above and O'Connor cited in Stevens, 2011) suggest that while transability calls more explicitly for a depathologisation, "BIID" could offer some benefits, including the possibility of a potential "cure" once a mental health label has been identified.[4] The "acceptance" of "BIID" from O'Connor's perspective (in Stevens, 2011) is important as he feels it will help society accept the fact the some people need their bodies to be disabled. This sentiment is shared in Davis's work (2012b) which shows how some transable individuals felt a medical label may help alleviate the moral stigma they experience and aid in developing their "condition" into a "consumable identity category" (p. 612). Goodley (2014) also explains how a diagnosis of disability may help give access to certain social and welfare support. Giving a clear indication of mental "disorder" by recognition of a diagnosis in *DSM-5* (and in the International Statistical Classification of Diseases (ICD)), also allows health insurance claims to be paid out in a straightforward manner (see APA, 2013b).

It is important to note, however, that despite transgender people having obtained a medical label (e.g. gender dysphoria), the acceptance of their experiences and indeed the obtainability of the treatments that they need, are still difficult to obtain (Baril, 2015). As Stevens (2011) documents many disability activists protest against the medicalisation of their lives and experiences, and the social model of disability (Oliver, 1990) has long campaigned against the individualisation of disability through the medical model. Often reliance upon a medicalised understanding of disability is seen to divert attention away from the responsibility of discriminatory practices and environments that result in the disabling of those with impairment.

---

[4] Although interestingly this "cure" would still be determined by the biomedical professionals and may not necessarily manifest as the allowance of surgery to help the transition to a bodily form consistent with the transable person's identity. For example it could be focused on the prevention of the need in the same way that psychiatry has focused on conversion therapy for transgender people.

Furthermore scholars such as Conrad (2007) and Szasz (2007) have provided a damning critique of the tendency to medicalise observed behaviours/lifestyles/tendencies as "illnesses" or "disorders" which are then defined, controlled and treated under medicine's name. According to these scholars such processes result in the individualising and isolation of symptoms and distress to the detriment of a more structural/cultural understanding. The person who is medicalised could also be seen as irrational, immoral and irresponsible which can then allow medicine to dehumanise and control the people under their "care" (Szasz, 2007). Stevens (2011) notes the logic, however, in utilising the medical model as a pathway for a "cure" for transable people. She states how without the body being constructed as "pathological" there would be no need for a cure and therefore transable individuals would not be able to legally obtain surgery to help transform their bodies.

For "BIID" to not be included in the *DSM-5* does not necessarily mean transable individuals have escaped the talons of medicalisation. Transable people are the subject of many articles and studies in which authors are debating the neurobiological (Giummarra, 2011; Vitacco, Hilti, and Brigger, 2009), psychological (First and Fisher, 2012; Oddo et al., 2009), legal (Tolmein, 2009), ethical (Bayne and Levy, 2005; Muller, 2009), theological (Song, 2013; Williams and Song, 2014) and sociological (Davis, 2014, 2012a, 2012b) significance. Some of the more biological/psychological research clearly pathologises the person with "BIID" with one example discussing their desires as potentially being caused by "deranged body processing" (Giummarra, 2011).

Writing in 1996, Joan Busfield explains how the ICD alongside the *DSM* seek to design a universally accepted classification of mental disorder yet the numerous revisions suggest this is quite difficult (the *DSM* is in its fifth revision and the *ICD-11* is due for release in 2017). The socially constructed nature of "mental disorder" can therefore be traced through the various changes, additions and omissions made during the lifespan of these two classification manuals. As Busfield (1996) notes, however, one needn't deny the ontological reality of physical symptoms when critiquing the way in which mental disorders and illness are classified. Through her critical realist perspective she contends that one can test and analyse the various discursive constructions of mental illness against lived experience.

A Poststructuralist Ambivalence?

The ambivalence in the language we use to define transable individuals allows a unique space to trouble perceptions about body "integrity" and the need for impairment. The scientific uncertainty in relation to "BIID" may potentially produce more of an inclination to listen to transable people's experiences and narratives. This appears to be the case within one of the most comprehensive texts about "BIID" (Stirn, Thiel, and Oddo, 2009), whereby a whole section is devoted to stories of transable individuals which consists of five chapters of different people's experiences. This may well be more common in the early stages of defining a new label; however, as there has been no agreed diagnosis for "BIID" the dialogue between personal narrative and biomedical terminology continues. Many papers on transableism also allude to the need for a cross-disciplinary understanding (Sedda and Bottini, 2014) and contain some research with more of a philosophical resolve which highlights how there is no clear directive in terms of how to best understand "BIID".

At this time of categorical ambivalence, a critical sociological perspective can help complement some of Davis's work that considers the impact of the wider social structure from the perspective of moral stigma (2014) and the "prosumption" (the blurring of production and consumption) of identity (2012a). Unlike Davis's work, this chapter will not engage with empirical data but will from the sociological perspective "crip" the conception of the body as "given", "natural" and "whole" and interrogate the boundaries of the work of psychiatry and neurobiology which looks for a stable, definable, reliable measurement of "BIID". The suggestion of the possibility of a straightforward, ontological biological certainty is troubled by highlighting contradictions and paradoxes within the practice of biomedicine and its treatment of transable individuals compared to those seeking to alter their bodies for varying purposes. Finally deconstructing the *social* understanding of "BIID" will help to understand better the public's reaction to transable people.

Normative Assumptions in Biomedicine and the Impact Upon Transable People

Within all understandings of disability lie strong assumptions of the notion of "normal" which is never defined clearly but exists as an assumed opposite of the categorisations of "other". Campbell's (2009) work discusses how disability continues to be understood and studied through the perspective of the "other". With this in mind, it may appear surprising that "BIID" has not been deemed a "mental disorder" within the dominant classification manuals. If the category of "disabled" is othered in the mainstream and within biomedicine then one might assume that healthcare professionals may deem transable individuals to be "othered" too. Nevertheless "BIID" is omitted from the *DSM-5*; as Sedda and Bottini (2014) state, a wider range of studies need to be conducted with transable individuals and results converged before the category of "BIID" can be validated and used as a diagnostic label. It appears that the diverse nature of

"BIID" (e.g. including people who pretend they are disabled,[5] those who need amputation and others who require blindness/ deafness or paraplegia) makes it difficult to develop a clear clinical classification and to conclude that all variants share a clear "pathogenesis". Sedda and Bottini (2014) call for a multi-disciplinary exploration of "BIID" that in addition to the "simple" clinical frame, incorporates social and ethical aspects.

Nettleton (2013) gives a useful outline of the assumptions of the biomedical model which, amongst others, include reductionist explanations of disease and the doctrine of specific aetiology. It appears that if a person presents themselves with a body or experience that makes it difficult to ascertain a specific (biological) cause, then they fall outside the scope of biomedicine's operations. Sedda and Bottini (2014) show also how the demand for operations to cause impairment specifically, would place medical professions in sticky ethical situations as there are restrictions imposed by law upon how one acts upon the body. Medical professionals are permitted legally to operate on the body frequently (following consent from the patient) for both clinical and aesthetic purposes, yet there would be legal implications if medical practitioners began to aid the transition to an impaired body for transable individuals. Medical professionals would prefer a clear evidence base for clinical classification if operations for transable individuals were to be carried out. Although narratives exist that document the cases of transable people becoming impaired (either through surgery or self-inflicted injury which eventually causes impairment) that

---

[5] As discussed at the beginning of the chapter, transable individuals experience a range of different needs but due to word constraints I have mainly limited my discussion of transableism to the group of people who need surgery to help them. Stevens's (2011) work explores this and further helps to trouble the definitions of dis/ability.

feel a sense of "completeness" (Blom, Hennekam, and Denys, 2012; Davis, 2014, 2012a, 2012b), biomedicine operates on the basis of conducting randomised controlled trials (RCTs) to collect a representative result on which treatment can be based. Therefore, these examples are dismissed. RCTs might be difficult to achieve, however, when transable individuals remain relatively small in number, heavily stigmatised (and therefore might keep their transableism to themselves) and varied in the way they relate to impairment. There is also "evidence" to show how amputation may not resolve (or may only temporarily resolve) the experience of mismatched identity between the self and the body (Bou Khalil and Richa, 2012), which is likely to be used to further justify medicine's unwillingness to conduct such operations.[6] Sedda and Bottini (2014) call for the need of systematic postamputation studies to further verify the success of this potential treatment.

So is it likely that the medical profession would offer treatment in the form of elective amputations or other operations for people with "BIID" if there was a clearer evidence base for firstly the nature and diagnosis of the category and secondly the success of operations? This debate will be extended further but instead of focusing on ethical considerations (such debate can be found elsewhere, see Bayne and Levy, 2005; Muller, 2009; Patrone, 2009; Tolmein, 2009), the remainder of this chapter intends to utilise some tools developed from post-structuralist and post-conventionalist approaches. This should help to demonstrate the potential ways in which transable people crip the biomedical model whilst simultaneously being denied an identity recognised within the field. It is felt that the first way in

---

[6] Although caution is needed, as "evidence" to support this is minimal and might be used to deny transable people access to surgery (as has been experienced by transgender people).

which transable people "crip" biomedicine is in the status of the patient before medical intervention (and their potential status after elective amputation).

Fixing What is Broken: Biomedicine and the Normal/Abnormal Divide

In the case of offering help to people with physical impairment, health professionals are used to dealing with people whose bodies are deemed not to be working "normally" (according to the problematic medical standards discussed above and by Nettleton, 2013). The visibility of their "failing" body depends on the particular impairment but the commonality is that a part of their body is not working "effectively" and this may present the patient with unpleasant symptoms that may disrupt their everyday life. Transable individuals are deemed fully functional physically although they experience extreme anxiety and pressure due to the incongruence between their bodies and identities. As one person with "BIID" states:

> During the times of high intensity "BIID", the need to be paralysed verges on obsessive. These thoughts invade my everyday, my every moments. Not only does it affect me when I am awake, but also during my sleep. It renders me unable to focus on simple tasks at times, even as simple as preparing dinner, or driving to work. (O'Connor, 2009, p. 91)

Stevens (2011) utilised McRuer's work on compulsory able-bodiedness to help understand society's (and biomedicine's) difficulty in accepting "BIID" as a label. Compulsory able-bodiedness according to McRuer (cited in Stevens, 2011), creates a view that able-bodiedness is a preference to which everyone has the choice to conform, although the regimes of compulsory able-bodiedness demonstrate there is no choice at all. The "non-normative" is still, however, understood in relation to able-bodiedness which helps create a hierarchy regarding ability (and sexuality). Professions in areas such as psychiatry are then able to privilege "normals" over those who are not. Transable individuals are already deemed to have "normally" functioning bodies to begin with and therefore their inclusion into psychiatry would demand an acceptance of their "non-normative" status, whereby some transable individuals would demand surgery to help them gain impairment (deemed non-normative in biomedicine).

Some papers attempt to draw a number of parallels between "BIID" and "gender identity disorder" (now referred to as "gender dysphoria" in *DSM-5*) (Lawrence, 2009) both labels which have been used by biomedicine to describe transgender people. Lawrence[7] (2009) discusses how both transgender and transable individuals experience a mismatch between their physical bodies and their own identity and some of these require major, irreversible surgery to remove a healthy body part. Roth (2009) argues that surgery highlights differences between transgender people and transableism, however, as in some cases transgender people have been able to obtain gender affirmation surgery in contrast to surgery for people with "BIID" where practitioners have been prosecuted for performing amputations in the past. Despite these arguments, it must be highlighted that there is still much medical discrimination experienced by transgender individuals (as well as social and economic discrimination) who often still have to fight for their rights (or do not have rights) to acquire gender affirmation surgery (Baril, 2015). This could result in transgender people modifying their bodies illegally (as with transable individuals). Biomedicine therefore appears focused on establishing "normalcy" and trans individuals (transgender and transable) crip medical ideas of

---

[7] An author who has been highly criticised in transgender literature and amongst transgender people.

norms by asking to have surgery performed that would result in a body classed as "lacking" or "othered" in medical discourse.

Baril's (2015) study more critically engages in the continuities between transsexuality[8] and transability and calls for further establishing an intersectional analysis, which may serve to create "alliances between trans and disability studies and movements" (Baril, 2015, p. 31). Baril's work focuses on how both trans communities are appropriated by biomedical discourse which serve to marginalise the experiences of trans people, how both transsexuality and transability focuses on issues regarding identity and sexuality and how they have both received similar stigmatisation and "definitional issues that have limited the trans phenomenon's visibility and justified its marginalisation" (Baril, 2015, p. 33). As in Szasz's (2007) work, Baril recognises how through processes of medicalisation, trans individuals are further criminalised and treated with suspicion. Despite these similarities Baril (2015) notes that there are particular historical constructions within transgender and transable understandings that disrupt the possibilities for intersection. He described these constructions as having been defined by cis* majorities. Cisgender, cissexual and cis(dis)abled, refers to staying within the birth assigned gender/sexuality/disabled/abled identities, rather than crossing their boundaries (Baril, 2015). Baril (2015) highlights that an ableist bias exists in trans studies whilst a cis(gender) normative exists in disability studies. This in fact disrupts attempts at intersectional analysis which could broaden debates on bodily freedom and disrupts ideas on body normalcy which are deeply embedded in medical discourse.

---

[8] A term that has been referred to as a psychiatric diagnosis, but is also a group that can be seen as part of the transgender community (or separate from it).

Crip theory (McRuer, 2006) is focused on critically analysing the dis/abled dichotomy and uses this to help understand any aspect of modern Western culture. When using this concept to look at transableism, the taken-for-granted assumptions of "health" can be troubled. Whereas the idea of the rationalised, unitary, objective human that can be individually examined and known has prevailed since the Enlightenment, transable individuals render this idea of the human limited and demand the disabled body (usually understood as the opposite to these qualities) to be regarded as the preferred, healthy body for them. Arguably the need for impairment questions questions the beliefs on which the biomedical practice is founded. The World Health Organization's definition of health is as follows: "a state of complete physical, mental and social well-being and not merely the absence of disease or infirmity" (WHO, 1948). If we can officially recognise health as being *both* mentally and physically healthy then it is necessary for biomedical scientists, policy makers, clinicians and the rest of society to consider that an impaired body can be a healthy one. Only then can the assertion of impairment being "lacking" be challenged, omitted from mainstream thinking and the possibilities of suitable treatment defined by, and for, transable individuals can be imagined. To deny a transable person access to impairment could be seen as leaving that person with "infirmity" which by definition renders the person "unhealthy" with biomedicine appearing to refuse to adequately treat this ailment.

Biomedicine might prefer to investigate the possibility of developing alternative therapies (potentially damaging) for transable individuals that might seek to alleviate their need to pretend to have or obtain an impairment. Patrone's work (2009) considers the similarity of "BIID" to anorexia nervosa "patients" and compares their treatment by health professionals. Anorexia nervosa is well established in medical discourse and recognised as a "mental disorder" (although this is contested in critical, feminist literature) and Patrone (2009) highlights within the treatment of anorexia that the practitioner does not engage with the "patient's" desire to make themselves thinner but instead encourages them to rethink their bodily perceptions and where necessary, may force-feed the patients as they are deemed incapable to make informed choices about their food. Patrone (2009) uses this argument to suggest that transable individuals' demands for amputation are not expressions of rational agency. Furthermore, he states that the specific demand for amputation is not just about the person's attempt to maintain identity but "is an expression of the disorder itself" (2009, p. 544). In short Patrone believes that demands from transable people cannot be taken seriously because these desires are connected to their transableism. This position does not merely overlook the success of performed surgeries in improving the lives of those desiring such action (as discussed above), it demonstrates the pathologising nature of biomedicine whilst ultimately acting in opposition to the convention of scientific empiricism. The APA has not included the label of "BIID" in the *DSM-5* as the scientific community cannot agree on the exact aetiology of this as a "mental disorder" yet Patrone (2009) uses "BIID" to claim it is the features of this illness that is creating the "irrational" desire for amputation/surgery. This example of the pathologising of transableism leaves us wondering if it was a "normalised" idea of the body requested by transable individuals, would it be deemed irrational? Patrone's work demonstrates a lack of ability to critically engage in problematic perceptions of bodily normalcy and demonstrates the problems of relying upon medicalised understandings of transableism.

Dis/abled: Rethinking "BIID" Socially and Culturally

Davis (2012a) feels that people with "BIID" "queer the categories of ability and disability, desirability and repulsion, health and illness, and mind and body" (p. 321) and turns to focus on how this manifests as moral stigma imposed upon those who feign/desire impairment. She refers to moral stigma particularly as this is imposed upon a category of people who are perceived to have some form of control over their stigmatising attribute. Indeed Davis (2014) uncovers the various attributions of immorality expressed by others towards transable people as seen on Transabled.org. The assumptions made were that transable people were: sexually perverted (probably carried over from the application of the term "apotemnophilia" which classified transable individuals with other paraphilia disorders including necrophilia and paedophilia), emotionally weak (the perception that transable people demand attention), dishonest (targeted at the "pretenders" and highlight the moral condemnation of deceiving others and the potential harm this may cause to an already disadvantaged group) and greedy (that they will require additional resources when impaired and these are scarce and should be allocated to the "real" disabled (Davis, 2014). These claims are intimately connected to the discourses surrounding disability in general that serve to socially construct a negative perception of what it is to be "disabled". Such discourses result in a general agreement that transable individuals should repress their thoughts and not be granted the right to surgery or to feign disability and could be said to demonstrate the cisabled dominance in our mainstream society that was highlighted by Baril (2015).

Goodley's (2011) work further shows how disabled people are hated, patronised, ignored, pitied or met with sympathy, curiosity or fascination. It can be understood that these attitudes are further proliferated when the emphasis is placed on an independent, economically efficient, productive subject in neoliberal times. As stated previously disabled people become "othered" in such a world and rejected as "non-normals". The outside perception of transable people therefore arises from a lack of ability to understand that people would wish to enter such a position, as ultimately the "other" is a definitive, static and ontologically real position that seems quite obviously undesirable. Transable individuals' need for impairment transcends the able/ disabled dichotomy and demands that biomedicine works for it in different ways than were first intended. One way that some people seem to deal with this challenge is to shame, degrade and ostracise transable people.

The level of opposition concerned with materiality centres around the assumption that transable individuals lack sensitivity towards the issues facing cis(dis)abled people (i.e. those with impairment from birth or due to life events). Thomas's concept of "impairment effects" allows us to understand that in obtaining an impairment transable individuals become in and of themselves a "complex bio-social phenomena" (2007, p. 137). It is likely that the person with newly acquired impairment will experience its effects socially as well as physically. Instead of consolidating the categories of able/ disabled, the acquirement or acting out of impairment serves to highlight the precarious boundaries between these categories through the transable body. In imagining the persons' experiences of impairment post-surgery, one is forced to think of the effect this has socially (as well as physically) which in this sense brings into view ableist and disablist practices and their unfair consequences. For those in Davis's study (2014) who regard transable people as "greedy" due to the assumption that they will create a position of dependency and require various governmental resources, their contradictory assumptions are also highlighted. There appears an assumption that there may be an actual need for welfare support for impaired individuals although much of the mainstream thinking in relation to disabled people and welfare rests on discrediting and demonising them for claiming benefits to which they are entitled (Aleksia, 2012). In thinking about the potential need to rely on welfare support it is important to consider how experiences of transability might be further impacted by an individual's class which may partially determine the extent to which care and additional equipment which may be required, could be obtained. Baril (2015) argues that by recognising intersectionality amongst transable individuals in this manner, it further develops alliances with other social movements which, in turn, could pave the way for further justice.

Critical disability studies has located the problem of disablism and ableism firmly in the hands of the social context, as opposed to the individual, and in doing so suggests that if society can change to accept anomalous embodiment then desire for impairment may not be as problematic. Shildrick (2009) reminds us that otherness occurs due to people's inability to deal with the connections between themselves and "others". Disability epitomises interdependency, instability and uncertainty which resonates with the reality of the "normal" citizen. "Insofar as the other in its alterity is always a possible threat to the integrity of self, then the radically different other – the one who … fails to observe the same boundaries – is doubly so." (2009, p. 84). Shildrick uses the term dis/ability to challenge the idea of ontological differences between the two, and draws attention to the transitory nature of both abled and disabled embodiment so there is a way to reimagine the way we think about bodies. Her postconventionalist approach not only demands engagement in the deconstruction of binary forms of thinking but further hopes that in emphasising the fluidity of the body, new negotiations and valuing of anomalous embodiment will be realised. Furthermore, Shildrick proposes that troubling dichotomous

166

thinking is an ethical necessity. The transable body highlights the transgressive possibilities of bodies and in a world where difference is only understood as a different set of connections between each other, an "elected" disabled person becomes just another example of a post-human and evidence of the limitations of imagining the body as a fixed entity. Yet one can turn to another example of the transgressive possibilities of bodies that is already being acted out in a much more culturally acceptable manner.

Un/desirable Dreams

Bordo's work (1993) explores why women engaged in extreme regimes of dieting, exercise and/or surgery to obtain slenderness and believes such behaviour can be explained by the "powerful normalising mechanisms of our century" (p. 186) which emphasise self-improvement and transformation to achieve bodily norms. Phipps (2014) continues this theme and believes the body has become a key location to practise self-control, blaming neoliberalism which "has become a normative framework based on the idea of citizens as rational and self-interested economic actors with agency and control over their own lives" (p. 11). So when humans engage in cosmetic surgery to obtain a body which fits in with society's construction of beauty, they are hailed as the perfect neoliberal subject who achieves their important aesthetic goals. People conveniently forget that this decision is based on pressures from the media and irrational ideas of gender norms which is interesting when considering the amount of scrutiny transable individuals are under to justify their needs in light of "rationality" (Bayne and Levy, 2005). Cosmetic surgery is also clearly a lucrative industry as Jones (2008) shows this drives people to increasingly utilise surgery to achieve the fictional utopia of "bodily perfection". In turn its initial use regularly results in continual engagement and multiple operations (Jones, 2008).

The difference in the case of the transable individual, is that despite them wishing to engage in the transformation of self to achieve their body ideal, the desire for an impaired body is not considered "normal". Kannen (cited in Goodley, 2014) states "social order is maintained through the constructed categorisations of privilege and power that we deem certain bodies to have, which then demarcate what is possible for those bodies and for bodies that are then considered to be Other" (p. 51). As Goodley (2014) continues, disabled people are often denied the right to the status of "human" as the world divides them away from "normal" peers. They are assumed therefore to stray from qualities of the "modernist human subject: bounded, rational, capable, responsible and competent" (p. 156). So as transable individuals desire entry into this neoliberal world, society appears to deny them agency as they are rendered irrational, precarious and incompetent. The decision not to allow transable individuals the right to perform impairment enhancing surgery then is a function of power which results in the normalisation of existence. It may appear an ableist decision to deny people to alter their body to become impaired, nevertheless people who are demanding the right for transable people to obtain elective surgery for the purpose of impairment appear to be reliant upon the merits of individual agency over and above the various structures and institutions that still continue to impose unfair conditions and rules on disabled people.

In critiquing feminist debates around the dis/empowering nature of sex work Phipps (2014) outlines and critiques the polarisation of feminist debates that are usefully applied to demonstrate the problems that emerge from binary arguments. Initially Phipps explores how in the debate surrounding the oppressing/empowering nature of the sex worker's identity, claims to authenticity have led to a "war on voice" (2014, p. 99). There can be seen to be a "war on voice" in the debate surrounding elective amputations as both transable individuals and disabled people themselves claim political capital and therefore can legitimise positions of anti/pro surgery. Baril (2015) shows the difficulty in claiming "authentic" identities (read cisnormative) as once again this limits understandings between different bodies and intersectionality. This war on voice has therefore led to a politicisation of the personal and individualises structural critiques of biomedicine and dis/ableism. Also, just as Phipps (2014) is critical of identity-focused celebration of "sex-radical" females, it appears that the heavily individualised focus on the transable individual "re-aligning" identity needs to be critiqued. If we apply the principle of intersectionality (as Baril, 2015 and Phipps, 2014 do) and consider the various different positions, identities and experiences of dis/abled and cis(dis/abled) people, then we may understand that "elective" impairment may create very different experiences. A person's class, age, gender, ethnicity, sexuality, etc., will impact differently upon how impairment is experienced. Baril (2015) asks us to consider for example the under-representation of cisgender women in transability studies (which may indicate bias in medical research), how racism might impact upon on how transable individuals are judged and how class might impact upon the "productivity" of the post-operative individual. Once again, the precarious existence of the transable "other" serves to crip ideas of "normalcy" and further highlights the interconnections between dis/ability.

Conclusion: Post/Human

When people are reacting with disgust at the thought of an able-bodied person needing to be or pretending to be disabled, they are reliant on the notion of the human as a stable, distinct and definable being. The transable body falls outside of their conception of "normal" and therefore is rendered "subhuman". As with her work on the monstrous body, Shildrick (2002) identifies that bodies rendered as such may evade classification as they occupy a liminal space. This appears to be the case with transable people, the label of "BIID" and the *DSM-5*. As with disabled people, society tends to treat transable individuals with abjection as the fragility of health and "ability" is ever more emphasised in the bodies of the transable and reminds the "able bodied" of their own precariousness. It is not necessary to conclude by deciding whether a transable person should be able to electively obtain impairment, but instead to continue to trouble and highlight the various contradictions within various arguments and interconnections of dis/ability. Through a post-conventionalist framework, one must conclude that humanity cannot manifest itself in one type of working body. Humanity is about desire for connection and a true acknowledgement of interdependence as opposed to any false notions of individual agency.

The connections between the dis/trans/abled communities in this chapter can be seen most obviously when considering some arguments' claims to "authentic" identities and the moral positions regarding transable communities' rights to feign or obtain impairment. Many positions from ethical perspectives to psychiatrists and neurologists to the lay public appear to rely upon the importance of rational agency to legitimise their particular argument. Indeed the transable individual also utilises discourses of essentialist realities as they seek to create a version of themselves that connects them to their ontologically "real" selves. It is integral to move beyond these constraining discourses and create more open dialogue about this topic which serves to crip, trouble, interrogate and problematise people's perception of the human in the twenty-first century.

References

Aleksia, A. (2012). *Why we're not benefit scroungers*. Woodstock, United Kingdom: Writersworld.

American Psychiatric Association (2013a). *Diagnostic and statistical manual of mental disorders* (5th ed.). Arlington, VA; American Psychiatric Association.

American Psychiatric Association. (2013b). *Insurance implications of DSM-5*. Retrieved 5 December 2014, from http://www.psychiatry.org/dsm5

Baubet, T., Gal, B., Dendoncker-Viry, S., Masquelet, A. C., Gatt, M. T., & Moro, M. R. (2007). Apotemnophilia as a contemporary frame for psychological suffering. *Encephale, 33*(4), 609–615.

Baril, A. (2015). Needing to acquire a physical impairment/ disability: (re) thinking the connections between trans and disability studies through transability. *Hypatia, 30*(1), 30–48.

Bayne, T., & Levy, N. (2005). Amputees by choice: Body integrity identity disorder and the ethics of amputation. *Journal of Applied Philosophy, 22*(1), 75–86.

Blom, R. M., Hennekam, R. C., & Denys, D. (2012). Body Integrity Identity Disorder. *PLoS ONE, 7*(4). doi: 10.1371/journal.pone.0034702

Bodyshock. (2004). London, UK: Channel 4. Retrieved from: http://www.channel4.com/programmes/bodyshock

Bordo, S. (1993). *Unbearable weight: Feminism, Western culture, and the body*. London, United Kingdom: University of California Press.

Bou Khalil, R., & Richa, S. (2012). Apotemnophilia or body integrity identity disorder: A case report review. *The International Journal of Lower Extremity Wounds, 11*(4), 313–319.

Busfield, J. (1996). *Men, women and madness: Understanding gender and mental disorder*. Basingstoke, United Kingdom: Palgrave Macmillan.

Campbell, F. K. (2009). *Contours of ableism: The production of disability and abledness*. Basingstoke, United Kingdom: Palgrave Macmillan.

Conrad, P. (2007). *The medicalization of society: On the transformation of human conditions into treatable disorders*. Baltimore, MD: The Johns Hopkins University Press.

Davis, J. L. (2014). Morality work among the transabled. *Deviant Behavior, 35*(6), 433–455.

Davis, J. L. (2012a). Narrative construction of a ruptured self: Stories of transability on transabled.org. *Sociological Perspectives, 55*(2), 319–340.

Davis, J. L. (2012b). Prosuming identity: The production and consumption of transableism on transabled.org. *American Behavioral Scientist, 56*(4), 596–617.

First, M. (2005). Desire for amputation of a limb: Paraphilia psychosis or a new type of identity disorder. *Psychological Medicine, 35*, 919–928.

First, M. B., & Fisher, C. E. (2012). Body Integrity Identity Disorder: The persistent desire to acquire a physical disability. *Psychopathology, 45*(1), 3–14.

Giummarra, M. J. (2011). Body Integrity Identity Disorder: Deranged body processing, right fronto-parietal dysfunction and phenomenological experience of body incongruity. *Neuropsychology Review, 21*(4), 320–333.

Goodley, D. (2011). *Disability studies: An interdisciplinary introduction*. London, United Kingdom: Sage.

Goodley, D. (2014). *Dis/Ability studies: Theorising disablism and ableism*. London, United Kingdom: Routledge.

Jones, M. (2008). *Skintight: An anatomy of cosmetic surgery*. Oxford, United Kingdom: Berg Publishers.

Lawrence, A. A. (2009). Parallels between Gender Identity Disorder and Body Integrity Identity Disorder: A review and update. In A. Stirn, A. Thiel, & S. Oddo (Eds.), *Body Integrity Identity Disorder: Psychological, neurobiological, ethical and legal aspects* (pp. 154–173). Lengerich, Germany: Pabst Science Publishers.

McRuer, R. (2006). Compulsory able-bodiedness and queer/ disabled existence. In L. J. Davis (Ed.), *The disability studies reader* (pp. 369–381). New York, NY: Routledge.

Muller, S. (2009). "BIID" – under which circumstances would the amputations of healthy limbs be ethically justified? In A. Stirn, A. Thiel, & S. Oddo (Eds.), *Body Integrity Identity Disorder: Psychological, neurobiological, ethical and legal aspects* (pp. 109–123). Lengerich, Germany: Pabst Science Publishers.

Nettleton, S. (2013). *The sociology of health and illness.* Cambridge, United Kingdom: Polity Press.

Oddo, S., Thiel, A., Skoruppa, S., Klinger, D., Steis, N., Markowitsch, H. J., & Stirn, A. (2009). Neurobiological and psychological aspects of "BIID" – an integrative approach. In A. Stirn, A. Thiel, & S. Oddo (Eds.), *Body Integrity Identity Disorder: Psychological, neurobiological, ethical and legal aspects* (pp. 238–245). Lengerich, Germany: Pabst Science Publishers.

O'Connor, S. (2009). Suffering from 'BIID'. In A. Stirn, A. Thiel & S. Oddo (Eds.), *Body Integrity Identity Disorder: Psychological, neurobiological, ethical and legal aspects* (pp. 88–93). Lengerich, Germany: Pabst Science Publishers.

Oliver, M. (1990). *Politics of disablement.* Basingstoke, United Kingdom: Macmillan.

Patrone, D. (2009). Disfigured anatomies and imperfect analogies: Body Integrity Identity Disorder and the supposed right to self-demanded amputation of healthy body parts. *Journal of Medical Ethics, 35,* 541–545.

Phillips, K. A., Wilhelm, S., Korna, L. M., Didie, E. R., Fallon, B. A., Feusner, J., & Stein, D. J. (2010). Body Dysmorphic Disorder: Some key issues for DSM-V. *Depression and Anxiety, 27,* 573–591.

Phipps, A. (2014). *The politics of the body.* Cambridge, United Kingdom: Polity Press.

Roth, R. (2009). Consent to an elective amputation: Response of students and experts. In A. Stirn, A. Thiel, & S. Oddo (Eds.), *Body Integrity Identity Disorder: Psychological, neurobiological, ethical and legal aspects* (pp. 139–53). Lengerich, Germany: Pabst Science Publishers.

Sedda, A., & Bottini, G. (2014). Apotemnophilia, body integrity identity disorder or xenomelia? Psychiatric and neurologic etiologies face each other. *Neuropsychiatric Disease and Treatment, 10,* 1255–1265.

Shildrick, M. (2002). *Embodying the monster: Encounters with the vulnerable self.* London, United Kingdom: Sage.

Shildrick, M. (2009). *Dangerous discourses of disability, subjectivity and sexuality.* Basingstoke, United Kingdom: Palgrave Macmillan.

Song, R. (2013). Body Integrity Identity Disorder and the ethics of mutilation. *Studies in Christian Ethics, 26*(4), 487–503.

Stevens, B. (2011). Interrogating transability: A catalyst to view disability as body art. *Disability Studies Quarterly, 31*(4), retrieved 5 December 2015 from http://dsq-sds.org/article/view/1705/ 1755

Stirn, A., Thiel, A., & Oddo, S. (Eds.). (2009). *Body Integrity Identity Disorder: Psychological, neurobiological, ethical and legal aspects.* Lengerich, Germany: Pabst Science Publishers.

Swindell, M., & Lawrence, J. S. (2009). Body Integrity Identity Disorder: An overview. In A. Stirn, A. Thiel, & S. Oddo (Eds.), *Body Integrity Identity Disorder: Psychological, neurobiological, ethical and legal aspects* (pp. 11–19). Lengerich, Germany: Pabst Science Publishers.

Szasz, T. (2007). *The medicalization of everyday life: Selected essays.* Syracuse, NY: Syracuse University Press.

Thomas, C. (2007). *Sociologies of disability and illness: Contested ideas in disability studies and medical sociology.* Basingstoke, United Kingdom: Palgrave Macmillan.

Tolmein, O. (2009). Are surgical solutions to "BIID" legally justified? In A. Stirn, A. Thiel & S. Oddo (Eds.), *Body Integrity Identity Disorder: Psychological, neurobiological, ethical and legal aspects* (pp. 124–132). Lengerich, Germany: Pabst Science Publishers.

Vitacco, D., Hilti, L., & Brigger, B. (2009). Negative phantom limbs? A neurological account of Body Integrity Identity Disorder. In A. Stirn, A. Thiel, & S. Oddo (Eds.), *Body Integrity Identity Disorder: Psychological, neurobiological, ethical and legal aspects* (pp. 201–210). Lengerich, Germany: Pabst Science Publishers.

World Health Organization (1948). Preamble to the Constitution of the World Health Organization as adopted by the International Health Conference, New York, 19 June–22 July 1946; signed on 22 July 1946 by the representatives of 61 States (Official Records of the World Health Organization, no. 2, p. 100) and entered into force on 7 April 1948. The definition has not been amended since 1948.

Williams, V., & Song, R. (2014). Defacing the image of God? Elective amputations and the Christian tradition; response to Vanessa Williams. *Theology, 117*(4), 256–268.

CHAPTER 7

PEOPLE OF SUBSTANCE: DISABILITY,
PROBLEMATIC DRUG USE AND NORMALCY

Jess Bradley and Greta Williams-Schultz

Summary
The experiences of the problematic drug user and the disabled person
intersect in multiple ways through discourses of rehabilitation,
institutionalisation, stigma and psychiatrisation. This chapter seeks to
put the disabled people's movement in conversation with the drug
users' movement to explore contemporary and historical intersections
between the two. We draw on disability theory to argue that both drug
use and disability can historically be seen through similar lenses of
moral, medical and social models of use, which may wax and wane in
dominance but are nonetheless synchronous and fluid. Informed by
interviews with drug user activists and disabled drug users, we then
discuss how "problematic drug use" is socially constructed through
various institutional and social factors, and weaponised punitively
against those with unruly bodies down gendered, raced and classed
lines. This leads us to question whether drug use can be considered a
disability or impairment. We argue that the lack of a widely understood
and accepted social model of drug use can be seen as a barrier to an
empowered and influential drug user community. We conclude by
calling for more collaboration between disability studies and the
fledgling field of drug user studies.

Introduction
The experiences of the problematic drug user and the disabled
person have many intersections. People from both groups might
find themselves institutionalised against their will,
psychiatrised, or feeling the sharp end of social stigma. Both
disabled people and people whose drug use is seen as
problematic may be reliant on the dwindling welfare system,

engaging with social services, or in some form of rehabilitation. Yet despite these similar experiences, engagements between disability studies and addiction studies/drug user studies are limited. There has to date been precious little cross-fertilisation between drug user activism and the disabled people's movement, despite many shared interests and approaches.

It is worth delineating here what we mean by "drug user studies". Drug user studies, as we understand it, is an underdeveloped field consisting of drug user activist perspectives on drug use, which we consider equivalent to disability studies perspectives informed by the disabled people's movement. As such, drug user studies views drug use through the lens of social oppression rather than seeing it as a socio-medical phenomenon to be managed by professionals. Just as the early disability studies literature was dominated by organisations of disabled people (UPIAS, etc.), this field is dominated by activist organisations of people who use drugs (such as the National Users Network, Respect Drug User Rights, VANDU (the Vancouver Area Network of Drug Users), the International Network of People Who Use Drugs, and *Black Poppy* magazine).

There is also a relevant body of literature in addiction studies and the sociology of drug use with a focus on policy, management, prevalence and adaption (e.g. Winstock et al. (2011), Nutt (2012) and Duff (2004)) which arguably comes from a similar positionality as medical sociologist perspectives on disability as they share common priorities. That is to say that they are both concerned with influencing government policy rather than community activism. For a detailed critique of medical sociologies of disability by disability studies scholars, please refer to Barnes and Mercer (1996) and Thomas (2007). For further critique of current sociologies of drug use, please see the section of this chapter titled "social understandings of disability and drug use".

This chapter explores the dominant historical and contemporary conceptualisations of drug use and disability. It goes on to explore how the categories of "problematic" and "non-problematic" drug users are unstable, precarious positions informed by intersections with disability, class, race and the legal status of the drugs in question. One of our participants articulates how we understand the figure of the problematic drug user well:

> the problematic drug user is someone who the state feels the need to interfere with, because they are seen as being a threat to themselves or society. So they need to be managed through prisons, courts, social services, rehab, etc. (John, 57, drug user rights activist, ex-heroin user)

We then go on to examine how the identities of drug users overlap with identities of disabled people and ultimately question if long-term drug use may be considered as disability.

Our study is based around 25 semi-structured interviews with UK-based drug user activists, disabled people who use drugs, and drugs service providers, as well as an analysis of historical sources around drug use and disability. Of the 25 participants, six were drugs service providers (who did not identify as either drug users or as disabled), seven were disabled drug users (who did not consider themselves to be activists), with the remaining 12 participants being drug user activists. Of the 12 drug user activists nine identified as disabled, although they were not recruited on this basis.

The authors have a background in both disability studies, especially the history of disabled people, and the drugs field; one has been heavily involved in drug user activism and drugs services more generally, whilst the other is an opiate addict (although crucially, as the drugs are prescribed in this case, they have not – yet – been labelled a problematic user). This background was utilised to recruit personal contacts in drug user activist groups and drug services in London, Leeds and Manchester.

The participants who used drugs were asked about their interactions with medical, legal and social support services. In all cases this led to unprompted discussions around the discrimination they had felt as drug users and the social role that this discrimination played. The participants who were recruited from the disabled drug users group were asked specifically to comment on the intersections of disability and drug use. The drug user activists were not asked specifically about disability but 10 of the 12 participants raised it in the discussion. The participants who were service providers were asked about their attitudes towards their work and their service users. They were not asked about disability and no service providers raised this in the discussion. The interviews were audio recorded and transcribed, and coded along major narrative themes that emerged from the discussion.

Normalcy studies seek to shift the attention from the construction of otherness towards the construction of norms which problematise the other (Davis, 1995). Just as constructions of physical, intellectual, and mental norms frame disabled people as problems, so do norms around socially acceptable drug use and behaviour frame some drug users as problematic. In both cases the construction of the norm represents hegemonic ideas around desirable and acceptable citizens, who are productive, rational, and individual. The disabled person and the drug user become unruly bodies; the focus of fascination, romantic objectification and revulsion. In this way they act as containers for society's anxieties about the acceptable ways to have a body (Fox and Lipkin, 2002).

Within disability discourse, it is possible to pick out three models of understanding disability: moral, medical and social. Similarly, moral, medical and social tropes are also present within drugs discourse. For both disability and drug use, these tropes act as controlling images. These controlling images are both generative and restrictive in their effects and shift in dominance. It is possible to ascribe each disability model a rough time-frame in which they were dominant in the UK. The moral model dominated up until the mid-nineteenth century, until medicalising discourses became popularised, with the social model developing in the post-war period onwards (Goodley 2011, pp. 7–13). However, these categorisations are not so neat; moral, medical and social disability tropes have existed and continue to exist simultaneously (Williams-Schultz and Bradley, 2013). Similarly, we will see how moral, medical and social drugs discourses, whilst waxing and waning in dominance, are also synchronous and fluid.

Moral Understandings of Disability and Drug Use

Moral understandings of disability frame sin as the cause of disability and associate piety and wholesomeness with bodily and mental perfection (Johnson, 2011). Similarly, drug use is framed as a moral issue and temperance associated with strength of character (Duff, 2004). The preamble of the UN Single Convention on Narcotic Drugs, upon which the UK Misuse of Drugs Act is based, called drugs a "serious evil" (UNODC, 1971). This framing establishes drug use and drug addiction as threats to a universal self which require state-led interventions (Crick, 2012).

Media representation of both drug use and disability reflect society's anxieties over the potential loss of social, physical or sexual control. These representations, such as "inspiration porn" of disabled people living relatively ordinary lives (Young, 2014), or "My Drug Hell" confessionals of reformed "addicts", are almost always framed in moral or spiritual terms. In 2014, NHS Choices, a government approved source of healthcare advice, ran a story which promoted a spiritual understanding of drug use (NHS Choices, 2014). The title was "My Drug Addiction Hell". Pearl Lowe was quoted as saying that her recovery from addiction was like moving along "a dark tunnel towards the light". She chose not to use medically researched treatments and instead describes herself as being part of a more "spiritual program" involving a "healing-circle". She also emphasises how leaving drugs behind allowed her to engage in paid work, which is presented as the ultimate aim of recovery. These cultural phenomena place the drug user and disabled person as "moral lessons for society", as inspirations for people to remain within, or strive towards, normalcy.

Disabled people and people who use drugs often become moral projects for charitable and religious organisations. As one participant, who runs a Christian agency supporting women who use drugs, said:

> I am not going to lie I do think my faith is what motivates me to work in this area, I see it as a spiritual calling. The church has a long history of supporting destitute and vulnerable women, and no doubt it will long continue. (Rachel, 32, charity support worker)

This framework commodifies the unruly body as a tool by which the normate can achieve salvation and gain social capital for doing "good works" (Striker, 1997). Bourke (2014) develops this idea through reference to nineteenth-century religious writings. She points out that as charity is a core principle of Christianity, it must follow that suffering is necessary so we might gain God's favour by relieving it (Bourke, 2014, p. 47). As one of our participants explained:

> These [charitable] organisations pat themselves on the back for deigning to work with us. It's not that we don't appreciate the support, it's just we see them being very loud about the small support they do give whilst being very silent on issues like decriminalisation [of drug possession]. Plus, the support we get rests on the fact that we live chaotic lives – the closer we get to appearing normal the quicker we fall "of" their lists, no matter what support we think we need. (Tascha, 38, harm reduction activist, ex-heroin user)

This relationship allows the charitable worker access to social capital, but by remaining silent on the issue of decriminalisation and discrimination, their service users are maintained in precarious positions. Moreover, the charitable dynamic relies on the unruly body being subordinate and remaining so in order to appear to the charity worker as suitably in need of help. Another example of this dynamic is how disabled people must present themselves as lacking agency during work capability assessments for Employment and Support Allowance, in order to receive necessary support. In other words, disabled people must prove themselves to be part of the deserving, rather than undeserving poor, as described by Stone (1984). One participant described her own experience of this:

> They make you go to these assessments ... interrogate you like you are on trial for something. It makes you feel like you've done something bad just by existing. And you have to buy into it, say please and thank you to them, talk about your worst days, let yourself be degraded by their questions ... cause if you don't you won't get the money you need ... But for them, they must go away thinking we are pathetic, because that's how we have to portray ourselves in this awful fucking system. (Laura, 29, harm reduction activist)

Both religious organisations and the state materially benefit from the continued oppression of disabled people and people who use

181

drugs. Religious organisations are reliant on the continued existence of the suffering of unruly bodies as means by which religious workers can achieve salvation, and more materially, to continue to appear relevant to the funding bodies which pay their wages (Williams-Schultz and Bradley, 2013). Similarly, neoliberal capital relies on the existence of a precarious and un(der)employed workforce in order to diminish the strength of labour as a mobilising force (Ross, 2009). This has, in various contexts, led to processes of neoliberalisation which have restructured the welfare state around socially regressive and politically volatile regulatory landscapes (Brenner and Theodore, 2002). Actions within this restructuring, such as cutting disability benefits and the partial privatisation of the NHS, has had a significant negative impact on those with unruly bodies, including disabled people and people who use drugs.

Medical Understandings of Disability and Drug Use

Foucault (1978) charts how the move of governments to seeing subjects as populations resulted in a regime change around bodily discourses. In the eighteenth century, populations started to be managed through the analysis of birth and death rates, marriage, contraception and fertility. For Foucault (1978), sex lay at the heart of this governance project. Arguably, the management of health, illness and death was equally central (Tremain, 2005, pp. 1–24). This continued throughout the nineteenth century which saw the growth of a new science which sought to define and categorise deviance, putting illness and disability increasingly in the hands of rationalist experts.

The passing of the 1834 Poor Law Amendment Act saw a huge growth in the institutionalisation of both disabled people and people who use drugs in the workhouse (Stone, 1984). Within this context disabled people and people who use drugs were often included within the crowd of vagrants alongside other unruly bodies. The New Poor Law (as the act came to be known) instigated a shift from "outdoor relief" (the giving of money, food and clothes to the poor) to "indoor relief" (economic exploitation within the workhouse).

The trend towards institutionalisation went hand in hand with the medicalisation of discourse around drugs and disability. The institutions established a class of professionals (doctors, psychiatrists, sexologists, etc.) who gazed upon and theorised unruly bodies with the aim of rehabilitating them back to normalcy (Foucault, 1975). This expert class were given increasing controls over the lives of those considered unruly. For example, the 1868 Pharmacy Act gave pharmacists exclusive control on the sale of opium, after moral concerns that working-class mothers and labourers were too dependent on the drug (Berridge, 1999).

The First World War was something of a turning point in our understandings of both disability and drug use. The 1914 Defence of the Realm Act represented a clamp down on drug users. The prohibition of cocaine, opiates and cannabis, initially criminalised only within the military, was soon enacted on the civilian population too (Berridge, 1999). The trend towards increasing legal restriction on drugs persisted after the war, with many widely available substances being banned. Criminalisation of drug use, leading to legal condemnation and punishment for users, represented a shoring up of moral narratives of drug use. Simultaneously, the use of medical evidence as rationale for the new laws, shows medical understandings beginning to take hold (Berridge, 1999).

We can also see shifts in understandings of disability during the war. Moral tropes were still applied in government policy, used as rationale for denying war pensions to those who were considered cowards or opportunists. In particular, those suffering from shell shock were often deemed unpatriotic, or faking symptoms in order to escape the front line. Ben Shepard describes the mood of the times well; "it is a tall order for the state to take on the liability to support a man who becomes a lunatic because he is a coward" (Shepard, 2000, p. xviii).

By way of contrast, medical narratives played a formative part in the new concept of "rehabilitation" which was born of the war. As a conference on the care of war wounded was told "we shall give the crippled soldier back functional ability, solidity of nerve or lung ... we shall re-create and fortify him" (Reznik, 2012, p. 185). The language of rehabilitation, echoing the post-war effort to rebuild damaged infrastructure, could only be applied to the more "deserving" war wounded rather than those disabled from birth (Williams-Schultz and Bradley, 2013). So we can see that access to the fruits of medical advancements was still regulated on a moral basis.

Similarly, medical understandings of drug use were restricted to more respectable, middle-class people who were seen as morally superior subjects. Whilst doctors who worked with working-class criminal populations had long argued from a moral perspective that heroin and morphine use caused criminality (Berridge, 1999), doctors of middle-class drug users argued for a strictly medical understanding of opiate use (South, 1998). People who used drugs were regulated based on who they were, rather than the drugs they took; a moral model for the poor and a medical model for the rich (Duster, 1970).

Since the 1960s, numerous studies have shored up medical understandings of drug use and addiction. One of the most influential is Dole and Nyswander's (1967) analysis of the effectiveness of methadone maintenance treatment for heroin addicts. In their study, 90% of the participants completed the programme, with 75% being "socially productive and living as normal citizens within 6 months of treatment". This study firmly established heroin addiction as a disease, for which the effectiveness of treatment is measured in economic or social productivity. It also impacted heavily on the lives of people who use drugs; the widespread adoption of methadone maintenance treatment resulted in a large increase in contact between people who use drugs and medical professionals. Although this shows a strengthening of medical understandings of drug use, here the medical and moral narratives are intertwined: the true meaning of "recovery" is not the absence of disease but the adoption of the moral imperative of paid labour.

Social Understandings of Disability and Drug Use

From the 1960s, we can see the development of new social understandings of both disability and drug use. The social model of disability defines disability as a construction of society rather than as a moral or medical deficiency of the individual (Oliver, 1986). This idea can also be applied to people who use drugs, when we view long-term drug use and addiction as produced by society rather than by individual disease or damnation. This user-centred social understanding of drug use is notably under-theorised within contemporary drugs discourse. Modern sociologies of drug use usually focus on how to manage the consequences of drug use, rather than looking at social understandings of user communities.

This is reflected in the aims of the major journals which typically publish sociological studies of drug use. The *International Journal of Drug Policy* (2015), for example, focuses squarely on how drug users can be managed by governments and clinicians. Drug and Alcohol Dependence (2015), another key publication, focuses on "treatment and prevention", again referring to management by authorities. As a final example, the *Journal of Drug Issues* (2015) positions itself as for those involved in "the struggle against the problem of drug use". Although it would not be fair to say that every article published by these journals aims to manage and control drug users, the stated scope of these and other key journals show that studies by and for drug users themselves are of secondary concern at best. This approach stands in marked contrast to the potential field of "drug user studies" suggested by this chapter.

The societal shift towards social understandings of disability can be demonstrated in the successful campaign for benefits to be granted based on degree rather than cause of impairment. From 1965, this campaign was headed by the Disablement Income Group, who also represented the UK's first pan-impairment organisation (Disablement Income Group, 1987). At this time, benefits were only awarded to people who had acquired their impairments in certain ways, with particular preference given to those impairments caused by a military incident or a workplace accident. The success of the campaign represents a shift from moral to social understandings of disability.

As disabled people's campaigning organisations developed in the second half of the twentieth century, we can also see a similar rise of politicised drug users' groups. As organisations such as UPIAS, which fought for disability rights, were founded in the UK in the 70s, in the Netherlands people who use drugs formed Junkiesbund, the Junkie's Union, which fought for drug users' rights (Southwell, 2009). Junkiesbund went on to establish the world's first needle and syringe exchange programme. Alongside this they also campaigned to drive up drug quality through consumer rights initiatives and ran a radio show which dispelled myths about drugs and drug users.

VANDU (the Vancouver Area Network of Drug Users) is a notable modern example of a Canadian drug user organisation whose work has received some academic attention (see Kerr et al., 2006; Wood et al., 2003). VANDU has managed to both appeal to local authorities (it is funded by local health authorities for its education, peer support, harm reduction and advocacy work), and engage in more radical actions such as establishing temporary and unsanctioned needle exchanges and occupying public spaces to draw attention to Vancouver's lack of social housing. VANDU is recognised internationally as a successful drug user organisation (Kerr et al., 2006), and the fact that only drug users or ex-users can vote on policy and in elections within the organisation align it well within the scope of what we characterise here as drug user activism.

Although the UK has adopted needle exchange programmes, they have been stripped from their original foundation in political organisations run by people who use drugs (Southwell, 2009). Instead, they are a part of the medical establishment and as such are not complemented with other campaigns which would benefit their users, such as pushing for higher quality drugs. Drugs discourse and drug user activism is severely limited by an unwillingness to consider "pleasure maximisation" next to harm reduction (Talkingdrugz, 2009). Although within recent years sociologists of drug use have begun to speak more openly about the benefits as well as risks associated with substance use, this discussion has yet to move beyond academic debate and into public policy and the media (Holt and Treloar, 2008). This taboo silences meaningful public conversations about how to improve the lives of drug users. The silence is enforced despite campaigns that focus on pleasure maximisation being proven more effective in preventing disease transmission than those that focus on harm reduction alone (Harris, 2014).

Disability and drug user activist movements have both suffered from people without lived experience speaking for and over those with. Both communities adopted the slogan "nothing about us without us", but in both cases it is still an ideal that needs to be fought for. As one of our participants noted: "In the late nineties we started organising around the phrase 'Nothing about us, without us', it's still a feature of the drug users' movement today although often it will just result in some token user being ignored on some committee somewhere" (John, 57, drug user rights activist, ex-heroin user). All too often, what is "best" for disabled people and drug users is decided by privileged politicians and professionals, perhaps after consulting "some token" oppressed person. The social model of disability has formed a rallying point for disabled people to fight against tokenisation and marginalisation and we can see a similar model would be beneficial to the drug user community. The current field of "sociologies of drug use" is equivalent to the field of "medical sociologies of disability", which the founders of the disability studies community have spoken against on the grounds that it failed to improve the lives of disabled people (Oliver, 1996, p. 45). The alternative is an academic movement equivalent to disability studies, firmly rooted in the drug user activist movement. We hope this chapter may be considered part of this alternative.

The Problematic Drug User

The UN narrative of drug use as a "serious evil" frames otherwise inanimate pills, powders and potions as a threat to the universal self. Yet the drug laws, medical treatments, and social programmes envisaged to combat this apparent evil are far from universally applied. According to the Crime Survey for England and Wales, the percentage of adults who self-report having used illicit drugs in their lifetime is 35.6% (Home Office, 2014). It is clear that not all people who use illicit drugs have come into contact with medical or legal authorities, nor would it be practical for them to do so.

Central here is the figure of the "problematic drug user". The distinction between perceived problematic and non-problematic drug use explains why, of the 35.6% who have used illegal drugs, few will ever be held to account by medical or legal authorities. People who are labelled problematic drug users are seen as being priorities for intervention over the non-problematic drug user. Often, those labelled as a problem will use heroin or crack.

What is considered "problematic" drug use is not legally defined. However, the drug classification system outlined in the Misuse of Drugs Act allows us some limited insight into how the authorities prioritise intervention by substance. According to the former chair of the Advisory Council for the Misuse of Drugs, Professor David Nutt (2012, pp. 18–19), current political thinking refuses to consider changing drug classification based on new scientific evidence. This points to moral understandings of drug use within the government; a medical understanding would classify drugs based on scientifically demonstrable harm. Nutt memorably compares the dangers associated with taking Ecstasy (Class A substance) to those associated with horse-riding, concluding that the latter may be considered more dangerous, depending on the calculations used (Nutt, 2012, p. 11). While moral understandings of drug use permeate government policy, and the government classification system helps determine who are "problematic" drug users, we must accept that that label is a moral rather than medical judgement.

As one drug user activist told us in reference to an earlier Nutt (2009) paper discussing Ecstasy and horse-riding:

> I think the paper showing that horse-riding is more dangerous than taking Mandy [MDMA/Ecstasy] tells us something interesting about the way society views drugs. We would never dream of locking people up for owning a horse-riding centre but we do not bat an eyelid when someone is sent down for possession or supply of Ecstasy. The obsession with drugs comes from the idea of control, it's not about harm and has never been about harm. Because the drug user is perceived to be giving up

> control of themselves they are in need of intervention. (Karen, 29,
> drug user activist, current user of various drugs)

Self-control is a central tenet of rationalist individualism (Oyserman, Coon, and Kemmelmeier, 2002). For Michalko (2002) and Oliver (1996), the problem of disability is fundamentally tied to the production of normate individuals and their alterity: the unruly bodies which threaten them. As such, those excluded from the rational human (disabled, raced, gendered or otherwise unruly bodies) are prioritised for punitive state intervention. This dynamic is shown in the disproportionate policing of minority groups, particularly black communities. In the UK, black people are 6.3 times more likely to be stopped and searched for drugs than their white counterparts (Eastwood, Shiner, and Bear, 2014) despite being less likely to use or supply drugs (Home Office, 2014). Similarly, disabled people (especially those with developmental disabilities) are disproportionately represented in the prison population, many for non-violent drug offences (Loucks, 2006).

The figure of the problematic drug user has an unruly body, the controlling image of an unattractive person living in poverty at the intersection of multiple oppressions (Dean and Rud, 1984). The exclusion from the rationalist default human is exacerbated by the perception that people who use drugs actively choose to abandon self-control. Free choice and autonomy is central to the rationalist paradigm (Braidotti, 2013), yet the choice to ingest certain substances which are seen to affect the ability to control one's actions is seen as unacceptable. It is this illusion of choice which accounts for the strength of the moralistic discourses of drug use. However, many drug user activists are interrogating the notion of choice with respect to drug use:

> I think we need to deconstruct this idea of drug use being a
> choice. I don't think many addicts have a choice as to whether

they are addicted. I guess you could argue that people chose to try drugs in the first place, but I think that needs to be seen in a wider social context, people choose from the options available to them. (Niel, 42, drug user activist, heroin user)

Production of Identity Amongst Drug User Activists

Despite falling short of what is understood as the rational normate individual, it was clear through the participants' self-presentations that many had internalised narratives of self-control and individualism. These narratives are felt in the work of sociologists of drug use as well as in the drug user community. Duff (2004) suggests that drug policy should be reconsidered with an emphasis on "limit setting" as a "virtue". Although Duff (2004) presents the move from prohibition to prescriptive moderation as a step forward, it actually encourages a very moral understanding of drug use. Indeed, he suggests that only those who do not have the moral strength to resist overindulgence should be subject to shame or punishment. Like Duff (2004), our participants assume that it is one's own responsibility to be in control of one's actions. From this position the majority of the participants argue that they should be allowed to choose for themselves which substances they wish to consume: "That is why I think it should be up to each and everyone to decide ... You have to place it on the individual's responsibility ... We are individuals and should be treated as such ..." (Laura, 29, harm reduction activist).

This appeal to rationalism is made evident by emphasising that their drug consumption is not a result of peer pressure or other external influences. Rather, drug consumption is an activity in which the informants themselves have chosen to engage, in their own self-interest. The informants present themselves as being "drug-wise": "after a while I got concerned about safety, started doing my research on sites like erowid [a crowd-sourced drugs information service]. But knowing yourself and your limits is just as important as knowing the drugs you are taking" (Jackie, 33, current user of various drugs). Thus the notion of being "drug-wise" includes both academic knowledge about drugs and their effects, and a reflexive ability to establish and respond to personal boundaries of acceptable and unacceptable behaviour. Knowing one's inner self, abilities and limitations were often mentioned as crucial factors for maintaining control over drug use. "I think that I haven't become addicted because I have a stable ground to stand on ... I reflect a lot about myself the whole time, ... so when it gets too much I back off ..." (Tomas, 31, harm reduction activist, current opiates user).

Due to the simplistic and moralistic characterisation of the drug user as a "bad person" within dominant drugs discourse, participants easily found elements of their own drug use such as knowledge and reflexivity which undermined the controlling images of drugs discourse in order to present a positive self-image. These controlling images provide an interpretive schema by which to evaluate their drug use. By presenting themselves as "drug-wise", the participants necessarily create a category of drug user who is not drug-wise. Informants had a tendency to self-evaluate by referring to the external figure of the problematic drug user, even if their own drug use has been labelled "problematic" by authorities. The authors would like to note that they are not assigning the label of "problematic" to any of the participants in this study, and indeed they question the usefulness of the label. As the term "problem drug user" is used by the state to control and institutionalise people, it should never be applied by academics to subjects against their wishes.

> There is a vast amount of drugs knowledge within the drug user activist scene. We know what we are doing with drugs and we help each other out ... in the most part I do not think we require much in the way of state intervention beyond harm reduction

and needle exchanges. Although outside of the activist scene there are a lot of chaotic individuals who need help, although obviously the current punitive policies don't help them one bit. (Jackie, 33, current user of various drugs)

Here the distinctions between the drug user activist and the problematic drug user are made clear. Good qualities such as knowledge and mutual aid were emphasised within the drug user activist community, whilst the chaotic nature of those outside the community was over-represented. Following Rødner (2005), the process of othering the problematic or chaotic drug user defines a desired group identity and has a functional role as a defence mechanism in surroundings which are hostile to people who use drugs. For many of the participants, this defence mechanism involved creating a positive self-presentation by normalising or naturalising drug use:

there is something primal in the desire to experiment with the senses ... our new drug rituals have replaced ancient pagan ones. To consider our drug using behaviour as the norm rather than the other, historical rather than contemporary, would be useful in informing practices of pleasure and control. (Tascha, 38, harm reduction activist, ex-heroin user)

Here the utilisation of the language of ritual is particularly interesting. The image of ancient rituals alongside discussion of primal desires makes drug use seem natural, pre-social and innate, offering an alternative moral understanding of drug use which may work better for people who use drugs. In contrast, prohibition and criminalisation seem unnatural, artificial and oppressive. As one participant explained:

I think that people who use drugs are oppressed. We are criminalised, harassed, stereotyped and demonised. The harms associated with drug use are not innately to do with the drugs themselves, but the context of their use – lack of access to good supply, clean needles, poverty, etc. (Karen, 29, drug user activist, current user of various drugs)

Drug Use as Disability

This understanding of people who use drugs as being oppressed chimes with the social relational understanding of disability. It positions disability as "the disadvantage or restriction of activity caused by a contemporary social organisation which takes no or little account of people who have [impairments] and thus excludes them from the mainstream of social activities" (UPIAS, 1976, p. 14). This understanding was built upon by Thomas (2004) to include the undermining of the psycho-emotional well-being of those with impairments.

It is clear that people who use drugs, especially those labelled as problematic users, face many restrictions – of movement, freedom, employment, etc., as well as stigma and discrimination which has an impact on their mental health. The key question, then, is whether long-term drug use and addiction is included in the realm of impairment. For most medical practitioners, long-term drug use is viewed as a medical condition and some authors such as McLellan, Lewis, O'Brien, and Kleber (2000) argue for addiction to be considered as a chronic illness. One of our participants, a disabled man with a mobility impairment and an opiate addiction, said: "both [my mobility impairment and my addiction] are part of my identity, it's impossible to separate them. Both of my impairments mean something different to society but they work in similar ways ... yes, I do consider my addiction a disability" (Joe, 34, current heroin user).

For some people, then, long-term drug use and addiction is both an impairment and a disability in and of itself. Many of our participants described drug use in terms of a "coping mechanism" or "self-medication". Many said they take drugs to "feel normal", implying a more complex relationship to disability and normalcy studies. In the eyes of some people who use drugs, taking drugs draws them closer to their perception of the normative ideal, whilst often society sees it as pushing them further away.

Participants located the "problem" of drug use as negative societal barriers and attitudes. However, when asked whether they would still have drug-related problems in a world where drug discrimination did not exist, a small minority thought they would:

> Most of my problems relating to heroin are in the way that society treats drug use, but I don't think it is honest to say that in this perfect world there would be no problems associated with heroin use, it's always going to have a health impact, even if some people in our community want to deny it. (Karen, 26, drug user activist, current user of various drugs)

This understanding of a pre-social negative impact associated with long-term drug use is similar to the understanding of impairment within the social model of disability. This highlights that some drug user activists focus too heavily on the social barriers that drug discrimination creates, to the detriment of embodied experiences of drug-related impairments. This dynamic is reminiscent of the critiques of the social model by those who feel their impairment doesn't neatly fit (i.e. Corker, 1993), or that the role of impairment is ignored (i.e. Thomas, 1999). These intersections mean that disability studies and drug user studies may have a lot to learn from each other.

Conclusions

The experiences of people who use drugs and disabled people mirror each other. Disability discourses and drug user discourses both incorporate moral, medical and social understandings. These three schemas defy neat division, they have all existed throughout the twentieth century and continue to exist today. The division between problematic and non-problematic drugs users echo that of the narratives of deserving and undeserving disabled people. Class and race are key factors in determining the experiences and identities of both disabled people and drug users. Despite these significant parallels, there is very little inclusion of drug user studies in disability studies or vice versa.

The social model of disability has provided a useful framework for organising and campaigning by disabled activists. Similarly, the lack of a widely understood and accepted social model of drug use can be seen as a barrier to an empowered and influential drug user community. There is also a clear case to be made that drug use, or at least some forms of long-term drug use, can be constituted as impairments. Under the social model of disability, aspects of drug user experience may be considered both disability and impairment. It is certainly the case that many drug users we spoke to consider themselves disabled, although this may not be the case for all people who use drugs.

The field of "drug user studies", as an equivalent to disability studies rather than to medical sociologies of disability, is so fledgling that its very existence can be debated. The development of this field by and for drug users is a matter of urgency. Potential new scholars would do well to look to the drug user activist movement, much as early disability studies looked to the disabled people's movement.

Whether we assign discrimination arising from drug use as a subset of disability in the social model sense, or as a related but distinct oppression, it is clear that increased dialogue and collaboration between the two communities is needed. Disabled people and drug users have shared histories and will benefit from pushing towards a shared future. We can suggest that the lack of a social model of drug use, and the persistence of a moral model may be a product of criminalisation. Whatever the cause, disabled people, drug users and their organisations would benefit from working together to push towards a future social model of drug use.

References

Barnes, C., & Mercer, G. (Eds.). (1996). *Exploring the divide: Illness and disability*. Leeds, United Kingdom: Disability Press.

Berridge, V. (1999). *Opium and the people: Opiate use and drug control policy in nineteenth and early twentieth century England*. London, United Kingdom: Free Association Books.

Bourke, J. (2014). *The story of pain: From prayer to painkillers*. Oxford, United Kingdom: Oxford University Press.

Braidotti, R. (2013). *The posthuman*. Cambridge, United Kingdom: Polity Press.

Brenner, N., & Theodore, N. (2002). Cities and the geographies of "actually existing neoliberalism". *Antipode, 34*(3), 349–379.

Corker, M. (1993). Integration and deaf people: The policy and power of enabling environments. In J. Swain, V. Finkelstein, S. French, & M. Oliver (Eds.), *Disabling barriers: Enabling environments* (pp. 145–154). London, United Kingdom: Sage.

Crick, E. (2012). Drugs as an existential threat: An analysis of the international securitization of drugs. *International Journal of Drug Policy, 23*(5), 407–414.

Davis, L. J. (1995). *Enforcing normalcy: Disability, deafness, and the body*. London, United Kingdom: Verso.

Dean, J. C., & Rud, F. (1984). The drug addict and the stigma of addiction. *Substance Use and Misuse, 19*(8), 859–869.

Disablement Income Group. (1987). *DIGS national disability income*. Retrieved from: http://disability-studies.leeds.ac.uk/files/library/disablement-income-group-dig.pdf

Dole, V. P., & Nyswander, M. E. (1967). Heroin addiction – a metabolic disease. *Archives of Internal Medicine, 120*(1), 19–24.

Drug and Alcohol Dependence (2015). http://www.journals.elsevier.com/drug-and-alcohol-dependence

Duff, C. (2004). Drug use as a "practice of the self": Is there any place for an "ethics of moderation" in contemporary drug policy? *International Journal of Drug Policy, 15*(5), 385–393.

Duster, T. (1970). *The legislation of morality: Law, drugs, and moral judgment*. New York, NY: Free Press.

Eastwood, N., Shiner, M., & Bear, N. (2014). *The numbers in black and white: Ethnic disparities in the policing and prosecution of drug offences in England and Wales*. Retrieved from: http://www.release.org. uk/sites/default/files/pdf/publications/Release%20-%20Race%20Disparity%20Report%20final%20version.pdf

Foucault, M. (1975). *Discipline and punish: The birth of the prison*. New York, NY: Random House.

Foucault, M. (1978). *The history of sexuality, volume 1: An introduction* (R. Hurley, Trans.). New York, NY: Vintage.

Fox, A. M., & Lipkin, J. (2002). Res(crip)ting feminist theater through disability theater: Selections from the DisAbility Project. *NWSA Journal, 14*(3), 77–98.

Goodley, D. (2011). *Disability studies: An interdisciplinary introduction*. London, United Kingdom: Sage.

Harris, M. (Jon Derricott). (2014, 24 November). *Pragmatics and pleasure in effective harm reduction* (video file). Retrieved from: https://www.youtube.com/watch?v= jDp SuFkxAOo

Holt, M., & Treloar, C. (2008). Editorial: Pleasure and drugs. *International Journal of Drug Policy, 19*, 349–352.

Home Office. (2014). *Drug misuse: Findings from the 2013/14 crime survey from England and Wales*. Retrieved from: https://www.gov.uk/government/publications/drug-misuse-findings-from-the-2013-to-2014-csew/drug-misuse-findings-from-the-201314-crime-survey-for-england-and-wales

The International Journal of Drug Policy. (2015). Retrieved from: http://www.journals.elsevier.com/international-journal-of-drug-policy/

Johnson, R. L. (2011). Introduction: health and disability. *Health and History, 13*(2), 2–12.

Journal of Drug Issues. (2015). Retrieved from: http://jod. sagepub.com/

Kerr, T., Small, W., Peeace, W., Douglas, D., Pierre, A., & Wood, E. (2006). Harm reduction by a "user-run" organization: A case study of the Vancouver Area Network of Drug Users (VANDU). *International Journal of Drug Policy, 17*(2), 61–69.

Loucks, N. (2006). No one knows: Offenders with learning difficulties and learning disabilities. *Review of prevalence and associated needs.* London, United Kingdom: Prison Reform Trust.

McLellan, A. T., Lewis, D. C., O'Brien, C. P., & Kleber, H. D. (2000). Drug dependence, a chronic medical illness: Implications for treatment, insurance, and outcomes evaluation. *Jama, 284*(13), 1689-1695.

Michalko, R. (2002). *The difference that disability makes.* Philadelphia, United States of America: Temple University Press.

NHS Choices. (2014). *Pearl Lowe: "My drug addiction hell".* Retrieved from NHS website: http://www.nhs.uk/Livewell/drugs/Pages/Pearllowe.aspx

Nutt, D. (2009). Equasy – An overlooked addiction. *Journal of Psychopharmacology, 23*(1), 3-5.

Nutt, D. (2012). *Drugs without the hot air.* Cambridge, United Kingdom: UIT Cambridge.

Oliver, M. (1986). Social policy and disability: Some theoretical issues. *Disability, Handicap and Society, 1*(1), 5-17.

Oliver, M. (1996). *Understanding disability: From theory to practice.* London, United Kingdom: Macmillan.

Oyserman, D., Coon, H. M., & Kemmelmeier, M. (2002). Rethinking individualism and collectivism: Evaluation of theoretical assumptions and meta-analyses. *Psychological Bulletin, 128*(1), 3.

Reznick, J. S. (2012). Work therapy and the disabled British soldier in Great Britain in the First World War: The case of Shepherd's Bush Military Hospital. In: D. A. Gerber (Ed.), *Disabled veterans in history* (pp. 185-203). Ann Arbor, MI: University of Michigan Press.

Rødner, S. (2005). "I am not a drug abuser, I am a drug user": A discourse analysis of 44 drug users' construction of identity. *Addiction Research and Theory, 13*(4), 333-346.

Ross, A. (2009). *Nice work if you can get it: Life and labour in precarious times.* London, United Kingdom: New York University Press.

Shepard, B. (2000). *A war of nerves: Soldiers and psychiatrists, 1914-1994.* London, United Kingdom: Pimlico.

South, N. (1998). Tackling drug control in Britain: From Sir Malcolm Delevingne to the new drugs strategy. In: R. Coomber (Ed.) *The control of drugs and drug users: Reason or reaction?* (pp. 87–106). Amsterdam, The Netherlands: Harwood Academic Publishers.

Southwell, M., (2009). Grassroots strategies to overcome legal barriers to drug user activism [slides] Retrieved from: http://www. slideshare.net/MatSouthwell/respect-presentation-grassroots-strategies-to-overcome-legal-barriers-to-drug-user-activism

Stone, D. A. (1984). *The disabled state.* Philadelphia, PA: Temple University Press.

Striker, H. J. (1997). *A history of disability,* Trans. by William Sayers. Ann Arbor, MI: University of Michigan Press.

Talkingdrugz. (2009, 10 July). *Canadian user rights activist on self medication, harm reduction and pleasure maximisation* (video file). Retrieved from: https://www.youtube.com/watch?v=9OIY9 JiiRd4

Thomas, C. (1999). *Female forms: Experiencing and understanding disability.* Buckingham, United Kingdom: Open University Press.

Thomas, C. (2004). Developing the social relational in the social model of disability: A theoretical agenda. In C. Barnes & G. Mercer (Eds.), *Implementing the social model of disability: Theory and research* (pp. 32–47). Leeds, United Kingdom: Disability Press.

Thomas, C. (2007). *Sociologies of disability and illness: Contested ideas in disability studies and medical sociology.* Basingstoke, United Kingdom: Palgrave Macmillan.

Tremain, S. (2005). *Foucault and the government of disability.* Ann Arbor, MI: Michigan University Press.

UNODC. (1971). *The single convention on narcotic drugs, 1961.* Retrieved from: https://www.unodc.org/pdf/convention_1961_en.pdf

UPIAS. (1976). *Fundamental principles of disability.* London, United Kingdom: Union of the Physically Impaired Against Segregation.

Young, S. (2014). *I'm not your inspiration, thank you very much.* Retrieved from TED website: http://www.ted.com/talks/ stella_young_i_m_not_your_inspiration_thank_you_very_much/transcript?language =en

Williams-Schultz, G., & Bradley, J. (2013, June). *Disabled people's emancipation through time and space.* Paper presented at Unoffical Histories Conference, Manchester Metropolitan University.

Winstock, A., Mitcheson, L., Ramsey, J., Davies, S., Puchnarewicz, M., & Marsden, J. (2011). Mephedrone: Use, subjective effects and health risks. *Addiction, 106*(11), 1991–1996.

Wood, E., Kerr, T., Small, W., Jones, J., Schechter, M. T., & Tyndall, M. W. (2003). The impact of a police presence on access to needle exchange programs. *JAIDS: Journal of Acquired Immune Deficiency Syndromes, 34*(1), 116–117.

CHAPTER 8

THE CULT OF HEALTH AND WHOLENESS: NORMALCY AND THE CHARISMATIC CHRISTIAN HEALING MOVEMENT

Naomi Lawson Jacobs

Summary

There is a preoccupation with health and healing in some Christian churches today. Physical healing is a central aspect of the charismatic-pentecostal Christian movement, which is one of the fastest-growing religious movements in the world. This chapter discusses the history and present-day practices of the faith healing movement in charismatic-pentecostal "new paradigm" churches, and the compulsory normalcy that may result from the Christian wholeness discourse that emerges from this movement. It then surveys some of the disability theology that has addressed these issues. Disability theologians have debated whether it is possible for disabled people to be agents, not objects, in Christian contexts where physical healing is a focus. They suggest new models and symbols for the representation of the body in Christian discourse. Rather than reinforcing normalcy, is it possible for healing practice to celebrate the diversity of embodiment? Can healing be experienced as liberatory for disabled Christians?

Introduction

There is a strong preoccupation with health and healing in many Christian churches today (Cox, 2011; Stolz, 2011). Unexamined and unchallenged, the specific use of concepts of "health" and "wholeness" within this healing movement has potential marginalising and oppressive effects for disabled people both within and outside the Christian churches – but especially within them. This chapter will consider the healing ideologies of the pentecostal-charismatic Christian healing movement, in the context of its history, and relate this to the ways in which these concepts have been challenged by disability theologians and disabled people within the churches.

Healing ministries are not always benevolent, particularly in their unintended effects. A number of disability theologians and biblical scholars have presented evidence of harm to disabled people as a result of healing and deliverance ministries. Kathy Black writes about a young Christian man who failed to take medication for a chronic condition, believing that he just needed to have faith that he would be healed, and dying as a result (Black, 1996). Nicole Kelley tells the story of Torrence Cantrell, who was eight years old and had autism, and died in 2003 at a prayer service in a church in Milwaukee. He had been restrained and wrapped up in sheets for several days before he finally died. The church's pastor said "We did what the Book of Matthew said … all we did is ask God to deliver him" (Kelley, 2011, p. 206). Yet there are also many examples of disabled people, and those with chronic illness, finding healing an empowering and useful experience (see Eiesland, 1994).

This situation may seem paradoxical, but it can be argued that much of the complex history between disability and Christianity has involved an inconsistent relationship. Christianity has variously exploited, marginalised and taken social responsibility for disabled people. While Christian churches have been recognised socially for their charitable and pastoral care of disabled congregants and parishioners, in fact the relationship between the churches and disabled people has been based as much on legitimation and exploitation, as on care and support (Betcher, 2007; Porterfield, 2005). One particular way in which some Christian movements have established their own legitimacy has been through the promise of healing for those who are ill or disabled (Kelley, 2011). While disabled people are unlikely to seen by Christians *only* as a site for healing, that is one prominent lens through which they are viewed, especially in churches where discourses and practices of healing are prominent, as this chapter will endeavour to demonstrate. This, I will argue, is rooted in essentialist concepts of wholeness and divine health that are not always received positively by those who are offered healing, and which have been resisted by some disabled people and disability theologians. I will argue that the preoccupation with health and healing in particular types of Christian churches today could be considered a cult of health and wholeness, and that this has a marginalising effect on those who cannot achieve this level of "health". Such Othering of disabled people, I will argue, is predicated on essentialist binaries around health and normalcy.

Healing and New Paradigm Christianity

Christianity's long history as a religion of healing, at least since the fourth or fifth century (Ferngren, 1992; Porterfield, 2005), is relevant to the relationship between disability and Christian traditions today. Within an apocalyptic cosmology where illness was considered the result of demonic activity, the early Christian movement established its own legitimacy by claiming "superior (if not unique) healing powers" over other belief systems (Kelley, 2011, p. 217), asserting a teleology of suffering and evil that only the Christian cosmology could defeat. These precedents helped to create a situation in which disabled people could be seen as sites for Christian healing and its legitimating power – as objects, rather than as agents in their own right.

In its modern form, the charismatic[9] Christian healing movement is a relatively recent phenomenon (Cox, 1996;

---

[9] Charismatic Christianity is associated with a revival of the New Testament gifts of the Holy Spirit, and is characterised by such phenomena as speaking in tongues (glossolalia) and supernatural healing.

Porterfield, 2005), closely related to the growth of Pentecostalism, particularly since the early twentieth century, and its influence on other forms of Christianity. Pentecostalism is one of the world's fastest-growing forms of religion (Stolz, 2011), and supernatural healing is "one of its main attractions" (Stolz, 2011, p. 456). Through the charismatic Christian movement, pentecostal-charismatic styles of healing have spread beyond the Pentecostal denominations into many other church contexts (Cox, 1996; Miller, 1997).[10] As the influence of pentecostal-charismatic Christianity spreads to other church contexts, so does the attraction of ritual healing.

Healing, furthermore, is a central aspect of the pentecostal-charismatic movement. Cox argues that not only is healing important in charismatic churches, it is often the very feature that draws people into the charismatic movement:

> [T]he practice that initially draws people to these groups, and the one that characterizes them more than any other, is that they offer healing – the "making whole" of mind, body, and spirit. Healing practices are not only integral, but they also often serve as the threshold through which new recruits pass into other dimensions of the movement. (Cox, 2011, p. xviii)

Furthermore, these healing practices have spread beyond the traditional charismatic Christian churches (Csordas, 1994, p. 30),

---

[10] The new paradigm Christian churches, Miller (1997) shows, are resistant to denominational categories; this is reflected in the decline in denominational loyalty that can be seen in European and North American Christianity in recent years. Brown (2011) uses a lower-case "p" to talk about Pentecostal Christians who may not be associated with the Pentecostal denomination. Rather, they may belong to one of many charismatic-influenced church denominations. It is the healing practices located in these new paradigm, pentecostal-charismatic churches that this chapter explores.

and even into the secular arena. An example of this can be seen today in the "Healing on the Streets" project, based in many charismatic Anglican churches, where passers-by are offered healing prayer by members of churches (Bromage, 2010; Marx, 2013). Projects such as this make it more urgent to establish a critical understanding of healing rituals in Christianity, particularly within disability studies. Healing practices may impact disabled people outside charismatic churches, rather than just being relevant to disabled Christians.

Yet despite their importance in the fast-growing charismatic Christian movement, the impact of healing practices in churches today is under-theorised (Cox, 2011; Pattison, 1989), particularly from a phenomenological perspective. Under-developed theology also characterises the internal landscape of charismatic Christian healing: "The imperative has been to heal, not to understand healing" (Pattison, 1989, pp. 11–12). On the whole, there is very little work in theology, religious studies, or – for reasons that will be explored in a moment – disability studies that critiques charismatic Christian concepts of the body and physical healing. The hegemonic dimensions of charismatic healing are rarely acknowledged, even when social aspects of embodiment in healing practices are considered (Lewis, 2007). This may be because these changing patterns of "new paradigm" Christianity (Miller, 1997, p. 11) fit with neither the expected developments of secularisation in Europe, nor existing categories of theology and denominational practice (Cox, 2011). This academic neglect of charismatic healing practices may prevent in-depth, critical explorations of the ritual healing experiences of many Christians, including disabled Christians.

It is not only religious studies that neglects the intersections of disability and religion. Disability studies is notoriously reluctant to engage with the subject of religion, and is often ill-informed when it does so:

> [S]ince social model theorists often focus on tracing legacies of discrimination, this approach may artificially homogenize religious practices and biblical texts. Attempts to use the social model, or a so-called religious model of disability, to trace the development of discrimination often pre-suppose that most religious authors, thinkers, and practitioners from a wide variety of religions essentially display similar enough views of impairments that they may be plugged into a common framework of discrimination. (Moss and Schipper, 2011, p. 11)

Moss and Schipper assert that there is neglect on both sides: neglect of disability from religious studies and related disciplines, and neglect of religion and the Bible from within disability studies. As a result, there is little critical research into the experiences of disabled Christians in relation to charismatic healing practices. This is a significant oversight, when disabled people are highly likely to encounter Christian healing practices.[11]

There is disagreement and controversy within the churches over the importance and function of supernaturally ascribed ritual healing in Christianity. This is not a new debate; ritual healing has been publicly contested in churches since the early nineteenth century (Robinson, 2011). Differences in the ways that Christians interpret scripture affect the ways in which the concept of "healing" is interpreted: literally or socio-symbolically, spiritually or physically (e.g. Goldingay, 1989). There are a number of types of healing in pentecostal-charismatic church contexts, including physical ritual healing, ministries of

---

[11] My current research, into disabled people's experiences in Christian churches, may go some way to addressing this. However, more detailed research into disabled people's experiences of healing practices is needed. At present, most studies of experiences of healing are not explicitly critical of power relations in healing practices.

deliverance from demonic influence (Twelftree, 1985), and "healing of memories" (Csordas, 1994, 2002; Poloma, 2003). In many theologies and pastoral guidance for churches on healing, these very different concepts of healing are often conflated, represented as contingent, mutually essential parts of one holistic healing process. It can therefore be difficult to establish what is meant by "healing" in any specific Christian context. The difference between holistic healing and individual physical cure has been emphasised by scholars of religion in the past few decades (Crossan, 1991; Ferngren, 2009; Gaiser, 2010; YaDeau, 1982). However, this scholastic separation of "healing" from "cure" does not tally with the experience of many pentecostal-charismatic Christians, for whom they may be considered one and the same, with physical healing an important aspect: "physical improvement is an essential component of what is often perceived as a more holistic healing process" (Brown, 2011). Furthermore, some anthropologists and sociologists have linked ritual healing to spiritual growth, the former sometimes considered dependent on the latter (Csordas, 2002).

To understand the prominence of ritual healing within the charismatic Christian movement, and the ideologies and theologies on which it is based, a brief socio-historical background of the modern healing movement is useful context.

A Brief History of Pentecostal-Charismatic Healing
The pentecostal-charismatic movement's beliefs and practices around healing are a specifically modern phenomenon, their success often attributed to modern technologies of travel and communication (Curtis, 2011; Lyon, 2000). Modern Pentecostalism, with its resurgence of the charismatic "gifts of the Spirit" as referred to in the New Testament, has been expressed in different forms over the past century. James Smith (2010) identifies three historical pentecostal-charismatic

movements, in the global north where these experiences have been prominent. What he calls the classical Pentecostal period began in the early twentieth century, when Pentecostalism was denominational, i.e. associated with particular church settings. The Asuza Street revival, mainly focused around the African-American community, initiated this period and led to the establishment of Pentecostal churches, including the Assemblies of God church. This was followed by the charismatic renewal in the 1960s and 70s, which included the beginnings of the Catholic charismatic movement and the informal house church movement. More recently, Smith identifies a neo-pentecostal movement involving many Christians who do not always identify with traditional denominations, some of whom have established new church networks.

However, the modern healing movement dates back before these developments and is associated with the roots from which Pentecostalism grew. In the late nineteenth century, the Holiness movement, which emerged from nineteenth-century Methodism, led to a resurgence of Christian interest in physical divine healing (Porterfield, 2005; Rack, 1982; Robinson, 2011). Elizabeth Baxter, a central figure in the movement, imagined Christ as a physician: "If you go on to God's side, you will take your body as well as your soul with you, and then sickness will have to take its departure" (Baxter, 1952 [1900], chapter 1, para. 12). Baxter linked healing directly to the atonement of Christ, believing that his death and resurrection provided for physical healing as well as spiritual – a theme that has continued through pentecostal-charismatic theology to the present day (Alexander, 2006). The promise of physical healing was often grounded in Isaiah 53:5, in a literal interpretation of the scriptural phrase "by his stripes we are healed" (Robinson, 2011), a concept sometimes referred to as the "full gospel". This theological development allowed a strong, successful focus on material salvation and

209

physical healing: "[B]y anchoring healing in the doctrine of the atonement, the radicals eased the opening of a floodgate that allowed a huge surge of expectation of healing that has today culminated in millions of people at the global scale being drawn to Christianity" (Robinson, 2011, p. 291).

This focus on physical healing was already present when the Azusa Street revival in the United States was building the foundations of modern Pentecostalism, drawing additional influences from African-American folk healing practices and spiritualism (Alexander, 2006; Porterfield, 2005). Prominent faith healers, including Aimee Semple McPherson and Carrie Judd Montgomery, helped to advance the phenomenon of divine physical healing in North America (Robinson, 2011). At the same time, James Moore Hickson and other travelling missionary faith healers influenced its reception in the UK (Robinson, 2014) and contributed to a reconsideration of charismatic healing practices in mainstream denominations including the Church of England (Mews, 1982).

Today, the concept of the full gospel continues to present healing as central to charismatic Christian experience, especially – but not solely – in the global south and in diasporic churches (Anderson, 2004; Curtis, 2011; Währisch-Oblau, 2011). The UK's charismatic revival of the 1960s to 80s saw some codification of healing rituals by a number of healers whose influence has continued to dominate charismatic healing discourse, including Morris Maddocks (1981, 1986), Agnes Sanford (1983 [1969], 1984 [1966]), and Francis MacNutt (1988, 1995).[12] While there are

---

[12] Although Maddocks and Sanford were writing mainly in the 1970s and 1980s, and MacNutt was writing primarily for a Catholic charismatic context, their influences have reached far beyond these specific contexts. The 1960s and 70s were a formative time for the pentecostal-charismatic movement (Smith, 2010); these prominent

varying models of healing in the charismatic and Pentecostal traditions (Alexander, 2006), the concept of healing through the atonement remains influential in charismatic Christianity, "connecting Jesus' crucifixion with believers' physical healing" (Bowler, 2011, p. 88). Charismatic spirituality is grounded in materiality, and accordingly in physical health; "the gospel is not just a tonic for souls" in charismatic Christianity (Smith, 2010, p. 42).

Wholeness, Charismatic Healing and Disabled People

Embedded in the charismatic Christian healing movement is a concept often referred to as "wholeness". In much charismatic Christian discourse of healing, wholeness is represented as an ideal and idealised physical state, a form of divine health to which Christians should aspire. Practical healing theologian Edwards writes: "Within the context and reality of God, being healthy is about becoming whole ... Healing then may be seen as bringing about a restoration to health and to purposeful living" (2011, pp. 2–3).

Many charismatic and evangelical theologians present whole, healthy and holy biblical exemplars as models for human health, particularly the model of Jesus in a post-resurrection state. Maddocks, for example, writes: "At the centre of the Kingdom stands the King. He alone is whole, the perfect pattern for our health ... of whose gift alone comes that wholeness and perfect health" (Maddocks, 1981, p. 16). Such a concept of wholeness is often essentialist, considering health as a divinely ordained,

---

writers from the period are regularly cited by those writing about practical healing theology, and by scholars examining influential voices in the charismatic healing movement. See, for example (Brooke, 2004; Goldingay, 1989; Howard, 2013; Lewis, 2007; Maddocks, Church of England, and Diocese of York, 1976; O'Malley, 2005; Pattison, 1989; Watts, 2011).

static reality that exists outside of the socio-historical contexts that have an influence on health. As McGuire argues, "'health" is an idealisation of a kind of self, and 'healing' is part of the process by which growth toward that ideal is achieved" (1988, p. 244).

Wholeness is also closely associated with holiness in many Christian contexts. Within a Torah (Old Testament) framework, Mary Douglas argues that only that which is whole can be holy (2002 [1966]). This model of perfection involves a paradoxical invisibility of the human body:

> In what is a rather interesting paradox within Christian symbolic logic, the body is often explicitly denied in importance, and then constructed through the necessity of only "perfect" bodies representing and approaching God. (Chopp, foreword to Eiesland, 1994)

Here, Chopp alludes to biblical precedent for the exclusion of the imperfect body from priesthood, assumptions that are embedded in the charismatic Christian cult of health and wholeness, where there is nowhere for unhealed, imperfect bodies to be situated. They are relegated to a liminal space, permanently waiting to be healed. To draw on Szakolczai's theories (2009), these imperfect bodies are dangerously liminal, threatening the charismatic Christian social order of wholeness and healing, since they cast doubt on the "full gospel" doctrine of the healing available to all Christians through the atonement. There is therefore little room for the exploration of the disabled body in these Christian contexts in anything but a negative sense.

An approach to healing that resists the social construction of health is likely to be individualised in its ideologies. Csordas's research shows a strong focus on personal, individual factors, such as the "need to forgive" on the part of the person receiving healing in charismatic healing ritual (1994, p. 65), but much less focus on social aspects of health. Rarely does Christian writing on health and healing address the need for socio-cultural factors, including oppression and health inequalities (Pattison, 1989). Accordingly, we see an individual approach to disability that recurs in much writing on charismatic Christian healing and disability. For example, the concept that some people are ill or disabled because they resist healing, or do not have enough faith, recurs frequently in theology and pastoral writing:

> Immediately I had the sense that lady did not really want me there ... Throughout the whole encounter I felt a strong resistance coming from this lady. (Edwards, 2011, pp. 111–112)

This approach to disability is also given biblical authority. The narrative of the man at the pool of Bethesda from the Gospel of John is often cited in theological writing. In the narrative, Jesus asks a mobility-impaired man whether he would like to be healed. His uncertain answer is often judged as a resistance to healing (see, for example, Arterburn, 2005; Edwards, 2011; Epperly, 2003; Jones, 2009). Guenther compares the experience of this man to a 24-hour illness that she once experienced: "Even as I declared my eagerness to be up and doing things, an inner voice whispered to me about the pleasure of dropping out, the luxury of unaccountability and the bland safety of relative helplessness" (1995, p. 507).

Guenther assumes that a similar pleasant irresponsibility was experienced by the man at Bethesda. Such a perspective, rooted in Parsons' sick role theory, is based on an individual model approach to disability. It acknowledges neither the historical and social context of biblical texts, nor the social oppression that disabled people experience in late modern society. While this is not the only approach to illness and disability within the pentecostal-charismatic movement, such ideologies are expressed frequently in charismatic healing theology.

However, despite this individualising of illness and disability, there is an important social aspect to the experience of charismatic Christian healing. In the context of the legitimating power of healing in Christianity, events such as healing services have performative and constitutive functions wherein a person who seeks healing – who may be disabled – becomes a central symbol of that reconstituted community and represents theological narratives (Csordas, 1994, 2002). In many systems of ritual healing, "candidates for healing often become symbolic objects in a ritual process of communal integration and group solidarity" (Porterfield, 2005, p. 9). In the Durkheimian collective effervescence of a healing service, the power of God, and the success and legitimacy of the charismatic healing ritual, is embodied in what Csordas calls a "Charismatic habitus" (1994, p. 80). In the process, theological order is re-established:

> Illness may be analyzed as a form of deviance, and healing is the corresponding form of social control ... Illness may be interpreted as a form of dis-order; healing constitutes re-establishing order. (McGuire, 1982, p. 163)

Church healing rituals, then, encompass the restoration of symbolic control over the social and theological deviance embodied in ill or disabled people. In this setting, healing is desired, assumed, and rarely critically examined. The disabled person becomes a symbol, either embodying the charismatic habitus or not. They become a site for healing.

It is at the intersection of individualised healing paradigms and community reconstitution that an absorption of a late modern concept of normalcy into charismatic Christian healing doctrine can be seen. As Eiesland argues,

> Healing has been the churchly parallel to rehabilitative medicine, in which the goal was "normalization" of the bodies of people with disabilities ... Failure to be "healed" is often assessed as a

personal flaw in the individual, such as unrepentant sin or a selfish desire to remain disabled. (Eiesland, 1994, p. 117)

Similarly, disabled minister Eric Gaudion writes that "I still receive letters to this day telling me that my faith must be deficient and that if I only believed more firmly in what Christ did for me on the cross, I would be healed" (2009, p. 83). The hegemony of normalcy becomes a moral imperative in charismatic Christian healing discourse, given that the body is a social symbol of the healing power of God. In this sense, the charismatic healing movement also has a eugenicist aspect, as Long has argued (2012). Ultimately, if a disabled person is not healed before they reach heaven, they will be after their arrival there (Baer, 2001; Berinyuu, 2005; Edwards, 2011; Tada and Musser, 1976; Yong, 2007)[13] – though it cannot be taken for granted that this is the perspective or the desire of disabled Christians (Freeman, 2002; Melcher, 2004). In this sense, disabled theologian John Hull argues, disability is associated with our intermediate fallen world, rather than with the final perfection of heaven:

Although disabled people may not necessarily have sinned or brought their condition on themselves ... their very existence is a continual reminder of the imperfect human condition, into which humanity has fallen and from which we hope to be redeemed. (Hull, 2003, p. 11)

---

[13] This assumption has begun to be questioned by disability theologians, such as Yong (2011), who debates which impairments will be healed in heaven, based on philosophies of the personhood of disabled people and drawing on disability rights perspectives. However, his assumption remains that because disability is associated with the fallen state of a sinful world, most impairments will be healed in heaven.

Hull argues that Christian healing practice and theology need to emphasise the plurality of bodies in order to move away from this hegemonic moral imperative of normalcy. Currently, however, it seems they rarely do so. Indeed, Hull attributes a lack of interest in Christianity from disabled people to these ideologies of healing:

> It is because of associations such as these that many disabled people have come to believe that far from being a power for their emancipation, Christian faith is a major source of the social and economic disadvantage that they suffer. Christian faith, to put it more bluntly, is not seen as part of the answer, but as part of the problem. (p. 12)

This also sheds lights on Moss and Schipper's comments (2011), outlined above, on the neglect of Christianity and the Bible by disability studies. In much Christian discourse, disability cannot be disentangled from the doctrine of the Fall, and is always located in a liminal space where it remains deviant from the non-disabled norm. Disabled people remain sites for healing, considered objects of healing rather than agents with the right of self-determination.[14]

Disabled People as Agents, Not Objects: Alternative Concepts of "Wholeness"

The wholeness paradigm has concrete implications for the inclusion and spiritual life of disabled Christians in a number of ways. A number of disability theologians have expressed concern about the focus of some Christian churches on healing, to the exclusion of oppression and justice (Eiesland, 1994; Lewis,

---

[14] Biblical scholars Melcher (2004) and Fontaine (1996) attribute this position of disabled people as objects in Christian discourse, rather than agents, to their representation and textual purpose in the Bible.

2007; Yong, 2011). For Pattison (1989), the concept of wholeness can trivialise and downplay the socio-political contexts of health and healing. Similarly, though the reconstitution of a community through healing rituals may be beneficial for some, those who fill the role of the symbols at the centre may be further marginalised, especially those who remain disabled or ill (Schumm and Stoltzfus, 2011).

The question of whether these issues are resolvable at all, for disabled people engaging with Christianity, is a contested one. Disability theologian Sharon Betcher argues that there may not be room for disability issues in liberation theology,[15] given the importance of wholeness in late modern Christian theology. For Betcher, Christian Fall discourse emphasises what disabled people are *lacking* in comparison to others. This lack in Christian discourse, is reinforced through the idea that it will be restored – either in heaven, or sooner through divine healing (2007, p. 118). This persistent deficit model may present a barrier to the development of liberation theology for disabled people. This is where a potential gulf between Christian discourses and a disability rights discourse becomes most apparent. Within the pentecostal-charismatic cult of health and wholeness, the only place left for unhealed disabled people is a maintenance position: care on this side of heaven, healing on the other side.

Yet there are other approaches to wholeness and healing, many of which have emerged from disability theology. Though I have argued that a charismatic theology of healing involves a static and essentialist approach to health, it does not necessarily

---

[15] Liberation theology is a school of theology that emphasises the liberation of the oppressed, and which began among those living in poverty in Latin America (Boff, 1996; Gutiérrez, 2001). It tends to be strongly concerned with the realisation of the justice of God in this world, rather than solely in heaven.

preclude the possibility of an understanding of the social construction of health, nor of the creation of impairment through social factors. A broader connection between health and a fallen world can be seen in the light of the health of entire communities, such as analysis of health inequalities. There is significant biblical precedent for such a concept of sin and fallenness as social injustice. Yet only rarely is the Fall related to disability in this way, with the state of the community judged on its treatment of disabled people. A rare example is Rennebohm and Paul's reflection on the social situation of people with mental health problems in churches (2008), which challenges the churches to aim for radical inclusion. Pattison explores some of the ways in which pentecostal-charismatic healing theologies and practices have humanised Christian responses to health and illness, such as through liberation theology, allowing people to resist the dehumanisation and alienation of capitalist structures that treat health as a commodity (Pattison, 1989). Betcher (2007) and Melcher (2004) relate disability to corporate sin, via postcolonial theology and liberationist biblical studies, respectively. However, while links between corporate sin, social oppression and injustice are important themes in liberation theology, this has rarely been explored in critical disability theology.

Many disability theologians are calling for a reimagined concept of wholeness and healing, drawing not on late modern normalcy discourses, but on concepts of liberation of embodiment and justice for all kinds of bodies. Eiesland has explored the possibility that healing rituals can allow agency for the object/subject of healing. She has not always found healing ritual a negative experience: some of it has involved embodied liberation:

> I have also experienced laying on of hands that was restorative and redemptive. These physical mediations of God's grace have often kept me related to my body at times when all of my

impulses pushed me towards dissociating from the pain-wracked, uncomfortable beast ... Their touch and tears were the body practices of inclusion. My body belonged in the church. (Eiesland, 1994, p. 117)

Hull argues that Christian healing practices have the potential to celebrate difference among bodies and reinforce concepts of justice for all bodies, beginning from the standpoint of the body as epistemic reality (2003, pp. 8–9). He suggests the biblical theology of St Paul as a resource for such a reformed healing practice, which emphasises the equal importance of both "weaker" and "stronger" members of the body of Christ. Schumm has challenged the churches to de-individualise concepts of the body in healing, suggesting that churches work towards a view of disability as "an opportunity for a deeper understanding of impermanence & interdependence" (2010, p. 135). This challenge has particularly been taken up by feminist disability theologians, including Creamer, whose "limits theology" focuses on the imperfect embodied experience of all humanity, with disability as a part of this limited experience of humanity (2003). Such a reimagining of bodily difference would present it not as distanced from perfection, nor as less than "whole", but as part of the diversity of humanity. It would allow space for social constructions of health and the body, presenting these not as static realities, but as culturally conditioned approaches to diverse human life.

These alternative concepts of healing and the body relate to a very different concept of wholeness, not presenting the disabled body as deficient in relation to the perfection of God, but as another expression of the good, embodied self, created in the image of God, which can experience well-being in diverse ways. This has theological precedent. Swinton has explored this through the biblical term *shalom*, a word that is often translated as *wholeness*, but which has different connotations from the concept of "wholeness" often cited in charismatic healing theology:

> The root meaning of the word *shalom* is *wholeness, completeness, and well-being. Shalom* is therefore a relational term that has primarily to do with the restoration of relationships ... To be at peace – to be healthy – is to be in right relationship with God. (Swinton, 2012, p. 233)

This biblical word that is sometimes translated as "wholeness", Swinton argues, is about something greater than our late modern biomedical concept of health. It is about relationship with God, and the well-being that comes with that relationship. Such re-examination of the ways that theological concepts are used within the healing movement can open up space for disabled people and disability theologians to create new theologies of healing and embodied existence.

However, there are barriers faced by disabled people and disability theologians who attempt to challenge the cult of health in pentecostal-charismatic settings. The reception of Nancy Eiesland's disabled God image is one example. Eiesland (1994) theorised that disabled people could not identify with a perfect God while they themselves were associated with imperfection, and therefore with distance from God, in Christianity. She thus imagined a God who used a wheelchair, showing that a perfect God could be disabled. Using this image, she called for new metaphors with which to understand God and human existence, a call which other disability theologians have echoed (Betcher, 2007; Black, 1996; Hull, 2002). It was a starting-point for a liberatory theology of disability: an approach based on disability rights discourse, which did not deny disability, did not focus excessively on the healing of impairment, and did not impose compulsory normalcy on marginalised disabled Christians. However, the response from some theologians has been to focus on the accuracy of concepts of God, to the exclusion of liberation theology that resonates with people's experiences (Edmonds, 2011; Swinton, 2011). Swinton, furthermore, has critiqued Eiesland's theology as one that is primarily aimed at a certain category of people (2011, p. 301) – an issue that in fact could apply to all liberation theologies, though Swinton only relates the criticism to this disability theology. This illustrates Betcher's comments, above, about the difficulty that disability liberation theology presents for Christian thought, mired as it often is in concepts of care and normalcy. The focus on accuracy of theology to the exclusion of social justice is an example of this resistance to disability liberation theology – a further marginalisation of the voices of disabled people. It ignores Eiesland and Hull's call for new symbols and transformation of current theological structures.

Christianity is not well equipped to deal with the paradox that has created particular liminality for the disabled people in its midst. As Willett and Deegan argue, disability itself "questions the meaning of a community when a member can be marginalized so easily. Because of the permanent liminality of disability, the arbitrariness and hostility of the disabling society can be revealed and shattered" (Willett and Deegan, 2001). Such a process can be seen today in a Christian paradigm where charismatic healing theologies and practices have a significant influence. Disability theologians exploring the issues associated with the cult of health and wholeness in many Christian churches are exposing an arbitrary, precarious normalcy at the heart of the application of much Christian theology. Christian churches may continue to have difficulty recognising their need to address inclusion and justice for disabled people while healing discourse and practices have such prominence in so many churches (Clapton, 1997). The persistence of disability, particularly in a society where many disabled people call as much for rights as treatment, demands an open examination of Christian discourses: of healing, wholeness, the atonement, and even the Fall and the nature of humanity in relation to God. However, until it deals with the cult of health at its centre, the discourses of normalcy that underpin much charismatic Christian thinking will not be addressed.

References

Alexander, K. E. (2006). *Pentecostal healing: Models in theology and practice*. Blandford Forum, United Kingdom: Deo.

Anderson, A. (2004). *An introduction to Pentecostalism: Global charismatic Christianity*. Cambridge, United Kingdom; New York, NY: Cambridge University Press.

Arterburn, S. (2005). *Healing is a choice*. Nashville, TN: Nelson Books.

Baer, J. R. (2001). Redeemed bodies: The functions of divine healing in incipient Pentecostalism. *Church History: Studies in Christianity and Culture, 70*(04), 735–771.

Baxter, M. (1952 [1900]). *Divine healing*. Bishop's Waltham, United Kingdom: Revival Library. (Kindle ed.)

Berinyuu, A. (2005). Healing and disability. *International Journal of Practical Theology, 8*(2), 202–211.

Betcher, S. V. (2007). *Spirit and the politics of disablement*. Minneapolis, MN: Fortress Press.

Black, K. (1996). *A healing homiletic: Preaching and disability*. Nashville, TN: Abingdon Press.

Boff, C. (1996). Methodology of the theology of liberation (R. Burr, Trans.). In J. Sobrino & I. Ellacuria (Eds.), *Systematic theology: Perspectives from liberation theology* (pp. 1–21). London, United Kingdom: SCM Press.

Bowler, C. (2011). Blessed bodies: Healing within the African American Faith Movement. In C. G. Brown (Ed.), *Global Pentecostal and charismatic healing* (pp. 81–106). Oxford, United Kingdom: Oxford University Press.

Bromage, E. C. A. (2010). *Evangelical Christian healing: An ethnographic study of identity in "Healing on the Streets" of Birmingham, UK.*

(Unpublished master's thesis), University of Birmingham, Birmingham, United Kingdom.

Brooke, A. (2004). *Healing in the landscape of prayer.* Harrisburg, PA: Morehouse Publishing.

Brown, C. G. (2011). Introduction: Pentecostalism and the globalization of illness and healing. In C. G. Brown (Ed.), *Global Pentecostal and charismatic healing* (pp. 3–26). Oxford, United Kingdom: Oxford University Press.

Clapton, J. (1997). Disability, inclusion and the Christian Church: Practice, paradox or promise? *Disability and Rehabilitation, 19*(10), 420–426.

Cox, H. (1996). *Fire from heaven: The rise of Pentecostal spirituality and the reshaping of religion in the twenty-first century.* London, United Kingdom: Cassell.

Cox, H. (2011). Foreword. In C. G. Brown (Ed.), *Global Pentecostal and charismatic healing* (Kindle ed., pp. xvii–xxi). Oxford, United Kingdom: Oxford University Press.

Creamer, D. (2003). Toward a theology that includes the human experience of disability. *Journal of Religion, Disability & Health, 7*(3), 57–67.

Crossan, J. D. (1991). The life of a Mediterranean Jewish peasant. *Christian Century, 108,* 1194–1200.

Csordas, T. J. (1994). *The sacred self: A cultural phenomenology of charismatic healing.* Berkeley, CA: University of California Press.

Csordas, T. J. (2002). *Body/meaning/healing.* Basingstoke, United Kingdom; New York, NY: Palgrave Macmillan.

Curtis, H. D. (2011). The global character of nineteenth-century divine healing. In C. G. Brown (Ed.), *Global Pentecostal and charismatic healing* (Kindle ed., pp. 29–44). Oxford, United Kingdom: Oxford University Press.

Douglas, M. (2002 [1966]). *Purity and danger: An analysis of the concept of pollution and taboo.* London, United Kingdom: Routledge.

Edmonds, M. (2011). *A theological diagnosis: A new direction on genetic therapy, "disability" and the ethics of healing.* London, United Kingdom; Philadelphia, PA: Jessica Kingsley.

Edwards, P. (2011). *The healing touch of God.* Aberystwyth, United Kingdom: Church in the Marketplace.

Eiesland, N. L. (1994). *The disabled God: Toward a liberatory theology of disability.* Nashville, TN: Abingdon Press.

Epperly, B. G. (2003). Healing and hospitality in Jesus' ministry. *Journal of Religion, Disability & Health, 7*(3), 81–93.

Ferngren, G. B. (1992). Early Christianity as a religion of healing. *Bulletin of the History of Medicine, 66*(1), 1–15.

Ferngren, G. B. (2009). *Medicine and health care in early Christianity.* Baltimore, MA: Johns Hopkins University Press.

Fontaine, C. R. (1996). Disabilities and illness in the Bible: A feminist perspective. In A. Brenner (Ed.), *A feminist companion to the Hebrew Bible in the New Testament* (pp. 286–300). Sheffield, United Kingdom: Sheffield University Press.

Freeman, D. (2002). A feminist theology of disability. *Feminist Theology, 10*(29), 71–85.

Gaiser, F. J. (2010). *Healing in the Bible.* Grand Rapids, MI: Baker Academic.

Gaudion, E. (2009). *Storm force: Winning the battle for the mind.* Milton Keynes, United Kingdom: Authentic Media.

Goldingay, J. (Ed.). (1989). *Signs, wonders and healing: Seven prominent Christians debate today's issues.* Leicester, United Kingdom: Inter-Varsity Press.

Guenther, M. (1995). Hazards of healing. *Christian Century, 112*(16), 10 May.

Gutiérrez, G. I. C. E. J. (2001). *A theology of liberation: History, politics, and salvation.* London, United Kingdom: SCM.

Howard, J. K. (2013). *Healing myth: A critique of the modern healing movement.* Eugene, OR: Cascade.

Hull, J. M. (2002). "Sight to the inly blind"? Attitudes to blindness in the hymnbooks. *Theology, 105*(827), 333–341.

Hull, J. M. (2003). The broken body in a broken world: A contribution to a Christian doctrine of the person from a disabled point of view. *Journal of Religion, Disability & Health, 7*(4), 5–23.

Jones, D. L. (2009). A pastoral model for caring for persons with diminished hope. *Pastoral Psychology, 58*(5–6), 641–654. doi:10.1007/s11089-009-0245-3

Kelley, N. (2011). "The punishment of the devil was apparent in the torment of the human body": Epilepsy in ancient Christianity.

In C. R. Moss & J. Schipper (Eds.), *Disability studies and biblical literature* (pp. 205–221). New York, NY: Palgrave Macmillan.

Lewis, H. (2007). *Deaf liberation theology.* Aldershot, United Kingdom; Burlington, VT: Ashgate Publishing.

Long, S. (2012). *The church: A eugenic moral coder?* Paper presented at the Disability Studies Conference 2012, Lancaster. Retrieved 1 June 2015 from http://www.lancaster.ac.uk/disability conference/

Lyon, D. (2000). *Jesus in Disneyland: Religion in postmodern times.* Cambridge, United Kingdom: Polity Press.

MacNutt, F. (1988). *Healing.* London, United Kingdom: Hodder & Stoughton.

MacNutt, F. (1995). *Deliverance from evil spirits: A practical manual.* Grand Rapids, MI: Chosen Books.

Maddocks, M. (1981). *The Christian healing ministry.* London, United Kingdom: SPCK.

Maddocks, M. (1986). *Journey to wholeness.* London, United Kingdom: Triangle.

Maddocks, M., Church of England, & Diocese of York. (1976). *The Christian ministry of deliverance & healing: A report from the York group.* York: Diocese of York.

Marx, M. (2013). Healing on the streets. Retrieved 13 November 2013 from http://healingonthestreets.com/

McGuire, M. B. (1982). *Pentecostal Catholics: Power, charisma and order in a religious movement.* Philadelphia, PA: Temple University Press.

McGuire, M. B. (1988). *Ritual healing in suburban America.* New Brunswick, NJ; London, United Kingdom: Rutgers University Press.

Melcher, S. J. (2004). *"I will lead the blind by a road they do not know": Disability in prophetic eschatology.* Paper presented at the Society of Biblical Literature 2004, Chicago, IL. Retrieved 10 April 2010 from http://www.sbl-site.org/

Mews, S. (1982). The revival of spiritual healing in the Church of England 1920–26. In W. J. Sheils (Ed.), *The church and healing: Papers read at the twentieth summer meeting and the twenty-first winter meeting of the Ecclesiastical History Society* (pp. 239–221). Oxford, United Kingdom: Basil Blackwell.

Miller, D. E. (1997). *Reinventing American Protestantism: Christianity in the new millennium*. Los Angeles, CA; London, United Kingdom: University of California Press.

Moss, C. R., & Schipper, J. (Eds.). (2011). *Disability studies and biblical literature*. New York, NY: Palgrave Macmillan.

O'Malley, B. (2005). *Lord of creation: A resource for creative Celtic spirituality*. Norwich, United Kingdom: Canterbury.

Pattison, S. (1989). *Alive and kicking: Towards a practical theology of illness and healing*. London, United Kingdom: SCM Press.

Poloma, M. M. (2003). *Main Street mystics: The Toronto blessing and reviving Pentecostalism*. Walnut Creek, CA: Alta Mira Press.

Porterfield, A. (2005). *Healing in the history of Christianity*. Oxford; New York, NY: Oxford University Press.

Rack, H. D. (1982). Doctors, demons and early Methodist healing. In W. J. Sheils (Ed.), *The Church and healing: Papers read at the twentieth summer meeting and the twenty-first winter meeting of the Ecclesiastical History Society* (pp. 137–152). Oxford, United Kingdom: Basil Blackwell.

Rennebohm, C., & Paul, D. (2008). *Souls in the hands of a tender God: Stories of the search for home and healing on the streets*. Boston, MA: Beacon Press.

Robinson, J. (2011). *Divine healing: The formative years, 1830–1890: Theological roots in the transatlantic world*. Eugene, OR: Pickwick Publications.

Robinson, J. (2014). *Divine healing: The years of expansion, 1906–1930: Theological variation in the transatlantic world*. Eugene, OR: Pickwick Publications.

Sanford, A. M. W. (1983 [1969]). *The healing power of the Bible*. New York, NY: Jove.

Sanford, A. M. W. (1984 [1966]). *Healing gifts of the spirit*. San Francisco: Harper & Row.

Schumm, D. (2010). Reimaging disability. *Journal of Feminist Studies in Religion, 26*(2), 132–137.

Schumm, D., & Stoltzfus, M. (Eds.). (2011). *Disability in Judaism, Christianity, and Islam: Sacred texts, historical traditions, and social analysis*. New York, NY: Palgrave Macmillan.

Smith, J. K. A. (2010). *Thinking in tongues: Pentecostal contributions to Christian philosophy*. Grand Rapids, MI; Cambridge, United Kingdom: William B. Eerdmans. (Kindle ed.)

Stolz, J. (2011). "All things are possible". Towards a sociological explanation of pentecostal miracles and healings. *Sociology of Religion, 72*(4), 456–482.

Swinton, J. (2011). Who is the God we worship? Theologies of disability; challenges and new possibilities. *International Journal of Practical Theology, 14*, 273–307.

Swinton, J. (2012). From health to shalom: Why the religion and health debate needs Jesus. In J. Levin & K. G. Meador (Eds.), *Healing to all their flesh: Jewish and Christian perspectives on spirituality, theology and health* (pp. 219–241). West Conshohocken, PA: Templeton Press.

Szakolczai, A. (2009). Liminality and experience: Structuring transitory situations and transformative events. *International Political Anthropology, 2*(1), 141–172.

Tada, J. E., & Musser, J. (1976). *Joni: An Unforgettable Story*. Grand Rapids, MI: Zondervan.

Twelftree, G. H. (1985). *Christ triumphant: Exorcism then and now*. London: Hodder & Stoughton.

Währisch-Oblau, C. (2011). Material salvation: healing, deliverance and "breakthrough" in African migrant churches in Germany. In C. G. Brown (Ed.), *Global Pentecostal and charismatic healing* (pp. 61–79). Oxford, United Kingdom: Oxford University Press.

Watts, F. N. (2011). *Spiritual healing: Scientific and religious perspectives*. Cambridge, UK; New York, NY: Cambridge University Press.

Willett, J., & Deegan, M. J. (2001). Liminality and disability: Rites of passage and community in hypermodern society. *Disability Studies Quarterly, 21*(3), 137–152.

YaDeau, R. E. (1982). Healing. *Word and World, 2*(4), 317.

Yong, A. (2007). Disability, the human condition, and the spirit of the eschatological long run: Toward a pneumatological theology of disability. *Journal of Religion, Disability & Health, 11*(1), 2–25.

Yong, A. (2011). *The Bible, disability, and the church: A new vision of the people of God*. Grand Rapids, MI; Cambridge, United Kingdom: William B. Eerdmans.

CHAPTER 9

RELATIONAL AUTONOMY AND DISABILITY: BEYOND NORMATIVE CONSTRUCTS AND POST-STRUCTURALIST DECONSTRUCTIONS

Steve Graby and Anat Greenstein

Summary

This chapter explores the concept of autonomy and its significance to disabled people's struggles for liberation. Autonomy has traditionally been associated with a concept of the "independent individual" which pathologises disabled people as inherently deficient, dependent and incapable. This has led many writers within Disability Studies, particularly those influenced by post-structuralism, to reject the concept of autonomy altogether as inherently ableist. However, this is problematic for disabled people as struggling for autonomy over the basic activities of daily life has been central to disabled people's movements.

We argue that, rather than being abandoned altogether, autonomy needs to be reconceptualised. The feminist concept of "relational autonomy", rooted in a recognition of material dependence as a fact of human life, but one which is not incompatible with self-determination, offers us a way out of the false dilemma between normative constructs of autonomy as independence (an impossible ideal which enables the oppressive systems of capitalism, ableism and patriarchy) and rejections of autonomy that fail to consider the desires, struggles and lived realities of disabled people.

In this chapter we examine how this concept of relational autonomy can be applied in areas including sexual consent, inclusive education and imagining possible futures. We argue that relations of care and attachment do not displace, but are a necessary condition for autonomy, and that people are not inherently either autonomous or non-autonomous, but instead become autonomous through engaging in relations that support our autonomy. We conclude by arguing that relational autonomy can be a key concept in building alliances between disabled people's struggles and those of other oppressed and marginalised peoples.

Introduction

Disability studies, which emerged in the late 1970s and early 1980s as a discipline for theorising the social oppression of disabled people with roots in Marxism and materialism, has incorporated over the last decade a lot of post-structuralist and post-conventionalist theory. Authors such as Gibson (2006), Goodley (2007), Shildrick and Price (2006) and Shildrick (2009) draw on queer and Deleuzian theory to challenge ableist modernist notions of the sovereign self as a rational and self-sufficient (white and male) adult, offering instead a rhizomatic model of profound connectivity, in which desire is seen as productive as it connects bodies and objects in surprising ways.

Such interventions have been highly productive in challenging philosophical and cultural notions of difference and disability as lack, which have been excluding disabled people from full social participation. However, over the last couple of years there has been a growing concern about the wholesale rejection of the concept of autonomy in post-structural theory (see Davy, 2014; Shuttleworth, 2014; Slater, 2015), which could be counterproductive to disabled people's long-lasting struggle to assert their subjectivity and gain control over their support, and which has often been incorporated into disability studies with little attention to disabled people's own views about such claims.

This chapter aims to contribute to the debate about the role of autonomy within disability studies. Our interest in the question of autonomy arose through our respective PhD projects, which explore how self-determination can be hindered or supported with inclusive education (Anat Greenstein, 2013) and personal assistance Steve Graby (in progress). While we reject the modernist model of the isolated rational man (gendered

229

language intended), we still maintain that agency and autonomy are crucial to social participation and social transformation. Our suggested reconfiguration of autonomy accepts as its basis the recognition that the human state is one of interdependence rather than independence, as we all rely on relations of care in order to live and flourish (Kittay, 2005). Further, we accept the post-structuralist claim that subjectivity is not given or innate, but rather is constantly constructed through social relations of power. Thus, as Davy (2014) argues, autonomy is not a static trait that resides wholly within the individual, but is continually *practised* within relations and wider social contexts.

We begin our discussion by exploring the concept of autonomy and its significance to the disabled people's struggles for liberation. We go on to explore critiques of autonomy from a feminist ethics of care and from post-structuralist theory, and argue that those critiques are better answered through adopting a relational view of autonomy (e.g. Barclay, 2000; Mackenzie and Stoljar, 2000; Mackenzie, 2000; Nedelsky, 1989). In the second part of the chapter we explore in detail how such a relational configuration of autonomy works in three different contexts – the connection between bodies, as in (but not limited to) sexual relationships; educational relationships and how these can support (disabled) students in becoming relationally autonomous; and the importance of collective imagining that can help to transform the social imagery. We then conclude by arguing that, as the denial of autonomy is intimately tied up with not just disablement but with many other forms of structural violence and oppression, the struggle to reclaim autonomy is a key component of the liberation struggles of all marginalised groups.

Autonomy

The word "autonomy" is derived from words meaning "self" and "rule" or "law" (Collopy, 1988; Nedelsky, 1989). As Mackenzie and Stoljar (2000, p. 5) note, its meaning is contested and the term is used differently by writers who espouse different political philosophies, but all uses share a basic concept of "self-determination or self-government". Aspects of autonomy that have been stressed by feminist writers include freedom from coercion and control over one's own body, actions and choices (Mies, 1986; Oshana, 1998; Davy, 2014).

"Autonomy" is often used interchangeably or conflated with "independence". This is in part because "independence" is also ambiguously defined, with some definitions being essentially the same as those just given of autonomy, while others more explicitly refer to material self-sufficiency (Fraser and Gordon, 1994; Vernon and Qureshi, 2000), but another reason for the conflation is that "independence" in the sense of self-sufficiency is often regarded as a prerequisite for autonomy (see for example Corbett, 1989). However, in the Disabled People's Movement (DPM) a vision of "independent living" (DeJong, 1983) has been articulated that is unambiguously based on a definition of "independence" as meaning autonomy rather than self-sufficiency (Oliver, 1989a; Barron, 2001; Leece and Peace, 2010). Brisenden (1986, p. 178), a pioneer of the Independent Living movement in the UK, argues:

> We believe fundamentally that all individuals have the right to live independently in the community regardless of their disability. But it is important to note the sense in which we use the word "independence", because it is crucial to everything we are saying. We do not use the term "independent" to mean someone who can do everything for themself, but to indicate someone who has taken control of their life and is choosing how that life is led.

231

Thus "independence" as seen in the DPM does not mean living without assistance, but having choice and control over what assistance one gets and how one receives it. Indeed, as many disabled writers and activists (for example Oliver, 1989a; Morris, 1991, 1993; Montgomery, 2001; Taylor, 2004; Withers, 2012) have said, true self-sufficiency is impossible for any person. Morris (1991, pp. 137–138) explains:

> In terms of the physical world, none of us – whether disabled or not – is completely independent in the sense that we rely on nothing and nobody. However, the meaning of our dependence on others and on the physical world is determined by both its socio-economic and its ideological context. For example, we all depend on water coming out of the tap when we turn it on, while a disabled person ... depends on someone to help her get dressed in the morning. However, when non-disabled people talk about water coming out of the tap, the issue is whether the water company is reliable; when they talk about [a disabled person] being dependent on an assistant, the issue for them is what they see as her helplessness created by her physical limitations.

The assumption that autonomy requires "independence" or "self-sufficiency" constructs disabled people as lacking and deficient, and justifies professional and parental interventions as acting in the "best interests" of disabled people; but the concept of autonomy, not as independence but as being given the support to control one's own life, remains central to the DPM's campaigns for the liberation of disabled people from oppression "justified" by paternalism (such as incarceration in nursing homes, long-stay hospitals and similar institutions).

Critiques of Autonomy
The concept of autonomy itself is not universally regarded as an unproblematic positive value. Mackenzie and Stoljar (2000, pp. 5–12) list symbolic, metaphysical, care, postmodernist and

diversity critiques as five separate "major feminist critiques of the notion of autonomy" (all of which, for them, have validity but do not justify rejecting the concept altogether). Of these, it is primarily care critiques and postmodernist critiques which have been prominent in discussions of autonomy in relation to disabled people.

Care critiques are associated with the development of an "ethic of care" by feminist writers in philosophy and psychology (e.g. Gilligan, 1982; Sevenhuijsen, 1998; Kittay, 1999, 2005). This ethic is defined in opposition to what is seen as a patriarchal and masculine-biased dominant ethical system based around "justice" and "rights", and is thus not based on rules or abstract principles, but "always a response to concrete situations" (Bubeck, 1995, p. 157). Many of its proponents argue that it is a distinctively feminine "moral voice", derived from the specific experiences and perspectives of women as carers (Gilligan, 1982; Bubeck, 1995), which emphasises interdependence and relationships rather than individualism, and focuses on action within the private rather than the public sphere (Erevelles, 2011).

Care ethicists have several (interconnected) critiques of the concept of autonomy. They tend to regard "notions of autonomy, independence, and individual rights" as "based on a masculine view of people as separate from each other" (Morris, 2001, p. 13), and thus biased in favour of men and traditionally "masculine" spheres of activity. Kittay (1999) argues that "the conception of society as constituted by free and equal autonomous agents" (p. 50), who are able to freely choose whether or not to remain in relationships, fails to recognise that the moral responsibilities of "dependency workers" towards their "charges"[16] prevents them

---

[16] Kittay here uses the term "dependency workers" to refer primarily to unpaid/informal carers, and "charges" to refer to people who receive

from acting as the equal and autonomous members of society that this prevailing conception presumes them to be. Some care ethicists, such as Lynch, Lyons, and Cantillon (2009), also make the claim that autonomy "may not be prioritised or desired" by some "severely dependent persons", because "it may involve too high a level of responsibility, energy and risk" (p. 115).

The ideal of autonomy has also been criticised by some postmodernist or post-structuralist writers within Disability Studies, such as Gibson (2006) and Shildrick (2009), who are inspired by the work of post-structuralist philosophers such as Deleuze and Guattari, whose organisational concept of the rhizome, consisting of "non-hierarchical networks which can be found in all aspects of life from politics to thought and desire" (Goodley, 2007, p. 149) is borrowed from its botanical usage meaning a type of root or underground stem which produces new shoots and can be separated from the parent plant. Deleuze and Guattari (1988) contrast this to the "arborescent" (resembling a tree growing from a single root) model of hierarchical thought, knowledge and social organisation, which they argue is paradigmatic of modernism and constitutes an attempt to impose artificial order on a reality which does not conform to hierarchical logic, but instead consists of multiple unpredictable, constantly splitting and recombining assemblages.

Gibson (2006), for example, argues that "individualism and autonomy" are arborescent modernist concepts which need to be transcended because they "limit desire by promoting independence and self-mastery as ends in themselves and rewarding their successes", and suggests that examining "dependencies", such as those of disabled people on assistive technology, service animals or personal assistance from other

---

"care", including non-disabled children as well as disabled children and adults.

people, in the light of such notions of connectivity could lead to a "radically altered ethics that is no longer premised on the rights of the generalised autonomous subject" (p. 188). Shildrick (2009) connects this destabilisation of individual autonomy and reinterpretation of desire to queer theory perspectives on the performativity of gender and sexuality, arguing that, because of the challenge presented by impaired and "dependent" bodies to modernist notions of sexual subjectivity, "the Deleuzian project will be realised at least in part through the medium of rethinking disability" (p. 142). Paralleling care ethicists such as Lynch et al. (2009), Shildrick also argues that disabled people who depend on other people's bodily assistance "may have less invested in the trope of sovereign subjectivity" (p. 140).

While we agree with the premise of feminist care ethics that interdependency rather than independence should be recognised and valued as the basis of subjectivity, and with the post-structuralist notion that subjectivity and personhood are socially constructed, we believe that the wholesale rejection of autonomy that is found both in some versions of the feminist ethic of care and in some post-structuralist and post-conventionalist critiques in disability studies has several major problems. Firstly, it is based on the flawed premise that autonomy and independence can be understood as the same thing (Mackenzie and Stoljar, 2000). It therefore ignores the conceptual distinctions made by authors such as Vernon and Qureshi (2000), Barron (2001), and Leece and Peace (2010) between self-determination and self-sufficiency. It is also problematic for disabled people because it appears to leave no justification for one of their most important political struggles, the independent living movement.

A particular problem of the arguments of post-structuralists such as Gibson (2006) and Shildrick (2009) is that they seem to celebrate impaired, "dependent" embodiments (and their surrounding assemblages of assistive technologies) as exemplars

235

of post-structuralist connectivity, while not considering either the subjective experience of impairment or the fact that another significant part of the context of these assemblages is disability as a system of oppression. For example, wheelchairs and Alternative and Augmentative Communication (AAC) systems – which Gibson (2006, p. 191) describes, among other assistive technologies, as making a disabled person into "a fluid body, not a subject, but a conglomeration of energies" – may be unaffordable to disabled people who need them for mobility or communication, due both to high prices charged by corporations that manufacture them and to the unwillingness of government bodies to provide funding for them. Physical and social environments may also not accommodate people who use such devices, meaning that needing them often results in serious social exclusion.

This failure to consider social context could be regarded as an objectification or fetishisation of disabled people's experiences by non-disabled theorists. As Siebers (2001, p. 745) says, "It is easy to mythologise disability as an advantage". Such theorists can be accused of drawing on disability for inspiration without stopping to consider what is actually valued by disabled people – which calls to mind another slogan of the DPM, "Nothing about us without us". For many disabled people, the supposedly radical idea of connectivity superseding individuality may look suspiciously like the threat of a return to a dehumanising lack of basic rights and freedoms, or a way to invalidate struggles against the oppressive aspects of "dependence". As Erevelles (2005) argues, disabled people would be entitled to "view with some suspicion ... the theoretical move to undermine the ontological status of the subject and proclaim it to be a fiction, at the very moment when they have made counterclaims for their subjectivity" (p. 59). Thus we argue in this chapter that while Western modernist conceptions of autonomy must be criticised, it is possible to do so without rejecting the concept altogether. It is such critiques to which we now turn.

Relational Autonomy

Feminist writers who also criticise the modernist construct of the isolated "autonomous" self, and take on some of the insights of care critiques, while still maintaining the value of individuals' right to control over their own bodies, desires and decisions have developed a concept of "relational autonomy" (see for example Nedelsky, 1989; Oshana 1998; Barclay, 2000; Mackenzie and Stoljar, 2000). Nedelsky (1989, p. 7) argues that the "prevailing conception" of autonomy "carries with it the individualism characteristic of liberalism" and therefore "cannot meet the aspirations of feminist theory", but the "basic value of autonomy is, however, central to feminism", meaning that feminists "must retain the value, while rejecting its liberal incarnation". Similarly, Mackenzie and Stoljar (2000, p. 5) claim that while it is important for feminists to challenge the (mis)conception of autonomy as embodied by a "caricature" of a "self-sufficient, rugged male individualist, rational maximising chooser of libertarian theory", "it is also imperative ... to reclaim and reconceptualise the concept ... and to articulate conceptions of choice and of political rights that are more adequate from a feminist perspective".

Barclay (2000) argues, in response to arguments against autonomy based on its opposition to family and other caring relationships, that "we cannot defend the value of relationships of attachment without qualification" (p. 60) because such relationships can be unwanted or oppressive, and that "to consider which particular attachments we should reshape, which to reject, which to choose, and which to promote, we need autonomy" (p. 68). This argument applies equally well to the uncritical valuation of dependence as transgressive, liberating "connectivity" by post-structuralists like Gibson and Shildrick, and to some of the stronger and less nuanced applications of the "ethics of care".

Responding as a disabled feminist to feminist care ethicists, Silvers (1995, p. 40) argues that "substituting the ethics of caring for the ethics of equality" can result in "an even more oppressive paternalism" for the recipients of "care", because "the very structure of helping or caring relationships invites the marginalization of whoever is consigned to the position of dependence". Universalising "caring" puts disabled people at a disadvantage because the relationship between "carer" and disabled person (or, as Kittay (1999) would put it, "dependency worker" and "charge") inevitably involves a power imbalance, and disabled people are denied equality on the grounds of their position as care recipients. Therefore, feminist care ethics shares with malestream modernist philosophy the assumption that dependence equates to non-autonomy and thus leads inevitably to social inferiority.

In contrast, relational autonomy offers a framework in which it can be recognised that dependence, as Barron (2001) argues, is not in itself necessarily oppressive, but only becomes so when the false assumption is made that autonomy requires self-sufficiency (and thus, a person can be "autonomously dependent" on another (Leece and Peace, 2010, p. 1850)). In fact, in a relational view of autonomy, its prerequisites can be seen in completely opposite terms to these; as Nedelsky (1989, p. 12) argues "relatedness is not, as our tradition teaches, the antithesis of autonomy, but a literal precondition of autonomy, and interdependence a constant component of autonomy".

This reframing of autonomy is consistent with the social model of disability, which, as Reindal (1999, p. 357) says, "needs an understanding of the subject as relational". Davy (2014, p. 13) makes the connection more explicit, arguing that her relational model of autonomy "draws on central features of the social model of disability" by focusing attention on social structures rather than individual capacities, and thus locating the "problem" of autonomy (or its lack) not in the individual but in a context of social conditions and relations. Reframing and reclaiming, rather than simply rejecting, autonomy also supports the struggles of the DPM for self-determination and freedom from the oppressively paternalistic systems of "care" which form part of the disciplinary power structure of capitalism. We will now turn to some specific cases to illustrate in greater depth how this vision of relational autonomy is particularly relevant to disabled people.

When Bodies Connect – Sexual Consent

Firstly, in the light of the focus of post-structuralist writers (especially Shildrick, 2009) on the interconnections of disability and sexuality as situations of profound connectivity, we will turn to the issue of consent in sexual relationships, which demonstrates the need for autonomy within connections. Shildrick (2009) articulates a vision of how disability can contest and subvert, or "queer", sexuality and sexual practices based on a Deleuzian analysis of desire. In this analysis, desire is not about lack but instead is "expansive, fluid and connective" (p. 134); this allows her to reject the normative view of disabled/impaired[17] bodies as undesirable, and to argue that the embodied experience of disability can lead to a liberating reconceptualisation of sexuality and sexual desire, beyond normative boundaries of what is (and is not) "sexual".

---

[17] Shildrick uses the term "disabled" when writing about bodies – where "impaired" might be considered more accurate – because, like many post-structuralists in Disability Studies, she does not accept the social model distinction between disability and impairment.

In contrast to the "modernist western conception of the sexual subject", which Shildrick argues values "precisely the qualities in which the universalised disabled body is deemed to be lacking" – i.e. autonomy, self-determination and the "wholeness" or "distinctness" of corporeal persons (p. 128) – Shildrick suggests that it is precisely the "dependence" of disabled people (on other people and/or on assistive technology), re-characterised as "profound interconnectivity" (p. 137), that exemplifies a Deleuzian model of "productive desire" that goes beyond the limits of the narrow modernist conception of the "autonomous individual".

In these discourses of revolutionary new forms of intimacy and connection, there is, however, a disturbing absence of any mention of consent – which is both central to feminist concerns around sexual relationships and closely connected to autonomy. Indeed, at times Shildrick strays dangerously close to declaring outright that consent, autonomy and agency do not matter. For example, when Shildrick argues that "most sexuality is inherently about intercorporeality, about a potential merging of bodies, wills and intentions", and thus in sex "the subject is never ... simply present as a sovereign self" (p. 129), a possible reading is that individual bodily autonomy and integrity is impossible in a sexual context. This would appear to blur, perhaps irrevocably, the boundary between sexual activity that is consented to by all parties involved and sexual assault, or even to imply that in a post-conventionalist paradigm of sex the question of consent is no longer relevant.

This post-conventional sexual future is uncomfortably similar to the "rape culture" that many feminist writers and activists (e.g. Buchwald, Fletcher and Roth, 1993; McEwan, 2009) argue is pervasive within actually existing patriarchal society. In this toxic culture, sexual violence is implicitly condoned, trivialised or treated as a normal and inevitable part of life, men are presumed to be entitled to touch or otherwise access women's bodies, and consent to sexual activity is not seen as important or necessary. In opposition to this, feminists argue for a "consent culture", in which consent to touch or sexual activity is never assumed, but must be explicitly negotiated. Importantly, this does not only apply to sexual interactions, but can be extended to non-sexual touching and to interpersonal relations more generally (Troost, 2008).

A significant contribution by feminist activists towards developing such a culture, both in theory and reality, is the edited book *Yes Means Yes* (Friedman and Valenti, 2008). In their introduction to this book, Friedman and Valenti explicitly link consent culture to autonomy, saying that their aim is "to claim a fundamental right to bodily autonomy for everyone" and create a world in which "each person's body, regardless of gender, is theirs to do with whatever pleases them – and to keep safe from whatever doesn't" (p. 8). In another chapter, Troost (2008, p. 171) links rape culture to a wider pattern of oppressive social structures denying bodily autonomy:

> Though the form and intensity vary, any oppression you care to name works at least in part by controlling or claiming ownership of the bodies of those oppressed – slavery and the prison-industrial complex being only the most extreme examples. In this sense, rape culture works by restricting a person's control of hir[18] body, limiting hir sense of ownership of it, and granting others a sense of entitlement to it.

---

[18] Troost here uses the gender-neutral third person pronouns "ze" and "hir" (instead of "he" and "him" or "she" and "her") to explicitly make no claim regarding the gender of the person being written about.

While disability is not directly addressed in *Yes Means Yes* – and is a problematic absence in feminist analysis of sexual culture in general (Ryan, 2014) – we would argue that disablement offers many examples of this aspect of oppression, and thus that sexual consent, sexual agency, and bodily autonomy are likely to be particularly important concerns for disabled people. For example, disabled people are disproportionately likely to be the victims of rape or other forms of sexual violence (Hollomotz, 2009; Davy, 2014), and disabled people, particularly disabled women and people with cognitive impairments, have also been denied the right to have consensual sexual relationships or have been treated as incapable of consenting to sex (Wilkerson, 2002; Hough, 2012; Monk, 2015).

Wilkerson (2002) argues that "sexual harms" such as these are significantly involved in the unequal treatment of all oppressed groups, and that sexual agency is central to political agency. For Wilkerson, therefore, sexual oppression is "an integral aspect of the oppression experienced by any group" (p. 38) – regardless of whether that group is defined by sexuality – and must be addressed as an urgently important part of any wider anti-oppression strategy. Similarly, Siebers (2012) argues that both sexual violence against disabled people and institutional denial of access to consensual sexual relationships can be seen as part of a wider pattern of denial of disabled people's privacy and autonomy, which is created at least in part by the medical model of disability as individual pathology.

Both Wilkerson and Siebers, like Shildrick, argue that the "polymorphous" sexuality of disabled people, in which – even in heterosexual relationships – heteronormative sex acts such as penis-vagina penetration are deprivileged, can expand the boundaries of the erotic in positive and productive ways. For all of them, bodily difference can productively open up routes to challenging and subverting restrictive sexual norms and

242

inventing new forms of pleasure. However, a crucial difference is that Shildrick sees individual autonomy as part of the normative to be transcended and discarded, whereas Wilkerson and Siebers – like activists in both feminist and disabled people's movements – regard it as central to struggles for personal and political liberation.

Of course, disabled people are also denied autonomy in a vast range of other ways – from incarceration in a wide range of institutions for those whose differences are regarded as too disruptive or whose "care needs" are regarded as too great to reasonably meet in the community (Ben-Moshe and Carey, 2014) to painful, humiliating and unnecessary medical practices such as public stripping of disabled children to demonstrate their impairments to medical students (Clare, 1999) or "normalising" interventions such as "conductive education" for those with physical impairments (Oliver, 1989b) or behaviourist "therapies" for autistic people (Bascom, 2012). The psychological effects of many of these have been described by disabled people who have experienced them as comparable to those of sexual violence (Giangreco, 2004; Bascom, 2012). We would argue that, just as the denial of bodily autonomy to disabled people goes beyond the sexual dimension, for it to be truly liberating and inclusive, "consent culture" must also go beyond sexual interactions, and also encompass, for example, the ways in which help and assistance – whether in acute medical situations or with ongoing daily needs – are provided to disabled people.

When People Connect – Social and Educational Relationships
In this section we will explore the role of educational relationships in supporting or hindering autonomy for (disabled) students in schools. As we have noted earlier, the liberal ideal of autonomy that is based on assumptions of rationality and (economic) independence excludes and oppresses disabled people who fail to satisfy such assumptions. Gore (2004) explores

how this understanding of autonomy constructs both children and "non-rational" people (e.g. people with "mental illness") as non-autonomous "property of the institutions" having many of their rights "delegated to legitimate 'owners' (doctors, teachers, parents and guardians) who decide on their charges' behalf what is good for them" (p. 148). In many cases students in schools are taught to obey authority without question, and are expected to abide by teachers' rules just because they occupy the respective social positions of "teacher" and "student" with no need for any further reason (Holt, 1983; Illich, 1971). The expectation that children will just "do as they are told" clearly denies them autonomy. It is based on the assumption that children do not possess the necessary information and cognitive abilities to make decisions on their own, and yet denies them such necessary information.

Many activists in the DPM who were interviewed in Greenstein (2013) argued that strict school hierarchies are disabling, because they hide the reasons and processes behind decisions, thus minimising students' opportunities to understand the social world and, crucially, try to change it. An example of this was discussed by Jennifer,[19] a mother of a disabled child:

> And then a member of staff told me "your child is like an animal the way he sits on the table and puts his shoes on". She gave me examples of things like he wouldn't put his shoes in the shoe bag. But she just decided to put her will over his, and unfortunately she had a strong willed child here, and he wouldn't do things until he was ready to do them or until he is approached in a particular way and then he does do them. Then she asked me "how do you ask him to do things?" I said, well, I explain what I want him doing. She said "do you just command him?" And I

---

[19] These names are pseudonyms.

> said no, I say "can you put that in because someone will fall over or it will get lost", I give him the reason why.

The approach described by Jennifer is an example of relations that are supportive of autonomy. By explaining to her son why she asks him to put his shoes away rather than just commanding him to do so, Jennifer has not only shown respect to her son as a person with thoughts, desires and ideas of his own, but has actually increased his capacity to make informed choices, object to arbitrary demands and negotiate solutions when conflict occurs. Such an approach sees the process of learning to live with one another as autonomous people within social relationships as always ongoing and changing according to the different participants. It enables children to experiment with relations of care and solidarity, thus learning about themselves in relation to others, understanding how to communicate and negotiate different needs.

Sinclair (2010) describes how "autistic-led spaces" (such as Autreat in the USA and Autscape in the UK) employ a similar approach to rule-making by always making the reasons behind rules explicit, in an attempt to support both autistic people who rigidly stick to rules and those who tend to object to any arbitrary external impositions. Explicitly explaining the reasons behind rules allows the autistic participants in those spaces to understand when and why to apply those rules, or how to object to them more effectively.

It is important to stress here that educational relations that support autonomy take interdependence rather than independence as its basis, and see obtaining assistance when and how one requires it as an essential aspect of autonomy. An example of what this might mean in practice is described by Lily (another of the activists I interviewed):

> Even someone who is quite mature and knows what they want, you still need support in making those decisions. You know, there is this thing about you making your own decisions, autonomous learning and blablabla, but actually you need, well first you need to feel really supported in doing that. [...] my support staff, they were reading for me and writing for me. But there was one woman who I actually stayed in touch with and she was teaching me how to dictate as well, how to better use my support.

What Lily describes is the process of becoming interdependently autonomous. It is not about becoming independent and providing one's own needs, nor about a view of needs as existing independently of social context. Rather, it is about understanding how needs and desires are always socially constructed in and through our relationships with others, and change as the context changes. Supporting people in developing relational autonomy means enabling them to negotiate their needs and desires within social contexts. To this end they need to be supported to understand their own needs and desires, society's norms and expectations, and how they can (independently or with support) negotiate the differences between them and work towards fulfilling their goals and aspirations. It is crucial to stress here that this means support must be available not only for aspirations which fall within current social conventions, but also for those which are still outside them, and for struggling to achieve social change.

Changing the Social Imagery

So far we have discussed how autonomy can be supported within intimate interpersonal relationships through a priori treating people with respect and recognition for their own authority over themselves, and through engaging in dialogue that provides information about the reasons behind social rules and expectations and opens up a space for negotiating those.

246

However, promoting relational autonomy means going beyond interpersonal relations that support people in making their own choices, as it is also necessary to challenge wider social contexts that work materially, culturally and discursively to hinder autonomy by limiting the range of possible choices. Autonomous decisions around seeking cure, passing as non-disabled or "coming out" as disabled are made by individuals and families against a cultural backdrop of what McRuer (2006) calls "compulsory able-bodiedness" which "assumes in advance that we all agree: able-bodied identities, able-bodied perspectives are preferable and what we all, collectively, are aiming for" (p. 9). This does not necessarily mean that such decisions are not "autonomous", but rather, it implies that in the struggle for increased autonomy we need to change the social imagery of which choices are possible or desirable.

Mackenzie (2000) stresses that the ability to "imagine otherwise", to consider the possibility of circumstances other than existing ones, is crucial for autonomy, as making choices requires considering alternatives; however, this ability to imagine otherwise is not located in isolation within an individual mind, but rather is produced through social and relational contexts. An example of how educational relationships can be used for changing and challenging the social imagery of what is possible comes from one of the authors' PhD research (Greenstein, 2013). As part of a series of creative workshops with students in a secondary school's special needs unit, we created a model of "the best teacher in the world" by drawing the outlines of students' bodies on a large sheet of paper which they later decorated (see Greenstein, 2014). As demonstrated by the dialogues in Table 1, the combination of a concrete task – creating a model of the teacher – with the fantastic orientation of describing an ideal reality rather than an existing one, provided a space for discussing complex and abstract ideas about bodies, normalcy and norms of beauty and gender.

Table 1: Dialogue from the Best School in the World Workshop.[20]

Dialogue 1	Dialogue 2
Anat: Ok, now let's use all this equipment and think what we want the best teacher in the world to have Jack: Green hair **Billy**: Leather jacket **Rachel**: Green hair, blue eyes and a leather jacket **Anat**: You want her to have green eyes? Jack: No, green hair blue eyes Jeff: Black hair **Billy**: Most definitely black leather jacket, Miss **Anat**: Why does she have green hair? Jack: I want her to look like a freak **Jeff**: We want to make a brilliant beautiful teacher, not a freak Jack: Not beautiful, she didn't say beautiful	Billy: that can be a moustache **Anat**: the ideal teacher has a moustache? Jack: yea (laughing) **Anat**: the ideal teacher is man or woman? **Rachel**: both, man and woman Jack: cool, freaking Jeff: I don't think I want to see that **Billy**: what? Jeff: a man and a woman **Rachel**: yea ... (laughing) Jack: what are they called, a man and a woman? What's the name? (Billy and Jack are gluing the felt piece) **Anat**: do we want the ideal teacher to be an androgynous or a trans ...? **Rachel**: (completing my unfinished word) gender

[20] All names here except Anat [Greenstein] are pseudonyms.

Anat: Well maybe someone likes being a freak, what does it mean if your teacher is a freak? **Rachel**: Pink eyes **Jeff**: Here you go **Jack**: She's a little bit different **Anat**: Is it nice to have a teacher that is a bit different and crazy, what do you think? **Jeff**: Yea, probably, you know, a bit more pizzazz.	**Jeff**: I think it's better for her to be straight, a woman **Anat**: the ideal teacher is a straight woman? **Jeff**: (at Jack) a weird looking lip, don't you think **Jack**: yea, well she'll be having a moustache in a minute **Jeff**: the ideal teacher, that? **Jack**: what? **Jeff**: teachers don't have moustaches **Rachel**: it might be a man and a woman **Billy**: that's just wrong **Anat**: what's wrong? **Billy**: a man in a woman's body

Both conversations moved between different contexts, starting with the very concrete task of choosing materials to produce the model, moving to interpreting the demands of the task and renegotiating the social meaning of "freak" and of gender boundaries. In these instances the students explicitly discussed social norms and expectations, and how their desires, understandings and wishes are framed within them (e.g. the desire to have a teacher who is "brilliant and beautiful", a "freak", or "both a man and a woman"). The students relied on the group relations to gain recognition of their choices and understandings as valid, to explore how these choices are limited, and to create a space that defies such restriction and opens up more possibilities. Thus, engaging in collaborative imagining broadened the scope of available options on the individual and collective level, positioning difference, freakiness and queerness (also) as productive possibilities. The utopian nature of the workshops, which entailed a sense of openness and an invitation to "go wild", was not only highly productive as a source of ideas, but also created a supportive space of becoming, in which students could experiment and expand their relations with the world, with themselves and with others in the world. As Mackenzie (2000) argues, such experimentation with possible relations and social imageries is crucial for practising relational autonomy, as it helps to challenge the wider norms and expectations that reduce people's ability to make autonomous choices.

It is true that abstract considerations of utopian alternatives will not, on their own, change much of the material conditions that limit autonomy. Yet as Halpin (2003) argues, collective utopian thought experiments are crucial for inducing change as they relativise the present and undermine the notion that the way things are is inevitable and unchangeable, and point towards desired avenues for change. Further, as Shuttleworth (2014) argues, individual imagination and social or collective imagination are in continual generative flux, both influencing each other but neither totally determined by the other. Therefore, in contrast to post-conventionalist writers like Shildrick (2009), Shuttleworth claims that "the maintenance of a critical space for autonomous subjectivity and the striving for political autonomy is crucial to assist both individuals and social movements in transforming social relations" (p. 83).

Conclusion

We have argued in the preceding sections that autonomy is a vital concern for everyone, but even more acutely so for disabled people, in areas of life as diverse as sexual (and other personal) relationships, education and imagining alternative futures. We do not wish to discredit post-structuralist perspectives on disability and embodiment altogether – in fact, we believe that they provide very valuable insights which counter unexamined assumptions about the individual subject which are still present in many of the more simplistic analyses of disablement based on the social model – but we do wish to articulate concerns about their (at best) neglect and (at worst) outright dismissal of disabled people's desires for self-determination.

We also believe that the normative (Western, liberal, modernist) model of autonomy as a property of the "independent", rational and self-sufficient individual is an impossible and harmful myth (Morris, 1991; Withers, 2012), that works to exclude disabled people from consideration as autonomous beings, rendering them what Davy (2014, p. 7) calls a "category of nonautonomous nonpersons". To resolve this dilemma, autonomy needs to be reconceptualised in a way that is explicitly designed to include everyone. Therefore, like Shuttleworth (2014, p. 77), we "want to provide a vision of disability that retains ... a critical space for agentic subjectivity, one that can work in productive tandem with a diversity of differently embodied disabled people together to transform the negative understanding of disability that permeates western societies".

We agree with the demand of feminist ethicists of care such as Kittay (2005) to promote relations of interdependency, which both ensure that people's dependency needs are met, and work to change social relations so that people are not made dependent in ways they need not be; however, we promote the value of relations of care and attachment not as a replacement, but as a necessary condition for autonomy. All of us, whether disabled or not, need autonomy to decide which relationships to pursue and nourish and which to abandon, and to negotiate our place and roles within the relationships that are needed and useful to us.

Our model of relational autonomy stresses that autonomy is always practised within relationships and is therefore essentially interdependent. People are not inherently either autonomous or non-autonomous, but instead become autonomous through engaging in relations that assume, recognise and support our autonomy. Achieving autonomy is not something that can be done by an individual for herself, but requires wider social support, in the forms both of cultural change that recognises and values diverse embodiments, subjectivities and identities, and of material support for people's needs which is provided in ways that recognise people's self-determination of their own needs and their right to choice and control over the way those needs are met.[21]

We recognise that a society that can achieve this will be a society with a fundamentally different political and economic system to that which exists now, as the capitalist economic system is founded on the denial of workers' autonomy; waged work is inherently non-autonomous as the sale of time and labour by workers to employers results in what work they do being determined by the employers rather than the workers themselves (Gorz, 1982). It is also capitalism that is largely responsible for much of the denial of autonomy that disabled people experience due to their exclusion from waged work and consequent construction as "dependent" in a supposedly qualitatively different way from non-disabled people (Oliver, 1989a; Withers, 2012), thus allowing state "welfare" systems to justify paternalistic restrictions on disabled people's lives

---

[21] We have not had space in this chapter to discuss this latter aspect of support for autonomy in detail, but it − in particular reference to personal assistance for disabled people − is the subject of ongoing research by one of us [Steve Graby].

(Russell, 1998), as well as those of other recipients of state funding or services, such as unemployed people or single parents (Fraser and Gordon, 1994). Therefore creating social relations that support autonomy must involve moving away from the position that liberation can be achieved through waged work (Abberley, 2002; Taylor, 2004) and exploring possibilities for alternative economies (for recent work by one of us addressing this in greater detail, see Graby, 2015). It is for these reasons that engaging in collective discussions and experimentation with such alternatives, held in inclusive ways that provide physical, cognitive and emotional support, is crucial for the development of relational autonomy.

Articulating a concept of autonomy that is rooted in the interdependence and the validity of all human subjects, regardless of individual dependency needs, can also help to connect disabled people's movements to, and build alliances with, many others, including anti-racist and anti-colonial (see for example Erevelles, 2011), queer (McRuer, 2006; Ben-Moshe, Nocella, and Withers, 2012), trans and intersex (Wilkerson 2012) and sex-positive/sex-radical (Wilkerson, 2002; Siebers, 2012) struggles, prison abolition and deinstitutionalisation movements (Ben-Moshe and Carey, 2014), feminists fighting for reproductive justice (Kafer, 2013; Ryan, 2014), and potentially others not yet imagined. Only with a relational concept of autonomy can we strive for a society in which autonomy is genuinely available to everyone.

References

Abberley, P. (2002). Work, disability and European social theory. In C. Barnes (Ed.), *Disability Studies Today* (pp. 120–138). Cambridge, United Kingdom: Polity.

Barclay, L. (2000). Autonomy and the social self. In C. Mackenzie & N. Stoljar (Eds.), *Relational autonomy: Feminist perspectives on autonomy, agency and the social self* (pp. 52–71). New York, NY: Oxford University Press.

Barron, K. (2001). Autonomy in everyday life, for whom? *Disability and Society, 16*(3), 431–447. doi:10.1080/09687590120045987

Bascom, J. (Ed.). (2012). *Loud hands: Autistic people, speaking.* Washington, DC: Autistic Press.

Ben-Moshe, L., Chapman, C., & Carey, A. C. (2014). *Disability incarcerated: Imprisonment and disability in the United States and Canada.* New York, NY: Palgrave Macmillan.

Ben-Moshe, L., Nocella, A. J., & Withers, A. J. (2012). Queer-cripping anarchism: Intersections and reflections on anarchism, queer-ness, and dis-ability. In C. B. Daring, J. Rogue, D. Shannon, & A. Volcano (Eds.), *Queering anarchism: Addressing and undressing power and desire* (pp. 207–220). Oakland, CA: AK Press.

Brisenden, S. (1986). Independent living and the medical model of disability. *Disability, Handicap and Society, 1*(2), 173–178.

Bubeck, D. E. (1995). *Care, gender, and justice.* Oxford, United Kingdom and New York, NY: Clarendon Press; Oxford University Press.

Buchwald, E., Fletcher, P. R., & Roth, M. (1993). *Transforming a rape culture.* Minneapolis, MN: Milkweed Editions.

Clare, E. (1999). *Exile and pride: Disability, queerness, and liberation.* Cambridge, MA: SouthEnd Press.

Collopy, B. J. (1988). Autonomy in long term care: Some crucial distinctions. *The Gerontologist, 28*(Suppl), 10–17.

Corbett, J. (1989). The quality of life in the "independence" curriculum. *Disability and Society, 4*(2), 145–163. doi:10.1080/02674648966780161

Davy, L. (2014). Philosophical inclusive design: Intellectual disability and the limits of individual autonomy in moral and political theory. *Hypatia.* Retrieved from http:// onlinelibrary.wiley.com/doi/10.1111/hypa.12119/full

DeJong, G. (1983). Defining and implementing the independent living concept. In N. M. Crewe & I. K. Zola (Eds.), *Independent living for physically disabled people* (pp. 4–27). San Francisco, CA: Jossey-Bass.

Deleuze, G., & Guattari, F. (1988). *A thousand plateaus: Capitalism and schizophrenia.* London:, United Kingdom: Athlone Press.

Erevelles, N. (2005). Signs of reason: Rivière, facilitated communication, and the crisis of the subject. In *Foucault and the Government of Disability* (pp. 45–64). Ann Arbor, MI: University of Michigan Press.

Erevelles, N. (2011). *Disability and difference in global contexts: Enabling a transformative body politic.* New York, NY: Palgrave Macmillan.

Fraser, N., & Gordon, L. (1994). A genealogy of dependency: Tracing a keyword of the U.S. welfare state. *Signs, 19*(2), 309–336.

Friedman, J., & Valenti, J. (Eds.). (2008). *Yes means yes!: Visions of female sexual power and a world without rape.* Berkeley, CA: Seal Press.

Giangreco, M. F. (2004). "The stairs didn't go anywhere!": A self-advocate's reflections on specialized services and their impact on people with disabilities. In M. Nind (Ed.), *Inclusive education: Diverse perspectives* (pp. 32–42). London, United Kingdom: David Fulton Publishers in association with The Open University. Retrieved 13 November 2012 from http://www.broadreachtraining.com/articles/arstairs.htm [no longer available].

Gibson, B. E. (2006). Disability, connectivity and transgressing the autonomous body. *Journal of Medical Humanities, 27*(3), 187–196. doi:10.1007/s10912-006-9017-6

Gilligan, C. (1982). *In a different voice: Psychological theory and women's development.* Cambridge, MA: Harvard University Press.

Goodley, D. (2007). Becoming rhizomatic parents: Deleuze, Guattari and disabled babies. *Disability and Society, 22*(2), 145–160. doi:10.1080/09687590601141576

Gore, J. (2004). In the eye of the beholder – child, mad or artist? In J. Purkis & J. Bowen (Eds.), *Changing anarchism: Anarchist theory and practice in a global age* (pp. 145–158). Manchester, United Kingdom; New York, NY: Manchester University Press.

Gorz, A. (1982). *Farewell to the working class: An essay on post-industrial socialism.* London, United Kingdom: Pluto Press.

Graby, S. (2015). Access to work or liberation from work? Disabled people, autonomy, and post-work politics. *Canadian Journal of Disability Studies, 4*(2), 132–161. doi:10.15353/cjds.v4i2.212

Greenstein, A. (2013). *Radical inclusive pedagogy: Connecting disability, education and activism* (PhD thesis). Manchester Metropolitan University, Manchester. Retrieved from http://www.e-space.mmu.ac.uk/e-space/handle/2173/ 326228

Greenstein, A. (2014). Today's learning objective is to have a party: Playing research with students in a secondary school special needs unit. *Journal of Research in Special Educational Needs, 14*(2), 71–81. doi:10.1111/1471-3802.12009

Halpin, D. (2003). *Hope and education: The role of the utopian imagination.* London, United Kingdom; New York, NY: RoutledgeFalmer.

Hollomotz, A. (2009). Beyond "vulnerability": An ecological model approach to conceptualizing risk of sexual violence against people with learning difficulties. *British Journal of Social Work, 39*(1), 99–112. doi:10.1093/bjsw/bcm091

Holt, J. (1983). *How children learn.* Delta, NY: Merloyd Lawrence.

Hough, R. E. (2012). Adult protection and "intimate citizenship" for people with learning difficulties: Empowering and protecting in light of the *No Secrets* review. *Disability and Society, 27*(1), 131–144. doi:10.1080/09687599.2012.631802

Illich, I. (1971). *Deschooling society.* Harmondsworth, United Kingdom: Penguin.

Kafer, A. (2013). *Feminist, queer, crip.* Bloomington, IN: Indiana University Press.

Kittay, E. F. (1999). *Love's labor: Essays on women, equality, and dependency.* New York, NY: Routledge.

Kittay, E. F. (2005). At the margins of moral personhood. *Ethics, 116*(1), 100–131.

Leece, J., & Peace, S. (2010). Developing new understandings of independence and autonomy in the personalised relationship. *British Journal of Social Work, 40*(6), 1847–1865. doi:10.1093/bjsw/bcp105

Lynch, K., Lyons, M., & Cantillon, S. (2009). Love labouring: Power and mutuality. In K. Lynch, J. Baker, & M. Lyons (Eds.), *Affective equality: Love, care and injustice* (pp. 114–131). Basingstoke, United Kingdom: Palgrave Macmillan.

Mackenzie, C. (2000). Imagining oneself otherwise. In *Relational autonomy: Feminist perspectives on autonomy, agency and the social self* (pp. 124–150). New York, NY: Oxford University Press.

Mackenzie, C., & Stoljar, N. (Eds.). (2000). *Relational autonomy: Feminist perspectives on autonomy, agency, and the social self.* New York, NY: Oxford University Press.

McEwan, M. (2009, 9 October). Rape culture 101. Retrieved from http://www.shakesville.com/2009/10/rape-culture-101.html

McRuer, R. (2006). *Crip theory: Cultural signs of queerness and disability.* New York, NY: New York University Press.

Mies, M. (1986). *Patriarchy and accumulation on a world scale: Women in the international division of labour.* London, United Kingdom; Atlantic Highlands, NJ: Zed Books.

Monk, L.-A. (2015). Intimacy and oppression: A historical perspective. In R. Chapman, S. Ledger, L. Townson, & D. Docherty (Eds.), *Sexuality and relationships in the lives of people with intellectual disabilities: Standing in my shoes* (pp. 46–64). London, United Kingdom; Philadelphia, PA: Jessica Kingsley.

Montgomery, C. (2001). Critic of the dawn. *Ragged Edge Online*, (2). Retrieved from http://www.ragged-edge-mag.com/0501/0501cov.htm

Morris, J. (1991). *Pride against prejudice: Personal politics of disability.* London, United Kingdom: Women's Press.

Morris, J. (1993). *Independent lives?: Community care and disabled people.* Basingstoke, United Kingdom: Macmillan.

Morris, J. (2001). Impairment and disability: Constructing an ethics of care that promotes human rights. *Hypatia, 16*(4), 1–16.

Nedelsky, J. (1989). Reconceiving autonomy: Sources, thoughts and possibilities. *Yale Journal of Law and Feminism, 1*(7), 7–36.

Oliver, M. (1989a). Disability and dependency: A creation of industrial societies. In L. Barton (Ed.), *Disability and dependency* (pp. 6–22). London, United Kingdom: RoutledgeFalmer.

Oliver, M. (1989b). Conductive Education: If it wasn't so sad it would be funny. *Disability and Society, 4*(2), 197–200. doi:10.1080/02674648966780191

Oshana, M. A. (1998). Personal autonomy and society. *Journal of Social Philosophy, 29*(1), 81–102.

Reindal, S. M. (1999). Independence, dependence, interdependence: Some reflections on the subject and personal autonomy. *Disability and Society, 14*(3), 353–367. doi:10.1080/09687599926190

Russell, M. (1998). *Beyond ramps: Disability at the end of the social contract.* Monroe, Maine: Common Courage Press.

257

Ryan, F. (2014, 20 May). "It's not only steps that keep us out": Mainstream feminism must stop ignoring disabled women. *New Statesman*. Retrieved from http://www.newstatesman.com/ society/2014/05/its-not-only-steps-keep-us-out-mainstream-feminism-must-stop-ignoring-disabled-women

Sevenhuijsen, S. (1998). *Citizenship and the ethics of care: Feminist considerations on justice, morality, and politics*. London, United Kingdom; New York, NY: Routledge.

Shildrick, M. (2009). *Dangerous discourses of disability, subjectivity and sexuality*. Basingstoke, United Kingdom: Palgrave Macmillan.

Shildrick, M., & Price, J. (2006). Deleuzian connections and queer corporealities: Shrinking global disability. *Rhizomes, 11/12*. Retrieved from http://www.rhizomes.net/issue11/shildrickprice/.index.html

Shuttleworth, R. (2014). Conceptualising disabled sexual subjectivity. In M. Pallotta-Chiarolli & B. Pease (Eds.), *The politics of recognition and social justice: Transforming subjectivities and new forms of resistance* (pp. 77–90). New York, NY: Routledge.

Siebers, T. (2001). Disability in theory: From social constructionism to the new realism of the body. *American Literary History, 13*(4), 737–754.

Siebers, T. (2012). A sexual culture for disabled people. In R. McRuer & A. Mollow (Eds.), *Sex and disability* (pp. 37–53). Durham; NC: Duke University Press.

Silvers, A. (1995). Reconciling equality to difference: Caring (f)or justice for people with disabilities. *Hypatia, 10*(1), 30–55.

Sinclair, J. (2010). Being autistic together. *Disability Studies Quarterly, 30*(1). Retrieved from http://dsq-sds.org/article/view/1075

Slater, J. (2015). *Youth and disability: A challenge to Mr Reasonable*. London, United Kingdom: Ashgate.

Taylor, S. (2004). The right not to work: Power and disability. *Monthly Review, 55*(10). Retrieved from http://monthlyreview.org/2004/03/01/the-right-not-to-work-power-and-disability

Troost, H. (2008). Reclaiming touch: Rape culture, explicit verbal consent, and body sovereignty. In J. Friedman & J. Valenti (Eds.), *Yes means yes! Visions of female sexual power and a world without rape* (pp. 171–178). Berkeley, CA: Seal Press.

Vernon, A., & Qureshi, H. (2000). Community care and independence: Self-sufficiency or empowerment? *Critical Social Policy*, *20*(2), 255–276. doi:10.1177/ 026101830002000204

Wilkerson, A. L. (2002). Disability, sex radicalism, and political agency. *NWSA Journal*, *14*(3), 33–57. doi:10.1353/nwsa.2003.0018

Wilkerson, A. L. (2012). Normate sex and its discontents. In R. McRuer & A. Mollow (Eds.), *Sex and disability* (pp. 183–207). Durham, NC; London, United Kingdom: Duke University Press.

Withers, A. J. (2012). *Disability politics and theory*. Halifax, Canada: Fernwood Publishing.

CHAPTER 10

IN PRAISE OF NORMAL:
RE-READING WOLFENSBERGER

Kathy Boxall

Summary
Discussions in critical disability studies have tended to downplay the positives of "normality" and have focused instead on difference and its challenges to "the norm". This chapter departs from this tendency by both highlighting the penalties of perceived difference which may be experienced by individual disabled people and arguing that normality may afford some protection from these penalties. The chapter begins by reflecting on the author's personal experience as someone who has survived the psychiatric system and also worked in services for people with intellectual disabilities. It then goes on to look at historical perspectives and Wolfensberger's ideas about Normalisation and Social Role Valorisation before discussing normalcy and penalties of difference. Finally, the chapter concludes by arguing that it may now be time to shift the emphasis back towards "the normal" and to focus attention on commonalties between human beings, rather than differences.

Introduction
In June 2012, I attended my first *Theorising Normalcy and the Mundane Conference* and found it engaging, lively, informative – and challenging. The most challenging aspect for me was the way in which the conference itself seemed to be founded on the assumption that "normal" was a "bad" thing, the implication being that there was nothing about normality that could be regarded as positive or helpful. This left me feeling decidedly uncomfortable as, although I would be the first to question notions of "normality" or "the norm", my own life experience has taught me about "the importance of being normal". Having

been diagnosed as "mentally ill" in my early twenties, thinking about normality and difference has been a personal preoccupation for much of my adult life and I've reached the conclusion that it's important to remain alert to the potential penalties of difference. I felt discomfort therefore at the way in which the positives of difference were highlighted in many of the *Theorising Normalcy and the Mundane Conference* presentations in 2012, with little reference to possible negatives. It seemed to me that these discussions of normalcy and difference were being undertaken from a position of privilege, which need not attend to penalties of difference. I use "penalties" here as a shorthand for the social economic and political responses to perceived impairment or difference which may be experienced by individual disabled people or, in social model terms, disablement (Oliver and Barnes, 2012).

My aim in this chapter (as in the *Theorising Normalcy and the Mundane Conference* presentation in 2013 upon which it is based) is to highlight the potential penalties of difference, and to argue that, far from being all "bad", normality can afford some protection from those penalties. I begin by outlining some personal and historical perspectives and go on to look at Wolfensberger's ideas about roles and normalisation. The chapter then moves on to discuss normalcy and penalties of difference, including institutional abuse and disablist hate crime. I conclude by arguing that it may now be time to shift the emphasis back towards "the normal" and focus attention on commonalities between human beings, rather than differences.

Personal Perspectives

I am a psychiatric system survivor. In my twenties, my life was controlled and dominated by psychiatrists and mental health professionals to the extent that I lost sight of my sense of self and identity and became the person prescribed by the diagnoses and labels I was given. I was constantly reminded of my abnormal status when admitted to hospital, at medical appointments, the dentist, the bank; when applying for jobs, driving licence, insurance, visas to work abroad and in interactions with everyone who was aware of "my diagnosis", or that I was – or had been – a mental health service user. My lack of normality was also reinforced through the media reports, television documentaries and popular psychology about "mentally ill people like me" to which I was subjected on an almost daily basis. During this period, I can remember repeating to myself a mantra: "All I want is to be normal. I just want an ordinary, normal existence." As someone who has been diagnosed "abnormal", I understand the desperate desire to join the ranks of the normal that people perceived as different may feel. However, I also acknowledge that not everyone feels this way; indeed, 30 years later I no longer place the same value on "being normal", now I have the trappings of a normal life around me. It is from this perspective therefore that I write this chapter.

My reflections on normality have not been restricted to my own experiences as a mental health service user/survivor. Since the 1970s, I have worked with children and adults with intellectual disabilities, including volunteering in a "mental handicap" hospital at the same time as I was a patient myself in the nearby psychiatric hospital. I volunteered on "Stanley Ward", a single storey "villa" on the outskirts of the hospital grounds, where the most severely and multiply impaired women patients lived; people who today would be described as having "profound intellectual and multiple disabilities". My role as a volunteer included pushing patients from Stanley Ward around the extensive hospital grounds in their wheelchairs. This left plenty of time to reflect on their lives – and my own – and to ponder the meaning of normality. Trying to think these things through on my own left me confused and frightened. It wasn't

until several years later that I was introduced to Wolf
Wolfensberger's (1972, 1983) work on normalisation and social
role valorisation. Wolfensberger was born in Mannheim,
Germany in 1934 and emigrated to the USA with his family in
1950. His ideas have been credited with achieving substantial
improvements in services and policy for people with learning
difficulties, but because they were susceptible to being viewed as
a "model" or "recipe" for practice, they were also sometimes
subject to rigid (mis)interpretation (Race, Boxall and Carson,
2005). Wolfensberger died in February 2011 and later that year a
special issue of the journal *Intellectual and Developmental
Disabilities* (Vol. 49, No. 6) reprinted several of his key
publications.

Wolfensberger's work highlights the historical mass
institutionalisation of people who were different; the next section
briefly outlines some of this history.

Historical Perspectives

During the first half of the twentieth century, mass
institutionalisation of those deemed "defective" or different was
evident throughout the Western world (Wolfensberger 1975;
Potts and Fido, 1991; Cocks, Fox, Brogan and Lee, 1996). When
I've asked students in the UK (and more recently in Australia
where I now work) why this was, very few are aware of the
eugenic policies which were in place at the time and most are
visibly shocked to learn about the practice of removing from their
family homes those deemed "fit persons to be removed" under
the Mental Deficiency Act 1913. These so called "defectives",
often still children, were placed in institutions hundreds of miles
from their families in order to discourage – and potentially sever
– family ties. Once in the institutions, the sexes were segregated
in order to prevent relationships that could lead to the birth of
further "mental or moral defectives". This practice of preventing

the formation of attachments to members of the opposite sex was not, however, restricted to the institutions. The Mental Deficiency Regulations 1935 allowed for some patients to be released from the institutions "on licence" (to work for a nominal wage as farmhands or similar where they could be under constant supervision), but there were particular requirements regarding their behaviour. Patients "on licence" were continually monitored and any evidence of their forming attachments to members of the opposite sex had to be reported to the superintendent of the hospital. Such was the fear that the "feebleminded", might procreate and proliferate that even the suggestion of the formation of such attachments led to their re-institutionalisation (Potts and Fido, 1991; Barron, 1996).

Mass institutionalisation during the first half of the nineteenth century was fuelled by concerns to protect society rather than those who were removed; as a consequence, institutionalisation was a permanent rather than temporary solution (Thomson, 1998). The Mental Deficiency Act 1913 did not just apply to people with intellectual disabilities; people who today would be understood as having physical or sensory impairments or mental health problems were also confined to the mental deficiency institutions alongside women who had children out of wedlock and other "moral defectives". The intention of the Act was to segregate and separate all "undesirable 'social inefficients'" and, to a large extent, this was achieved" (Race, 1995, p. 49). During this period therefore, penalties for not being "normal" included incarceration – for life. There were also penalties within the institutions in that some patients were "neglected, treated with callousness and even deliberate cruelty" (Martin, 1984, p. xi).

In the UK a series of official inquiries into scandals in mental handicap and psychiatric hospitals in the late 1960s and 1970s revealed overcrowding, squalid conditions and abuse. The inquiry reports were reviewed by J. P. Martin in his 1984 book

Hospitals in Trouble which explored the "corruption of care". In addition to shocking instances of objective and tangible abuse, Martin's review found wider more pervasive attitudes and practices which indicated "that the primary aims of care – the cure or alleviation of suffering – [had] become subordinate to what are essentially secondary aims such as the creation and preservation of order, quiet and cleanliness" (Martin, 1984, p. 86). The deviant or devalued status assigned to the patients was identified as contributing to this corruption of care. Martin (1984, p. 98) suggests that "human beings do not harm or treat others callously unless they can justify this in some way"; by viewing them as less than human, hospital staff justified or rationalised violent behaviour towards the patients in their care, perhaps believing that they did not understand or feel and therefore did not suffer. This theme of justified or rationalised violence towards deviant groups has also been explored elsewhere. For example, Kelman argued that victims of sanctioned massacres, "provoked the violence by what they are, ... not what they have done"; extreme dehumanisation which permits sadistic behaviour becomes possible when the target group can be identified as a separate category of people who have historically been stigmatised, the use of labels helping to "deprive the victims of identity or community" (Kelman, 1973 p. 32; Keith and Keith, 2013). There are parallels between Martin and Kelman's ideas about devaluation and dehumanisation and Wolf Wolfensberger's work which I explore below.

Roles

Wolfensberger (1975; 1998) identified a number of deviant roles assigned to people with intellectual disabilities: these included sick; subhuman; menace; object of pity; burden of charity and holy innocent which, he suggested, led to particular models of institutional care. For example, patients viewed as subhuman were, like animals, denied the right to privacy, property or

265

individuality. Viewing patients as objects of pity led to a model of welfare, which sheltered the individual from injury and risk, and made few demands for growth, development or personal responsibility. The menace perception led to segregation from the community and segregation of the sexes and as Wolfensberger (1975, p. 13) argued, "Since the menace model may ascribe a certain wilfulness and even intent to the retarded individual ... an element of vindictiveness and persecution may enter into his management". As an object of charity, the patient was entitled to food and shelter but not "luxuries" and residential provision based on this model left few opportunities for privacy or personal possessions.

For Wolfensberger therefore, the person with intellectual disabilities' deviant status or "role" was a direct determinant of the institutional model and the "care" provided therein; a view not wholly shared by Alaszewski (1986, p. 133) who argued that in the mental handicap hospital he researched terms like "animal" and "vegetable" were used metaphorically by nurses to classify patients, not metonymically, and were a means of relating different groups of patients to each other in the same way that terms like "high grade" and "low grade" were used to differentiate between the same groups of patients. Alaszewski's study demonstrated how the patient classification system was a sophisticated and powerful "ideological control of reality"; the classification providing prescriptive norms or "rules" for staff/patient relations. However, Alaszewski (1986, p. 249) concluded that these "rules" justified, rather than caused staff behaviour towards patients. Given that he also argued that ideological power within the hospital was "implicit, unconsciously exercised and pervasive", had "insidious and sophisticated effects" upon the classifiers and excluded any alternatives (Alaszewski, 1986, p. 236), it is difficult to see how this differentiation between cause and justification was made.

Kelman, Wolfensberger, Alaszewski and Martin appear to be in agreement, however, that the way in which people are perceived influences the way they are treated by others. This work on the roles assigned to people with intellectual disabilities informed Wolfensberger's version of the normalisation principle as well as his later work on social role valorisation.

Normalisation

The origins of normalisation are often mistakenly attributed to Wolfensberger, but Wolfensberger (2000) himself acknowledges that he was inspired by Bengt Nirje's (1969) paper. Wolfensberger's original (1972) formulation of the principle of normalisation (which was itself a re-formulation of Nirje's (1969) Scandinavian version) was: "Utilization of means which are as culturally normative as possible, in order to establish and/or maintain personal behaviors and characteristics which are as culturally normative as possible" (Wolfensberger, 1972, p. 28).

Translated into the everyday language of what were then mental handicap services, this was explained to me in the 1980s in the following terms. Rather than teaching mentally handicapped people how to cross a road by using a life-size, roll-out zebra crossing and plastic Belisha beacons inside the confines of a mental handicap hospital (as was usual practice in many hospitals), it's better to go out with patients and help them to use the real zebra crossings outside. In other words we were told that we should be doing "ordinary", "normal" things with the mentally handicapped people with whom we were working. Being shut away inside a mental handicap hospital was not "culturally normative"; being outside, as a visible part of the local community, wearing "culturally normative" (rather than hospital issue) clothing, was.

But "visibility" came at a cost if you had behaviours or characteristics that were not deemed "culturally normative".

Although Wolfensberger (1983) argues that he never advocated this, his normalisation principle was subject to the (mis)interpretation that it was about "making people normal". It can also be viewed as shoring up, rather than challenging, prevailing social attitudes and negative ideas about the "acceptability" of people with learning difficulties (Brown and Smith, 1992; Culham and Nind, 2003; Yates, Dyson and Hiles, 2008). Wolfensberger felt that the term "normalisation" was particularly susceptible to misinterpretation because people assumed they already knew what it meant and in 1983 he proposed a new term for his principle of normalisation: "Social Role Valorisation" or "SRV":

> The highest goal of the principle of normalisation has recently been clarified to be the establishment of enhancement, or defence of the social role(s) of a person or group, via the enhancement of people's social images and personal competencies. In consequence, it is proposed that normalisation be henceforth called "social role valorization". (Wolfensberger, 1983, p. 234)

He argued that if people with intellectual disabilities occupied valued social roles (for example, having a job or being a tenant and living in their own home) then other people's perceptions of them would be enhanced and good things may follow. On the other hand, if they are congregated with other people with intellectual disabilities in segregated settings, they will be perceived negatively by others and will be denied the "good things in life" (Wolfensberger, 2000). Drawing on Wolfensberger's work, David Race (2002, p. 203) offers a list of "good things in life" that may follow from socially valued roles – these include:

> Absence of imminent threats of extreme privation;
> A place to call home;
> Work, especially meaningful work;

Opportunities and expectations to discover and develop skills,
abilities, gifts and talents;
Access to most of the "sites of everyday life".

The patients I worked with when I was a volunteer on "Stanley Ward" were routinely denied all of these "good things", as were many of the people with intellectual disabilities I later worked with "in the community". Wolfensberger's ideas on normalisation/social role valorisation alerted managers and staff working with people with intellectual disabilities to the possibility that the people with whom they were working could (and should) be offered greater opportunities. My experience was that Wolfensberger's ideas gave staff and volunteers working in mental handicap hospitals "permission" to treat people with intellectual disabilities as human beings; they provided a "set of guidelines" as to how they could begin to work with people they had previously understood as "subhuman" and had treated accordingly. Viewed in retrospect, this need to treat people as human beings may seem obvious; however, to have acted without this "permission" at that time (late 1970s, early 1980s) would have entailed going against a working culture of deprivation and degradation (with all its in-built sanctions). This served to both deny people with intellectual disabilities individual humanity and worked to maintain a system upon which the denial of their collective humanity depended (Martin, 1984; Ryan and Thomas, 1987; Jones, 1996). Wolfensberger's ideas encouraged a service-level response that, for the first time, viewed people with intellectual disabilities as human beings.

Wolfensberger's ideas on normalisation changed and developed over the years but there is little doubt that his work had substantial influence on deinstitutionalisation policy in the UK. The late 1980s and 1990s saw the mass "resettlement" (to community services) of people with intellectual disabilities and mental health service users who had spent many years of their lives living in long-stay hospitals in the UK. Wolfensberger's influence on this major change in public policy was also evident in Australia, Scandinavia and the USA (Cocks et al., 1996; Mansell and Ericsson, 1996).

Normalisation was, however, criticised because it was the staff, not patients, who determined what was "culturally normative" and there was little space for self-advocacy or self-determination (see, for example, Chappell, 1992). In response to these critiques, Wolfensberger (1995) argued that he had merely pointed to the likely consequences of non-normative behaviours or characteristics for the people with intellectual disabilities (or members of other "devalued groups") who displayed them and had outlined the possible consequences of affording them valued social roles; he had not advocated specific courses of action, or the overruling of self-determination. Normalisation has also been criticised for advocating change at the level of the individual, rather than the political or social change demanded by social model understandings of disability (Chappell, 1992; Oliver, 2009). Making links with the oppressive practices to which disabled people have historically been subjected, Michael Oliver (2009, p. 96) suggests that the discourse and practices of normalisation "both construct and maintain the normal/ abnormal dichotomy". He argues that normalisation with its commitment to prevailing life conditions, environments and values may itself justify the continued oppression of "abnormal" disabled people; through both acting on them and acting on their behalf.

Claire Tregaskis (2004, p. 144) also argues that Wolfensberger's approach can never be completely successful. For Tregaskis, a disabled researcher, and the manager she worked with when undertaking her research:

> ... full assimilation on the basis of our approximation to normative standards of appearance and behaviour was simply

not possible, because at the end of the day he was a black man and I was a disabled woman, and no amount of dissembling would change the fact that we face ongoing discrimination on the basis of those aspects of our identities ... For both of us, the simulation route was not acceptable. Instead, embracing those apparently socially devalued aspects of identities was the only logical approach, because it enabled us to be proud of who we are, as we are, rather than attempting to engage in a constant struggle for self-regulation in the hope that we might just get away with fitting in as a result. (Tregaskis, 2004, p. 144)

Wolfensberger's adherence to dominant views about what counted as "culturally normative" has also been questioned in relation to people with intellectual disabilities from minority ethnic communities and other minorities (Bano, Crosskill, Patel, Rashman, and Shah, 1993). However, Wolfensberger (1972, p. 28) was clear from the outset that the term "normative" was intended to have statistical rather than moral connotations, and could be equated with "typical" or "conventional"; it may be helpful here to explore in more detail those statistical understandings.

Normalcy

Lennard Davis (1995) argues that the concept of "normal" that permeates our everyday lives in contemporary times is the product of a particular historical moment: nineteenth century industrialisation. Indeed, terms such as "normal", "normalcy", "norm" and "abnormal" did not enter European languages until around this time. Since then, norms and averages, that are the currency of statistics or "political arithmetic", have been used by governments to administer policy. If a particular human characteristic (for example, weight) is plotted against frequency, a bell-shaped curve or "normal distribution" results in which most members of the population fall into the central part of the bell, and those with characteristics that deviate from the norm (for example, extreme light or heavy weight) fall in the outer extremities of the curve. Davis (1995) and Goodley (2011) point to the way in which the early statisticians reframed this normal distribution so that the outer extremities of the bell-shaped curve were described in terms of "standard deviations from the mean", rather than "errors" and the superiority of one extremity over the other could be maintained. In relation to intellect, for example, "at one end speed is desirable and superior, while at the other end slow intellect is to be avoided as self-evidently pathological" (Goodley, 2011, p. 46). Contrary to Wolfensberger's (1972) assertion that "statistical" need not have moral connotations, both Davis (1995) and Goodley (2011) argue that statistical norms firmly underpin the social processes of disablement. Davis (1995, p. 30) also notes the striking coincidence that all the early statisticians were eugenicists – but regards this as unsurprising since "the central insight of statistics is the idea that a population can be normed", and the next step "is for the state to attempt to norm the nonstandard – the aim of eugenics".

As noted earlier, Davis's own work challenges the hegemony of the normal. In the introduction to the fourth edition of his *Disability Studies Reader* (an edited collection), he argues that the authors of the essays in that volume move beyond eugenics as they:

> ... are not simply trying to include disability under the rubric of normal but to question the idea of normality ... It's less a question of segregating the normal from the abnormal, the old eugenic game, as it is to describe, detail, theorize, and occupy the category of disability. (Davis, 2013, p. 12)

The difficulty I have with this is that we cannot simply set aside the normal. Feminist researchers have long argued that "experience is not gender-neutral in societies in which gender matters because it is the experience of gendered persons" (Bar

On, 1993, p. 83). It can similarly be argued that experience cannot be "normalcy-neutral" in societies in which normalcy matters. However much we strive to challenge and overturn the dominance of the norm, we live out our lives in contexts in which, at present, difference and deviation from the norm are negatively valued. When Mark Sherry (2010) researched disability hate websites on the internet in August 2009, he found that what Davis refers to as "the old eugenic game" was very much alive. Sherry cites numerous shocking examples of vitriolic hatred towards disabled people on disability hate sites; many of which included:

> ... a direct statement linking hatred and disability; the use of insulting, demeaning and hateful language such as "pet cripples", "human pretzels", "a mangle of flesh", "a gimp" and "tard and his owner"; ... a recitation of social Darwinist themes about "survival of the fittest"; and an assumption that the "quality of life" of all disabled people is so low that their lives are barely worth living ... another common theme is that disabled people should not reproduce. (Sherry, 2010, pp. 37–38)

Sherry raised the question, "Does anyone really hate disabled people?" After reviewing disability hate sites on the internet, he concluded that disability hatred and eugenic intent were widespread. However, Sherry's research was not limited to disability hate websites; his wider research found evidence of crimes towards disabled people in both the US and the UK. For example, the UK report *Getting Away with Murder* (Quarmby and Scott, 2008), documented a number of shockingly brutal direct physical assaults on disabled people. Sherry's (2010) research supports the view that there can be penalties for perceived difference. The following section reviews some of those penalties.

Penalties

As mentioned previously, the 1913 Mental Deficiency Act led to the institutionalisation of people who were different, many for life. The inquiry reports of the 1960s and 1970s provided evidence of penalties faced by incarcerated mental handicap and psychiatric hospital patients at the time (Martin, 1984). The documentary film *Silent Minority* which was broadcast on national television in the UK on 10 June 1981 provides graphic footage of the appalling conditions in mental handicap hospitals in 1980–1981 (see https://www. youtube.com/watch?v=az2f TYud0us). One of the most shocking scenes is of people with intellectual disabilities locked in a wire compound (a large outdoor cage) on a hot sunny day. That such a method of corralling human beings under lock and key should be employed by a hospital in the UK in the 1980s is shocking enough, but the camera then pans towards a plaque which states that the wire compound was, "Donated by the League of Friends of Borocourt Hospital", thus signalling a wider social acceptability of caging by those who raised the funds.

Thirty years later, similarly graphic footage was shown on British television on 31 May 2011, when BBC *Panorama* broadcast "Undercover Care: the Abuse Exposed". This included scenes (filmed by an undercover journalist) of staff at Winterbourne View Hospital mistreating and physically assaulting adults with intellectual disabilities (see https://www.youtube.com/playlis t?list=PLtiPZ6fpvjnL9zOyda5xLVNQXrcerBwTC); six members of staff were subsequently jailed and the Serious Case Review report which followed found evidence of a culture of intimidation and cruelty towards patients at Winterbourne View (Flynn, 2012). But this was not an isolated incident; in 2013, two people were jailed for assaulting patients at the Solar Centre, a day centre for people with intellectual disabilities run by

Rotherham, Doncaster and South Humber NHS Foundation Trust (Stothart, 2014).

However, deinstitutionalisation has not ended abuse against disabled people. Dan Goodley and Katherine Runswick-Cole's (2011, p. 606) research with parents of disabled children discusses "The real of violence … pain inflicted by one body on another" and provides shocking disclosures of violence experienced outwith institutional settings. For example:

> She's had her moments, she got bullied by a girl on the school bus, they pinned her down and were putting tampons in her mouth but you know you don't always get the, but then I think well you can't fight against that can you? We stuck out on the bus a bit longer and then I thought no, so that's why we give her the lift. (Lesley in Goodley and Runswick-Cole 2011, p. 606)

> The youth worker called me into her office. She looked dreadful, shocked. Eventually she told me that there had been an incident in the toilet. A group of girls had been teasing Isobel and they tried to get her to lick the toilet seat. There was a rumour that the whole thing had been videoed on a camera phone and posted on You Tube. (Alex in Goodley and Runswick-Cole 2011, p. 606).

There are also numerous other examples of abuse against people with intellectual disabilities in community settings and, for many people with intellectual disabilities, violation of their human rights is "a normal part of their everyday lives" (JCHR, 2008, p. 16; EHRC, 2011; McCarthy, 2014). In recent years hate crime against disabled people has been recognised in the UK and elsewhere (Sherry, 2010; Quarmby, 2011; Roulstone and Mason-Bish, 2013). People with intellectual disabilities living in the community in the UK have lost their lives in circumstances where they were being harassed or physically assaulted because of their intellectual disabilities or visible difference: Steven Hoskin (July 2006); Christine Lakinski (July 2007); Brent Martin

(August 2007); David Askew (March 2010) and Gemma Hayter (August 2010). People with mental health diagnoses also report discriminatory treatment in the community. A study by Rose et al., (2011) that interviewed 75 people with a diagnosis of schizophrenia across 15 different countries found transnational patterns of negative discrimination, with reports of humiliation and abuse. Interviewees were, however, able to provide examples where they did not experience discrimination but couched these in terms of "gratitude" for being treated similarly to people who did not have a mental illness diagnosis. As Rose et al. (2011, p. 203) note, "In the absence of discrimination that was expected, people with mental illness feel grateful. Other members of society see no need to be grateful if they are treated with civility" (Rose et al., 2011, p. 203). Mental health service users also experience isolation and rejection from the communities of which they are a part; a key finding of Hamilton et al.'s (2014) telephone survey of 537 people who used mental health services in England was that friends, employers and family had distanced themselves from the people with mental health problems who were interviewed (Hamilton et al., 2014, p. 92).

These are the penalties of difference to which I refer.

Conclusion

If Wolfensberger's ideas on normalisation have been so heavily criticised, why am I advocating a re-reading of his work? I am not suggesting that we should all become advocates for normalisation and cease from critiquing the hegemony of the normal, quite the reverse. I would be the first to argue that ideas of normality need to be questioned and shaken up. However, I also believe that it is important to attend to the social and political contexts in which disabled people live out their everyday lives and in which their experiences are also theorised. We know from history what happened when attention was focused on people's visible differences – their characteristic appearance, facial features, abnormal gait and lack of intelligence – they were congregated and segregated in long-stay institutions. It is in our very recent past in the United Kingdom that scenes such as those broadcast in the 1981 film *Silent Minority* were commonplace. Wolfensberger's ideas may seem uncomfortable, for there is no doubt that they prop up the prevailing ideology which does not value people who are different; what they also do, however, is draw attention to contemporary social responses to perceived difference and the sometimes devastating impact such responses can have on individuals. This needs to be acknowledged. Just as it is important to "imagine otherwise" and move away from stereotypical understandings of impairment and difference, so too is it important to temper such imaginings with an acknowledgement of the potential penalties of difference.

It seems to me that there are two key ways of doing this. The first is to acknowledge the positives of normal in our everyday lives. The second is to balance discussions of difference with a focus on commonalities between human beings. Referring to the essays he edited in his *Disability Studies Reader*, Davis (2013) notes that, "If anything, this collection of essays serves to render complex the simple fact of impairment *while rendering simple the ideological screen of normality*" (Davis, 2013, p. 12, emphasis added). I would argue, however, that the ideological screen of normality is far from simple as it serves both to reinforce hegemonic understandings of normality and, for those who fall within its bounds, to afford protection from the penalties of not being "normal". Rather than simply challenging the hegemony of the normal, we need also to harness its power; the challenge is to do this in ways that do not "construct and maintain the normal/abnormal dichotomy" (Oliver, 2009, p. 96).

*

For many disabled people normality – as it is conventionally constituted and understood – may be unattainable (Tregaskis, 2004). If the protective functions of normality are to be extended to those who fall outwith its bounds, we may need to rethink those bounds and to institute alternative ways of understanding people's differences so that they are not framed in terms of abnormality, deficit or lack. Contrary to Davis (2013, p. 12), therefore, I would argue that we should continue "trying to include disability under the rubric of normal". One of the ways in which this might be achieved is through increasing emphasis on commonalities between all human beings. None of us are totally "normal", we all differ in some way from the "ideal" type. We are all also, in some ways, "normal" as we all have commonalities with other human beings; the recognition of these commonalities and their acceptance as "normal" has the potential to afford protection from the penalties of difference.

Wolfensberger's work achieved considerable positive change in the lives of people with perceived impairments; it did this by minimising their visible differences in order to offer them the protection of normal. The challenge now is to achieve this protection through the acknowledgement and celebration of everyone's normality.

References

Alaszewski, A. (1986). *Institutional care and the mentally handicapped*, London, United Kingdom: Croom Helm.

Bano, A., Crosskill, D., Patel, R., Rashman, L., & Shah, R. (1993). *Improving practice with people with learning disabilities: A training manual* (Antiracist Social Work Education: No. 5), London, United Kingdom: CCETSW.

Bar On, B. A. (1993). Marginality and epistemic privilege. In L. Alcoff & E. Potter (Eds.), *Feminist epistemologies* (pp. 83–100). London, United Kingdom: Routledge.

Barron, D. (1996). *A price to be born: My childhood and life in a mental institution*. Harrogate, United Kingdom: Mencap Northern Division.

Brown, H., & Smith, H. (1992). *Normalisation: A reader for the nineties.* London, United Kingdom: Routledge.

Chappell, A. L. (1992). Towards a sociological critique of the normalization principle. *Disability, Handicap and Society, 7,* 35–51.

Cocks, E., Fox, C., Brogan, M., & Lee, M. (Eds.). (1996). *Under blue skies: The social construction of intellectual disability in Western Australia.* Perth, Edith Cowan University.

Culham, A., & Nind, M. (2003). Deconstructing normalisation: clearing the way for inclusion. *Journal of Intellectual and Developmental Disability, 28*(1), 65–78.

Davis, L. (1995). *Enforcing normalcy: Disability, deafness and the body,* London, United Kingdom: Verso.

Davis, L. (2013). *The Disability Studies Reader.* (4th ed.), New York, NY: Routledge.

EHRC. (2011). *Hidden in plain sight: Inquiry into disability-related harassment.* London, United Kingdom: Equality and Human Rights Commission.

Flynn, M. (2012). *Winterbourne View Hospital: A serious case review.* South Gloucestershire Council/South Gloucestershire Safeguarding Adults Board.

Goodley, D. (2011). *Disability studies: An interdisciplinary introduction.* London, United Kingdom: SAGE.

Goodley, D., & Runswick-Cole, K. (2011). The violence of disablism, *Sociology of Health and Illness, 33*(4), 602–617.

Hamilton, S., Lewis-Holmes, E., Pinfold, V., Henderson, C., Rose, D., & Thornicroft, G. (2014). Discrimination against people with a mental health diagnosis: qualitative analysis of reported experiences. *Journal of Mental Health, 23*(2), 88–93.

JCHR. (2008). *A life like any other? Human rights of adults with learning disabilities, Seventh Report of Session 2007–08.* London, United Kingdom: House of Lords/House of Commons, Joint Committee on Human Rights.

Jones, C. (1996). Anti-intellectualism and the peculiarities of British social work education. In N. Parton, (Ed.), *Social theory, social change and social work* (pp. 190–210). London, United Kingdom: Routledge.

Keith, H., & Keith, K. (2013). *Intellectual disability: Ethics, dehumanization and a new moral community.* Oxford, United Kingdom: Wiley.

Kelman, H. G. (1973). Violence without moral restraint: Reflections on the dehumanization of victims and victimizers. *Journal of Social Issues, 29*(4), 25–61.

Mansell, J., & Ericsson, K. (1996). *Deinstitutionalization and community living: Intellectual disability services in Britain, Scandinavia and the USA.* London, United Kingdom: Chapman & Hall.

Martin, J. P. (1984). *Hospitals in trouble.* Oxford, United Kingdom: Blackwell.

McCarthy, M. (2014). Brick by brick: Building up our knowledge base on the abuse of adults with learning disabilities. *Tizard Learning Disability Review, 19*(3), 130–133.

Nirje, B. (1969). The normalization principle and its human management implications. In R. Kugel & W. Wolfensberger (Eds.), *Changing patterns in residential services for the mentally retarded* (pp. 179–195). Washington, DC: President's Committee on Mental Retardation.

Oliver, M. (2009). *Understanding learning disability: From theory to practice.* Basingstoke, United Kingdom: Palgrave Macmillan.

Oliver, M., & Barnes, C. (2012). *The new politics of disablement.* Basingstoke, United Kingdom: Palgrave Macmillan.

Potts, M., & Fido, R. (1991). *"A fit person to be removed": Personal accounts of life in a mental deficiency institution.* Plymouth, United Kingdom: Northcote House.

Quarmby, K. (2011). *Scapegoat: Why we are failing disabled people.* London, United Kingdom: Portobello.

Quarmby, K., & Scott, R. (2008). *Getting away with murder: Disabled people's experiences of hate crime in the UK.* Report by Scope, Disability Now and the United Kingdom's Disabled People's Council.

Race, D. (1995). Historical development of service provision. In N. Malin, (Ed.), *Services for people with learning disabilities.* (pp. 46–78). London, United Kingdom: Routledge.

Race, D. (2002). The "normalisation" debate – time to move on. In D. Race (Ed.), *Learning disability – a social approach.* (pp. 191–208). London, United Kingdom: Routledge.

Race, D., Boxall, K., & Carson, I. (2005). Towards a dialogue for practice: Reconciling social role valorization and the social model of disability. *Disability and Society, 20*(5), 507–521.

Rose, D., Willis, R., Brohan, E., Sartorius, N., Villares, C., Wahlbeck, K., & Thornicroft, G. (2011). Reported stigma and discrimination by people with a diagnosis of schizophrenia. *Epidemiology and Psychiatric Sciences, 20*(02), 193–204.

Roulstone, A., & Mason-Bish, H. (Eds.). (2013). *Disability, hate crime and violence.* London, United Kingdom: Routledge.

Ryan, J., & Thomas, F. (1987). *The politics of mental handicap.* London, United Kingdom: Free Association Books.

Sherry, M. (2010). *Disability hate crimes: Does anyone really hate disabled people?* Farnham, United Kingdom: Ashgate.

Stothart, C. (2014). Serious case review of abuse scandal highlights lack of regulation of day centres. *Community Care,* 23 July.

Thomson, M. (1998). *The problem of mental deficiency: Eugenics, democracy, and social policy in Britain c.1870–1959.* Oxford, United Kingdom: Clarendon Press.

Tregaskis, C. (2004). *Constrictions of disability: Researching the interface between disabled and non-disabled people.* London, United Kingdom: Routledge.

Wolfensberger, W. (1972). *The principle of normalization in human services.* Toronto, Canada: National Institute on Mental Retardation.

Wolfensberger, W. (1975). *The origin and nature of our institutional models.* New York, NY: Human Policy Press,.

Wolfensberger, W. (1983). Social role valorization: A proposed new term for the principle of normalization. *Mental Retardation, 21*(6), 234–239.

Wolfensberger, W. (1995). An "if this then that" formulation of decisions related to social role valorization as a better way of interpreting it to people. *Mental Retardation, 33*(3), 163–169.

Wolfensberger, W. (1998). *A brief introduction to social role valorisation.* Syracuse NY: Training Institute on Human Service Change Agentry, Syracuse University.

Wolfensberger, W. (2000). A brief overview of social role valorization. *Mental Retardation, 38*(2), 105–123.

Yates, S., Dyson, S., & Hiles, D. (2008). Beyond normalization and impairment: Theorizing subjectivity in learning difficulties – theory and practice. *Disability and Society, 23*(3), 247–258.